Library of
Davidson College

Archeological Explanation
The Scientific Method in Archeology

ARCHEOLOGICAL EXPLANATION

The Scientific Method in Archeology

**Patty Jo Watson
Steven A. LeBlanc
Charles L. Redman**

Columbia University Press
New York   1984

Library of Congress Cataloging in Publication Data

Watson, Patty Jo, 1932–
Archeological explanation.

Bibliography: p.
Includes index.
1. Archaeology—Philosophy. 2. Archaeology—Methodology. I. LeBlanc, Steven A. II. Redman, Charles L. III. Title.
CC72.W37 1984   930.1′01   84-5014
ISBN 0-231-06028-9 (alk. paper)

Columbia University Press
New York   Guildford, Surrey
COPYRIGHT © 1984 COLUMBIA UNIVERSITY PRESS
ALL RIGHTS RESERVED

PRINTED IN THE UNITED STATES OF AMERICA

Clothbound editions of Columbia University Press Books are Smyth-sewn and printed on permanent and durable acid-free paper

Contents

	Preface	*vii*
	Acknowledgments	*xiii*
1.	The Logic of Science, the Nature of Explanation, and Archeology as Science	*1*
2.	Systems Theory and Archeology	*67*
3.	Ecology and Archeology	*113*
4.	The Archeological Record and the Designing of Archeological Research	*155*
5.	Archeological Analysis	*187*
6.	Archeology and Society: Problems and Prospects	*233*
	References	*277*
	Name Index	*303*
	Subject Index	*307*

Preface

Archeology is the study of human societies through examination and interpretation of their material remains; thus it occupies an area of overlap between the humanities and the sciences. It began in the Old World as an avocational and antiquarian (object-oriented) pursuit that was divided during the mid-nineteenth century into two subdisciplines: paleolithic and early post-Pleistocene prehistory with a natural history/natural science emphasis; and archeology of the ancient, literate civilizations with a classics/fine arts emphasis. In the New World, archeology of the American aborigines north of Mexico was by definition prehistoric because there were no pre-Columbian writing systems there. By the late nineteenth century there was a strong interest—subsidized heavily by the U.S. government—in the arts and life ways of these native Americans. Historically documented knowledge about them came largely from ethnography and ethnohistory, whereas archeologists working closely with ethnographers and their data provided information about the pre-Columbians before the time of European contact. Ethnographers, ethnohistorians, and archeologists all were identified as anthropologists: scholars who study nonliterate, non-European, exotic, and primitive human societies.

Anthropology, as practiced in the United States, was and is a very broadly conceived discipline. It includes prehistoric archeology together with numerous other subfields and sub-subfields and is usually ranked with the social sciences in American educational institutions. In contrast, the purposes and objectives of classical archeologists and art historians have traditionally been, at least in part, significantly different from those of prehistorians or anthropologically trained archeologists. Until recently, only anthropological archeologists have considered themselves to be primarily social scientists, and it is the work of this group with which we are concerned. Hence, in this book we do not discuss humanistically oriented or classical archeology, but rather anthropological archeology.

The goals of anthropologically oriented archeology are to provide understandings of past cultures, and explanations of the differences and similarities among them. During the 1960s, under the stimulus of a controversial theoretician, Lewis Binford (1962, 1972), Americanist archeologists became overtly dissatisfied with the traditional emphasis on detailed particularistic descriptions of excavated or collected prehistoric materials and with the lack of attention paid to theoretical frameworks that could give context and meaning to these materials. As Walter W. Taylor indicates in considerable detail (Taylor 1948), the focus of most pre-1960s archeology was on the chronological and spatial distribution of artifact types, or "time–space systematics," as it is now often called. (For a clear exposition of the differences between traditional archeologists and the rebels of the 1960s as the latter viewed the situation, see Hill 1972.)

Those archeologists most vocal in urging drastic changes in archeological theory and method were called "new archeologists" or sometimes "processualists." One of their key concerns was to explain cultural processes by testing generalizations about how cultures function and evolve. This approach utilizes but goes beyond the rather narrow time–space systematics characteristic of "old" or "traditional" archeology or culture history (Flannery 1967).

Some of the most hotly debated issues during the late 1960s and early 1970s concerned the nature of explanation in archeology and the appropriateness of applying scientific methods to interpretation of archeological materials: What is the logical structure of the explanations archeologists provide to interpret the materials they recover? How are those explanations supported or confirmed? Is archeological explanation scientific or not? Do archeologists discover laws of human behavior? Can or should archeology be a science? Can or should archeology be a nonscientific kind of history? Archeologists discussed these and related questions intently (Adams 1968; Bayard 1969; Binford 1968a; Hawkes 1968; Isaac 1971; Trigger 1968, 1970, 1973; Watson 1973, 1974b; Watson, LeBlanc, and Redman 1971).

Preface   ix

Our main reasons for writing *Explanation in Archeology* (1971; (referred to hereafter as EA) were to provide an introduction to these theoretical issues and to produce a formulation of what an explicitly scientific approach to archeology entails. In this second book we again aim to provide a relatively comprehensive account of what science in archeology entails. We believe—as we say more fully in chapter 1 and elsewhere here—that familiarity with some aspects of the philosophy of science is highly beneficial for archeologists. Thus, although like Brown (1963:2), we do not wish to become so immersed in philosophical disputes that we are unable to carry on our scientific work, we also wholeheartedly agree with the philosophers of science Merrilee and Wesley Salmon:

> It does seem important to bring analytic tools to bear in an effort to discern the logical features which characterize successful explanations, in the hope that such knowledge may have value in the construction and criticism of actual explanations. Perhaps philosophers of science can play a useful role in this enterprise. As John Venn, a nineteenth century philosopher, wrote in his epoch-making work on probability (1866),
>
> "No science can safely be abandoned entirely to its own devotees. Its details of course can only be studied by those who make it their special occupation, but its general principles are sure to be cramped if it is not exposed occasionally to the free criticism of those whose main culture has been of a more general character (p. ix)."
>
> The principle is reciprocal. While philosophers may supply logical criteria, scientists provide the hard cases against which philosophical models of explanation must be tested (Salmon and Salmon 1979:72).

In chapter 1 of this book we summarize the rudiments of the logic of science, stressing especially models of explanation, the possible differences between history and science, and the general relevance of these topics to archeology. In chapters 2 and 3 we discuss the two most popular methodological orientations in contemporary prehistoric archeology: systems theory and the ecological approach. We view them from the perspectives of the theoretical framework established in chapter 1 and of archeological practice.

Chapters 4 and 5 contain a summary account of the methods and techniques of scientific archeology in the field and in the laboratory.

In the sixth and last chapter, three topics are considered: (1) the nature of archeological publications; (2) the relationship of conservation or contract archeology to noncontract or academic archeology; and (3) archeology conceived and practiced as a social science.

Americanist anthropological archeology has undergone numerous changes since we wrote EA. Much of the strife reflected here and there in EA has long been resolved, although some of the discussions initiated at that period continue intermittently (Bamforth and Spaulding 1982). The massive advent of contract archeology in the wake of the Archeological Conservation Act (passed in May 1974) has altered the direction and shaped the content of contemporary U.S. archeology in ways not foreseen in 1970 when we wrote EA, yet much Americanist archeological research is now being carried out with the aid of concepts and techniques first adopted or publicized by the new archeologists of the 1960s. Hence, current attitudes to many of the subjects treated in EA are very different from those of 1970.

The extent and direction of major changes in North American professional archeology over the past twelve to fifteen years are indicated by the organizations that have risen in the late 1960s and the 1970s: American Society for Conservation Archaeology, Society of Professional Archaeologists, Association for Field Archaeology, Society for Archaeological Sciences. There are also a number of new state-level professional organizations across the country, as well as numerous private firms engaged in full-time contract archeology. New archeological programs have also appeared, most of them strongly interdisciplinary and not especially anthropological in orientation: for example, the Center for Ancient Studies at the University of Minnesota, the Program in Archaeological Studies at Boston University, the Departments of Archaeology at Calgary and Simon Fraser universities; the Institute of Nautical Archaeology at Texas A & M. Other indicators of current trends are the two new theory/method-oriented periodicals (*Advances in Archaeological Method and Theory* and *Journal of Anthropological Archaeology,* established in 1978 and 1982, respectively). However, even a cursory reading of titles and abstracts in *American Antiquity* and in the Society for American Archaeology program announcements for the past five years indicates how far the pendulum has swung from the predominantly theory-and-method phase of the late 1960s and early 1970s. Some observers attribute this shift in emphasis to the impact of contract archeology; others see it as a reaction to and rejection of the new archeology program. A third opinion (in which we share) is that the majority of practicing field archeologists are absorbed in implementing or operationalizing those parts of the new archeology program they believe to be most productive, while others (for example, Hall 1977, Hodder 1982, Leone 1982b) are concerned with a variety of supplementary, complementary, or alternative ("post-processual") approaches.

We have changed somewhat since 1970 ourselves, but we still adhere to the fundamental framework we expressed in EA. We have written the present volume because the primary issues treated in the first book will always be essential elements in discussions of archeological theory, and continuing development of the field necessitates continuing examination of these issues. In this new book we have considerably expanded our discussion of the philosophy of science as it relates to archeology (in chapter 1 primarily, of course, but also in parts of other chapters), and we have also greatly increased the scope and content of the sections on archeological research design and analysis of archeological materials (chapters 4 and 5). These expansions reflect our opinions about the crucial importance of two matters: the conceptual foundations of archeological inference and interpretation; and the relationships among interpretation, data recovery, and analysis.

Acknowledgments

We wish to thank the many people who have helped us prepare this book although we are responsible for its final form. Portions of various drafts were read and commented upon by Robert Dunnell, Merrilee Salmon, Wesley Salmon, Keith Kintigh, David Browman, George Cowgill, Alison Wylie, Mark Leone, William Marquarolt, and an anonymous reviewer for Columbia University Press.

We are especially indebted to Richard A. Watson for discussing the entire project with us on innumerable occasions, for line editing the penultimate manuscript, and for seeing the final draft through the word processor.

Much of the expense incurred in the early stages of manuscript preparation was met by Washington University faculty grants. Also at Washington University, Sue Cunningham, Marcella Waddell, Mary Kennedy, David Lake, Fuki Hisama, and Douglas Givens aided materially in the manuscript production process.

The final draft was completed at the Center for Advanced Study in the Behavioral Sciences, Stanford, California. We are grateful to the Center, to its genial and efficient Director Gardner Lindzey, and to its patient, cheerful typists Deanna Dejon, Anna Tower, and Barbara Witt.

PJW
SAL
CLR

Archeological Explanation
The Scientific Method in Archeology

CHAPTER ONE

The Logic of Science, the Nature of Explanation, and Archeology as Science

Writing in the 1940s, Walter W. Taylor found Americanist archeologists to be narrowly concerned with particulars of chronology and trait distributions to the virtual exclusion of any other kinds of information obtainable from the archeological record. He expressed his views in a detailed analysis published in 1948, *A Study of Archeology*, in which he also described scientific methods of testing archeological explanations.

Taylor's critique had little immediate effect. In a paper published in 1962, Lewis Binford complained about the same narrow focus on description of specific sites and artifacts. Most archeologists still gave little thought to functional contexts or to the processes that resulted in patterned distributions. However, Binford, his students, and other Americanist archeologists of the mid- to late 1960s did begin to examine the rationales and justifications for archeological interpretations and explanations. Because most of these archeologists had been trained in anthropology departments, nearly all their discussion took place within a context of archeology viewed as anthropology, and hence as a social science. Once attention was explicitly turned to theoretical issues, these archeologists found themselves participating in some of the oldest debates in the intellectual history of the Western world: What is knowledge? In particular, what is archeological knowledge? Is there an objective, real world of past human behavior that can be empirically perceived, described, and explained, as physical scientists perceive, describe, and explain the behavior of nonhuman entities? What is science? Are the human sciences, that is, the social sciences, logically different from the natural sciences (physics, chemistry, biology)? What are the significant differences and similarities between archeology and history? Is historical research logically distinct from scientific research? Are there laws of human behavior, and if so how can they be discovered or established? Are the patterns of human behavior now or in the archeologically documented past sufficiently regular so that they can be explained and predicted? Do explanations and predictions of the social and cultural behavior of human beings have the same logical form as explanations and predictions of processes and events in the nonhuman physical world?

Attempts to answer these and related questions drew archeologists into philosophical discussions new to most of them. The issues were complicated because archeology seemed to be neither solidly one of the humanities nor one of the natural sciences. Rather it is a distinctive kind of social science that relies on data and uses methods from both the humanities and the natural sciences.

To help make the scientific framework of archeology explicit we wrote *Explanation in Archeology* (1971). There we emphasize scientific method, especially the formulation and testing of hypotheses about past human behavior. Confirmed hypotheses are incorporated into a body of knowledge about past social and cultural processes to enable us not only to describe the archeological record as we uncover it but also to devise broadly based explanations of it.

Although some of our opinions and perspectives have changed since publication of *Explanation in Archeology*, we believe that these formal or philosophical matters are as important now as they were then. However, our basic concern is still with the practical aspects of those issues that are most relevant to practicing archeologists, and we make no attempt to summarize the total range of discussion on topics treated in chapter 1. We present our views as clearly and forthrightly as possible, with reference to basic bibliographic sources, so that the subjects in question can be pursued further by anyone who wishes to do so.

The Logic of Science

In philosophical terminology, the issues that concern us are epistemological; that is, they have to do with how we know and with how we justify or confirm our knowledge claims. How do we acquire knowledge of archeological subject matter? How do we justify the use of our methods and confirm our conclusions? How do our colleagues know when we have made a genuine contribution to archeological knowledge? How can we assure ourselves or anyone else that we are advancing knowledge?

Epistemology—or the theory of knowledge—is a traditional concern of philosophers of science, among the best known and most widely respected of whom is Carl G. Hempel. Hempel's writings on the logic of science (in particular, Hempel 1965 and 1966) are one of the primary sources for the discussion presented here. However, we also refer to the work of other theorists (not all of whom agree with Hempel) who concern themselves with the philosophy of the physical, biological, and social sciences, for example, Dray, Popper, Rudner, Wesley Salmon, and Merrilee Salmon. Although our own orientation is primarily Hempelian, our concern with the logic of science, once again, is that of practicing archeologists, not aspiring philosophers. For our purposes, the crucial epistemological issues referred to above can be summarized under three headings: Knowledge of the World; Truth; and Hypotheses, Explanations, General Laws, and Theories.

Knowledge of the World

Two basic working assumptions of practicing scientists are that there is a real, knowable world that can be empirically perceived and described and that the empirically observable behavior of the entities making up this real world is orderly. The behavior of the phenomena in the real world is often complex and seemingly random or haphazard, but the practicing scientist assumes that regular patterns are present in natural phenomena and that these patterns can be observed and described. The presence of this ordered or patterned structure is confirmed by means of observations made to test hypotheses that describe suspected relationships and regularities. Thus, hypothesis formulation leads to tests and the acceptance, alteration, or rejection of the hypotheses. Once fundamental relationships are understood, prediction and explanation of the phenomena are possible. Given some knowledge about relationships and classes of relationships characteristic of the subject matter being investigated, scientists can formulate theories to subsume available data. One way to confirm a theory is to show that it can be used to predict other, as yet unobserved phenomena. The most important tasks of the scientist, then, are to observe and describe regularities that can be incorporated in theories useful for the explanation and prediction of the phenomena being investigated. Descriptions of regularities that have withstood repeated testing can sometimes (see the discussion of empirical generalizations in the next section to see why we must qualify this statement) be expressed as universal or statistical laws. But, as Hempel says, "Quite broadly speaking, an opinion as to what laws hold in nature and what phenomena can be explained surely cannot be formed on analytic non-empirical grounds alone but must be based on the results of empirical research" (Hempel 1965:425, n. 17).

Whether all (or most) empirical phenomena *really are* incorporated in a system of regularities that can be described in terms of universal and/or statistical laws is a philosophical issue that has been debated—without resolution—for a long time. This philosophical problem about the uniformity or regularity of nature and the status of knowledge claims about nature based on induction from past experience was formally described more than two hundred years ago by David Hume:

> Let the course of things be allowed hitherto ever so regular; that alone, without some new argument or inference, proves not that, for the future, it will continue so. In vain do you pretend to have learned the nature of bodies from your past experience. Their secret nature, and consequently all their effects and influence, may change, without any change in their sensible qualities. This happens sometimes, and with regard to some objects: Why may it not happen always, and with regard to all objects? What logic, what process of argument secures you

against this supposition? My practice, you say, refutes my doubts. But you mistake the purport of my question. As an agent [for example, a practicing scientist], I am quite satisfied in the point; but as a philosopher, who has some share of curiosity, I will not say scepticism, I want to learn the foundation of this inference. (Hume, *An Enquiry Concerning Human Understanding*, section IV, part II, in Selby-Bigge 1902:38)

Induction here is to be strictly distinguished from deduction. Deduction is nonampliative inference. The conclusion of a deductive inference contains no more information than do the premises, and the conclusion follows from the premises with logical certainty. If the premises are true, the conclusions must also be true. On the other hand, induction is ampliative inference. The conclusion of an inductive inference contains more information than do the premises, and the truth of the conclusion does not necessarily follow from the truth of the premises. Thus, it is possible for the premises of an inductive argument to be true and the conclusion to be false.

Hume's problem of induction has not been solved. That is, philosophers of science are unable to provide a logical demonstration of why or how it is possible to apply the results of past observations to unobserved phenomena. There is no logical justification for the prediction that the sun will rise in the east tomorrow morning, or that an apple released from the bough will fall down and not up. Simply because similar events have followed these courses in every known instance in the past does not mean one can say with the force of logical certainty that similar events will continue to do so in the future. Hence, although plausible generalizations can be used to explain past events and to predict previously undetected or unsuspected phenomena, no matter how rigorously, extensively, and intensively we test, we cannot attain certainty about future, as yet unobserved, events. We leave this problem to the philosophers, after presenting it to indicate one fundamental reason why we should not expect absolute certainty from scientific research. Nevertheless, science *is* based on the working assumption or belief by scientists that past and present regularities *are* pertinent to future events and that under similar circumstances similar phenomena will behave in the future as they have in the past and do in the present. This practical assumption of the regularity or uniformity of nature is the necessary foundation for all scientific work. Scientific descriptions, explanations, and predictions all utilize lawlike generalizations hypothesized on the presumption that natural phenomena are orderly.

Some philosophers of science continue to work on the problem of induction that Hume first described in detail. One such philosopher is Wesley Salmon, who says:

> I, too, have faith that the scientific method is especially well suited for establishing knowledge of the unobserved, but I believe this faith should be justified. It seems to me extremely important that some people should earnestly seek a solution to this problem concerning the foundations of scientific inference. (Salmon 1967:56)

Truth

Although scientists must and do assume that there is a real, orderly, knowable world, they do not believe and cannot prove that any pattern, regularity, or law is necessarily the final or certain truth about reality. Scientists do not seek absolute certainty but must, again logically speaking, base their explanations on theories and hypotheses that—with reference to currently known data and appropriate tests—are most adequately confirmed. Just what constitutes "adequate confirmation" or an "appropriate test" must be implicitly or explicitly agreed upon within each particular scientific discipline but will always involve comparison of *expected* results (that is, predictions made on the bases of theories, laws, and hypotheses) with *observed* results (the situation as actually observed among the phenomena being investigated), and an evaluation of the fit between the two (expected versus observed). Such evaluation is dependent upon the state of knowledge in the field in question, on the scope and adequacy of the theory, and on the precision of observational techniques. Obviously, hypotheses and theories can be altered in the light of new data and new tests. This means, in turn, that accepted scientific theories and laws (and all explanations and predictions based on them) are hypotheses most probably descriptive of regularities in the real world as far as is known at a given time. As scientists, we attempt to increase the scope and application of this knowledge and leave the question of its certainty to philosophers.

Hypotheses, Explanations, Laws, and Theories

In attempting to understand observed phenomena, scientific investigators formulate trial or tentative explanations that are called hypotheses. The word *hypothesis* is also used to mean any unconfirmed but testable proposition (as in Hempel 1966:19). Such hypotheses state that in given circumstances particular events are covered by—that is, are particularizations of and thus are explained by— suspected and/or confirmed laws or lawlike generalizations. The last sentence comprises a brief description of a very general covering law (CL) conception of explanation (see below, and tables 1.1, 1.2). The explanation consists of a statement more or less like this: "In these given circumstances and considering this given set of relevant suspected and/or confirmed laws, it is reasonable to expect P (the phenomenon to be explained)."

Table 1.1.

Model	Type of Law	Scope	Use
General Covering Law CL* (as used in this book)	Universal and Statistical	Classes and Particulars	Wherever appeal is made to any lawlike generalization
Deductive-Nomological CL: D-N (Hempel 1965)	Universal	Classes and Particulars	In supportive deduction of general and particular knowledge claims
Deductive-Statistical CL: D-S (Hempel 1965)	Statistical	Classes	In supportive deduction of statistical knowledge claims
Inductive-Statistical CL: I-S (Hempel 1965)	Statistical	Classes and Particulars	In supportive inference of statistical and particular knowledge claims
Statistical Relevance CL: S-R (Salmon 1967, 1971, 1973)	Statistical	Classes and Particulars	In support of knowledge claims

*All CL explanations depend ultimately on induction.

Table 1.2.

Model of Scientific Explanation	Advantages	Limitations	Test
General CL	1. Forces one to recognize that even narrative explanations ("plain story") are supported implicitly by appeals to lawlike generalizations, truisms, etc., that function as laws and that imply higher-level formulations (minitheories or macrotheories). 2. Content of conclusion can exceed that of the premises. 3. Conclusions can be drawn about particulars. 4. Can include systems theory.	1. Is very general. 2. Provides no way to distinguish causal laws from accidental regularities. 3. Requires external criteria of relevance.	Empirical checking
CL: D-N	1. If premises are true and argument form is valid, the conclusion is true. 2. Seems to fit some patterns of causal relations in nature. 3. Conclusions can be drawn about particulars. 4. Can include systems theory.	1. Conclusions can be true even if premises are false. 2. Content of conclusion cannot exceed content of premises. 3. Provides no way to distinguish causal laws from accidental regularities. 4. Requires external criteria of relevance. 5. The laws of nature it models are not logically necessary.	Empirical checking

CL: D-S	1. If premises are true and argument form is valid, the conclusion is true. 2. Seems to fit some patterns of causal relations in nature. 3. Can include systems theory.	1. Conclusions can be true even if premises are false. 2. Content of conclusion cannot exceed content of premises. 3. Cannot explain particulars. 4. Cannot be used to determine prior probabilities that must be assigned. 5. Requires high probabilities for explanation. 6. Requires total or nearly total information (maximal specificity). 7. Provides no way to distinguish causal laws from accidental regularities. 8. Requires many cases. 9. Requires external criteria of relevance. 10. The laws of nature it models are not logically necessary.	Empirical checking
CL: I I–S	1. Seems to fit some patterns of causal relations in nature. 2. Content of conclusion can exceed that of premises. 3. Can include systems theory.	1. Premises can be true and argument form correct, but the conclusion false. 2. Cannot be used to determine prior probabilities that must be assigned.	Empirical checking

Table 1.2. (Continued)

Model of Scientific Explanation	Advantages	Limitations	Test
CL: I-S		3. Requires high probabilities for explanation. 4. Provides no way to distinguish causal laws from accidental regularities. 5. Requires total or nearly total information (maximal specificity). 6. Requires many cases to establish laws.	
CL: S–R	1. Can explain particulars. 2. Can provide explanations of low probabilities. 3. Does not allow irrelevant explanatory principles. 4. Allows determination of prior probabilities that must be asigned. 5. Requires maximal specificity. 6. Can include systems theory.	1. Does not fit all patterns of causal relations in nature. 2. Provides no way to distinguish causal laws from accidental regularities. 3. Requires many cases. 4. Requires criteria of relevance.	Empirical checking

Archeology as Science

To test an explanation, an archeologist compares the proposed explanation systematically with the empirical data of, and relating to, the situation to be explained (see the discussion of testing below). Archeologists rarely test the suspected or confirmed general laws upon which their explanations depend, but such tests are similar to tests of proposed explanations (table 1.2).

Logically speaking, hypothetical explanations or possible laws can be derived from any source whatever, although practically speaking they are usually inferred from observations made on the available data in combination with the observer's knowledge of related data (and/or related laws).

There is no precise agreement among philosophers of science as to the best technical definition of "law" or "general law" (Dray 1957; Hempel 1965:264–270, 1966; chapter 5). We use the word *law* or the phrase *general law* to mean a confirmed statement describing a regularly recurring universal ("It always happens") or statistical relationship among two or more types of observable phenomena ("It happens *x* percent of the time"). A lawlike generalization is such a statement that may or may not be confirmed as a law. That is, all laws are lawlike generalizations, but all lawlike generalizations are not (confirmed) laws. Finally, not even highly confirmed laws are certain; all laws are open to modification or disconfirmation.

The difference between lawlike generalizations and empirical generalizations is also important. Hempel notes, "Lawlike sentences, whether true or false, are not just conveniently telescoped summaries of finite sets of data concerning particular instances" (Hempel 1965:377). Lawlike generalizations are general claims about phenomenal regularities, the instances of which are at least potentially infinite, whereas empirical generalizations simply describe the sum of a finite series of specific observations. Empirical generalizations are necessary and very useful in all sciences. In the initial stages of organizing a body of observations or other data, we inevitably produce a good many of them as we attempt to find patterns and regularities in the phenomena being studied. Obvious archeological examples of empirical generalizations are the traits and trait complexes prehistorians isolate to define phases or horizons as they work out the time–space systematics of a previously uninvestigated region.

Empirical generalizations are notoriously vulnerable to even a single counter example, however (Yellen 1977:8–11), and it is far more interesting and significant scientifically to explain them than simply to accumulate them. This is the issue at the heart of Binford's recent critique of Yellen (Binford 1978a:358–361).

Nevertheless, philosophers cannot adduce clear-cut criteria to distinguish empirical from lawlike generalizations, any more than they (or anyone else) can solve Hume's problem of induction (described above) or demonstrate with logical certainty that processes and events in this world really are as orderly as scientists operationally assume them to be. On the level of day-to-day work in a science, the difference between lawlike and empirical generalizations is important, but philosophically the difference is impossible to characterize precisely (see also Wylie 1981:178–179). And it must be kept in mind that even repeatedly tested and seemingly well-confirmed laws may eventually require revision, or even rejection (Hempel 1965:433).

The crux of scientific procedure is that hypotheses (that is, the possible explanations or the possible laws) are formulated tentatively and then tested empirically. To test these trial explanations or possible laws, one first infers implications from them. These implications are statements describing particular things or events that should pertain if the hypothesis is correct. Then one checks to see whether or not what these statements describe is actually the case.

In the archeological literature this procedure is often referred to as "the hypothetico-deductive (H-D) method," although as M. Salmon has pointed out (1975), this descriptive phrase is only approximately correct (see below).

If it appears that the implications *do* describe what is actually the case, then the hypothesis is so far confirmed. Ideally, the investigator tests several alternative hypotheses by checking their implications (the method of multiple working hypotheses) and devotes his or her best efforts toward falsifying the hypotheses rather than attempting merely to confirm them. The reasoning here is that if a hypothesis cannot be disconfirmed even after repeated attempts to do so, it is stronger than a hypothesis one is simply trying to confirm. This falsification approach to hypothesis testing has been developed in some detail by Karl Popper (1959) and is often identified with him.

Archeology as Science

In archeological practice, however, hypothesis testing is usually far from straightforward. Merrilee Salmon describes some of the complications and difficulties that arise in testing archeological hypotheses:

> The problem here is that hypotheses can rarely be isolated for testing. Auxiliary hypotheses regarding the likelihood of preservation of artifacts, the correctness of dating techniques, the care with which field work is undertaken, etc. are almost always intertwined with the hypothesis which is under consideration. Because of this, a false implication statement shows only that at least one of the set of hypotheses being tested jointly is false. The test gives us no clue as to which of the joint hypotheses is false. (Salmon 1976:378)

In spite of such difficulties, justification of a knowledge claim by formulation and testing of its implications ("It's so because these tests did not disconfirm it") is essential. One should not simply assert the truth of a knowledge claim ("It's so because I say so"). Formulation and empirical testing of hypotheses justify knowledge claims about the subject matter; untested assertions of knowledge claims do not.

Most archeologists would probably agree that one of their major goals or purposes is to explain some portion of the past. We believe that archeologists should understand the fundamentals of scientific procedure for testing their knowledge claims. Otherwise they cannot separate fact from fiction. We believe further that the generalized covering law (CL) conception of explanation referred to at the beginning of this section is useful because it presents the knowledge claims (trial explanations) made by archeologists as hypotheses, shows how these claims can be tested and justified, and emphasizes the necessary dependence of such claims on general statements descriptive of lawlike relationships, and on theories that subsume laws and particular explanations.

> To justify knowledge claims, one must test them: In trying to appraise the soundness of a given explanation, one will first have to attempt to reconstruct as completely as possible the argument constituting the explanation or the explanation sketch. In particular, it is important to realize what the underlying explanatory hypotheses are, and to appraise their scope and empirical foundation. A resuscitation of the assump-

tions buried under the gravestones "hence," "therefore," "because," and the like will often reveal that the explanation offered is poorly founded or downright unacceptable. In many cases, this procedure will bring to light the fallacy of claiming that a large number of details of an event have been explained when, even on a very liberal interpretation, only some broad characteristics of it have been accounted for. (Hempel 1965:238–239)

In other words, if one is aware of the logical structure of successful explanatory arguments in general, then one will be much better equipped to construct and evaluate explanations in archeology (or elsewhere). What, exactly, is to be explained? What processes are involved? What data are presented and pertinent? What laws or postulated general relationships functioning as laws are referred to? What is the status (explicit or implicit, weak or strong) of the theoretical framework subsuming these laws?

Successful explanations and the laws or possible laws to which they refer may all be subsumed by a theory. Explicit examples are models of series of relationships such as central place theory. Implicit theories underlie hunches or speculations such as, "It's my theory that that noise is caused by a jackhammer."

The ultimate goal of any science is construction of an axiomatized theory such that observed regularities can be derived from a few basic laws as premises. Such theories are used to explain past events and to predict future ones. Good theories lead to prediction of previously unsuspected regularities. Logical and mathematical axiomatic systems are essential as models of scientific theories, but no empirical science has yet been completely axiomatized. As Hempel indicates, it may ultimately turn out for any science, or for all sciences, that the goal is actually unattainable. This is a question to be determined empirically. In terms of practice, even models that are only partly axiomatized are of great utility in science. The value of a model, or of a hypothesis or a lawlike generalization or a theory does not necessarily depend on the detail with which it represents the data but on how well it supports explanations and predictions of phenomena at a given level of investigation and interest.

The Nature of Explanation

Models of Explanation

Few students of archeology acquire formal training in philosophy, but they do need basic familiarity with at least a few philosophical topics if they are to understand the debates about theory and method in the literature of the past twenty years and in current journals and books. Accordingly, in the following section we provide an introduction to the vocabulary and concepts necessary for comprehending this literature—old and new—on the philosophical underpinnings of what we do as archeologists and why.

Hempel's work on scientific explanation is central to the debates about new archeology. We begin with a summary discussion of his account of explanation, then make comparative reference to an alternative (but very closely related) model of explanation presented by Wesley Salmon. We continue with a consideration of an account of explanation that differs markedly from Hempel's (Dray's discussion of historical explanation), and conclude by discussing archeological theory with reference to these various analyses of explanation.

The Hempelian Covering Law (CL) Models of Explanation

Hempel gives the essence of his analysis as follows: "All scientific explanation involves, explicitly or by implication, a subsumption of its subject matter under general regularities; . . . it seeks to provide a systematic understanding of empirical phenomena by showing that they fit into a nomic [lawful] nexus" (Hempel 1965:488).

The phrase, "covering law model of explanation" was introduced by Dray (1957:1) and refers to the subsumption (or covering) of the particular phenomenon to be explained (the *explanadum*) by the general relationships (lawlike generalizations or general laws) cited to explain it. The laws, together with the particular circumstances in which they apply to the explanadum, are referred to as the *explanans*.

Before summarizing the Hempelian CL models of explanation, we emphasize that Hempel does not claim that these models are ethnographically descriptive of the way in which scientists either discover or present explanatory accounts. Rather his interest is in "the logical structure and the rationale of various ways in which empirical science answers explanation-seeking why-questions" (Hempel 1965:412). That is, Hempel's concern is with what is known as the logic of justification, not with the logic of discovery or with the history of actual research or discovery.

Hempel discusses two basic kinds of logical structure characterizing scientific explanation: deductive-nomological (D-N) and statistical. D-N explanations are best exemplified in the physical sciences. According to Hempel they take the form of a deductive argument which he diagrams as follows:

$$\frac{C_1, C_2, \ldots C_k}{L_1, L_2, \ldots L_r} \quad \text{Explanans}$$
$$E \quad \text{Explanandum}$$

$C_1, C_2, \ldots C_k$ are sentences that describe relevant antecedent conditions or particular facts of the phenomenon to be explained; $L_1, L_2, \ldots L_r$ are universal general laws (relevant to the kind of phenomenon to be explained); and E is the description of the empirical phenomenon to be explained. This sort of explanation

> effects a deductive subsumption of the explanandum under principles that have the character of general laws. Thus a D-N explanation answers the question *"Why* did the explanandum-phenomenon occur?" by showing that the phenomenon resulted from certain particular circumstances, specified in $C_1, C_2, \ldots C_k$, in accordance with the laws $L_1, L_2, \ldots L_r$. By pointing this out, the argument shows that, given the particular circumstances and the laws in question, the occurrence of the phenomenon *was to be expected;* and it is in this sense that the explanation enables us to *understand why* the phenomenon occurred. (Hempel 1965:337)

The example used by Hempel to illustrate the D-N form of explanation is a charming one that describes the philosopher, John Dewey,

Archeology as Science

washing dishes at the kitchen sink. Dewey notices that when he places a newly washed glass upside down on a plate, soap bubbles grow out from under the rim of the glass, hold their shapes for a brief interval, and finally recede under the rim. He wonders why this happens. The explanation he arrives at is a D-N explanation as follows: The dishwater is considerably hotter than the surrounding air. The glass is heated by this dishwater, but on being transferred to the plate it traps cool air inside it. The cool air is warmed by the hot glass, expands into the soap film beneath the rim, and blows bubbles out from under it until the glass and the air inside it cools to room temperature. Then the air inside the glass contracts and the bubbles collapse.

With reference to the diagram presented above: $C_1, C_2, \ldots C_k$ are the particular relevant facts about Dewey's dishwashing arrangement (the glasses had been submerged in soapy dishwater hotter than the air in the kitchen, they were turned upside down on a plate so that a puddle of soapy water formed under them, etc.). $L_1, L_2, \ldots L_r$ are physical laws about behavior of gases and of soap bubbles and about transfer of heat between bodies of different temperatures. E is the conclusion Dewey drew after considering these two groups of facts together.

An example of D-N explanation more familiar to archeologists is the revelation of the Piltdown forgery (Weiner, Oakley, and Clark 1953; Weiner et al. 1955). The famous "Piltdown Man" fossils found in Sussex, England, in 1912 were disputed or ignored by some students of human biological evolution but completely accepted by others for decades until definitely identified as fakes by shrewd analytical work performed at the British Museum of Natural History in the early 1950s. The explanandum is a description of an association in the same ancient geological horizon of an undeniably (indeed, nearly modern) human cranium with an undeniably apelike mandible. Some scientists explained this fossil find by saying it was the remains of a "missing link" kind of protohuman or half-human creature, just the sort of thing to be expected if *Homo sapiens* did indeed evolve from primitive, apelike ancestors. An alternative explanation that was suggested from time to time, then finally tested and shown to be correct by J. S. Weiner and his colleagues, was that the fossil was a hoax. Weiner et al.'s explanation of the Piltdown specimens rests on relevant facts ($C_1, C_2, C_3, \ldots C_K$) about the discovery of the bones by the amateur paleontologist, Charles Dawson, about their condition (found by accident in a jumbled and poorly documented geological rather than archeological context in the same general area as fragments of bone from nonhuman animals, the alleged ancient human bones—on being closely examined and tested for mineral and organic content—showed traces of dye and indications of nonrandom mechanical abrasion on the jaw and teeth, as well as a large and statistically significant difference in chemical composition between cranium and jaw, etc.); and on laws ($L_1, L_2, L_3, \ldots L_r$) about the nature and behavior of ground water; about the behavior of ground water and animal bone in long-term contact; about the relationship between the detailed morphology of mammalian teeth and jaws and the gross anatomy and functioning of those body parts in the living animal, etc. E is Weiner et al.'s conclusion after considering these two sets of facts together: the Piltdown find is a fake.

The other form of explanation described by Hempel is *statistical explanation,* in which reference is made to one or more laws describing statistical probabilities. Radiocarbon dating, for example, makes use of statistical laws.

Statistical laws differ from the laws of D-N explanations in that D-N laws attribute a certain characteristic to *all* members of a particular class (hence, they are called universal laws), whereas statistical laws attribute a certain characteristic to a specific *percentage* of class members only. According to Hempel, statistical laws are used in two kinds of explanation: deductive-statistical (D-S) and inductive-statistical (I-S).

D-S explanation is illustrated by the classic probability exercise of flipping a fair coin. It is wrong to say that after a long run of heads the next toss will be more likely to yield tails than heads. Why? The explanation involves a premise comprising two laws of probability: (1) flipping a fair coin yields heads 50 percent of the time (heads occur with a probability of one-half); and (2) the result of each coin toss is independent of every other coin toss. These two laws imply deductively that the probability for tails to come up after a long run of heads is still one in two. Hempel says,

Archeology as Science

> D-S explanations . . . involve the deduction of a statement in the form of a statistical law from an explanans that contains indispensably at least one law or theoretical principle of statistical form. . . . What a D-S explanation accounts for is thus always a general uniformity expressed by a presumptive law of statistical form. (Hempel 1965:381)

The most familiar example to archeologists of events and processes governed by D-S laws is radiocarbon dating. The rate of decay of 14_C atoms (a rate that is independent of the age of any one such atom at any one time) has been determined with such precision that physicists utilizing this D-S law can determine the age of archeologically recovered carbon samples with great accuracy.

I-S explanation differs from both D-N and D-S explanation in that an I-S explanandum is not deductively implied by I-S premises but is only indicated with some degree of inductive support. If a jar contains 999 black marbles and 1 white marble, one could explain why a blindfolded person drew a black marble by specifying those facts and coming to the conclusion that anyone reaching into the jar for a marble would almost certainly come up with a black one because the probability of drawing a black marble is close to one and the probability of drawing a white marble is close to zero. Nevertheless, a person reaching into the jar *could* get a white marble; hence, as stated above, the explanatory conclusion does not follow deductively from the premises but only with (in this case quite strong) inductive support.

There are other characteristics of I-S explanation that distinguish it from D-N and D-S explanation. Foremost among these is what Hempel refers to as the *epistemic ambiguity* of I-S explanation. This ambiguity arises because statistical or probabilistic laws by their very nature partition phenomena into classes. An individual event may fall into any one of several such classes. The consequences resulting from the presence of the event in one class may be quite different from the consequences of the presence of the event in a different class. Hempel illustrates the epistemic ambiguity of I-S explanation by referring to a man who suffers from a streptococcal infection. If he is given penicillin treatment, then the chances of his recovery are very high, *unless* the particular streptococcal strain he harbors is resistant to penicillin. In that case, his chances for recovery as a result of penicillin treatment are very low.

Similarly, if the man is highly allergic to penicillin, then a massive dose of it may kill him rather than cure him. Thus, the specific individual event (this man's illness from streptococcal infection) may fall into any one of the three reference classes mentioned: treatment with penicillin in normal circumstances, so chances of recovery are very high; treatment with penicillin but streptococcal strain is penicillin-resistant so chances for recovery are very low; treatment with penicillin but the patient is highly allergic to penicillin and dies from the reaction.

An archeological example of the sort of epistemic ambiguity to which Hempel is referring arises from the fact that the physicochemical properties of different plant species affect their radiocarbon determinations differently. Suppose that an archeologist is excavating a series of Mississippian house structures. The roofs of several of these are found to have been burned in a brief, very hot fire so that great masses of thatch from each of them are completely charred. The chances for abundant and accurate radiocarbon determinations on this series of individual structures are excellent unless some or all of the thatching material consists entirely or in part of C4 pathway grasses (Browman 1981:268–279). Uncorrected determinations of C4 pathway grasses are significantly too young. Here, then, there are three reference classes: normal radiocarbon determination of non-C4 pathway organic materials yielding valid results; normal radiocarbon determination of C4 pathway organic materials yielding invalid results; corrected radiocarbon determination of C4 pathway organic materials yielding valid results.

Because of the ambiguity of I-S explanations, Hempel stresses that the total information potentially of explanatory relevance should be considered before a decision is made about the acceptability of a proposed probabilistic explanation. To make this task as easy as possible, one should define as narrowly as possible the reference class to which the specific individual event belongs. For example, to evaluate the radiocarbon determinations on the Mississippian house, we need to know not just that the determinations come from a burned house roof but also whether the roofing material is grass or some other substance and, if grass, whether or not the grass is a C4 pathway species.

Salmon's Statistical Relevance Model of Explanation

The philosopher Wesley Salmon believes that statistical laws are of central importance in scientific explanation. He offers a statistical-relevance (S-R) model of explanation (W. Salmon 1967, 1971b, c, 1975b). Although Salmon's model, like Hempel's, characterizes explanations as nomological, that is, as being based on laws (Salmon 1971c:78), Salmon's statistical-relevance model differs from Hempel's CL model in a number of ways. First, in the case of inductive explanation (Hempel's I-S model), Salmon believes that the required relationship between the explanans and the explanandum need not be one of high probability as Hempel does, but rather can be of low probability. Salmon says that statistical relevance is a significant relation between explanans and explanandum; it is not an attribution of a specific degree of probability to either. Further, "To say that a factor is *statistically relevant* to the occurrence of an event means, roughly, that *it makes a difference to the probability of that occurrence*— that is, the probability of the event is different in the presence of that factor than in its absence" (Salmon 1971c:11).

Salmon contrasts his S-R model to Hempel's I-S model in two respects by saying that the I-S model (1) characterizes explanation as an *argument* and (2) renders the explanandum highly probable, whereas the S-R model characterizes an explanation not (1) as an argument but (2) as *an assembly of facts statistically relevant to the explanandum,* regardless of the degree of probability of the results (Salmon 1971c:11). Salmon also does not require that S-R explanations be arguments in which the conclusion (the explanandum or event to be explained) follows logically from the premises (the explanans), and thus his S-R model differs fundamentally from Hempel's CL model. Elsewhere Salmon says that "relations of statistical relevance must be explained on the basis of causal relevance" (Salmon 1973:400; this position is further discussed in W. Salmon 1975a and b). It is perhaps difficult at first to understand how causal relevance can be exhibited in the absence of an argument that describes the effect as a result of the cause. And, in fact, causality is a difficult philosophical issue. For Hume, specifying causal relations is a part of the whole problem of induction:

> There is no object, which implies the existence of any other if we consider these objects in themselves, and never look beyond the ideas which we form of them. . . . 'Tis therefore by *experience* only, that we can infer the existence of one object from that of another. The nature of experience is this. We remember to have had frequent instances of the existence of one species of objects; and also remember, that the individuals of another species of objects have always attended them, and have existed in a regular order of contiguity and succession with regard to them. . . . In all those instances, from which we learn the conjunction of particular causes and effects, both the causes and effects have been perceiv'd by the senses, and are remember'd: But in all cases, wherein we reason concerning them, there is only one perceiv'd or remember'd, and the other is supply'd in conformity to our past experience. . . . [But] From the mere repetition of any past impression, even to infinity, there never will arise any new original idea, such as that of a necessary connection. . . . If reason determin'd us, it wou'd proceed upon that principle, *that instances, of which we have had no experience, must resemble those, of which we have had experience, and that the course of nature continues always uniformly the same.* . . . There can be no *demonstrative* arguments to prove *that those instances, of which we have had no experience, resemble those, of which we have had experience.* . . . For 'twill readily be allow'd, that the several instances we have of the conjunction of resembling causes and effects are in themselves entirely independent, and that the communication of motion, which I see result at present from the shock of two billiard-balls, is totally distinct from that which I saw result from such an impulse a twelve-month ago. (Selby-Bigge 1888:86, 87, 88, 89, 164)

Hempel considers causal explanation as a kind of deductive explanation:

> *Causal explanation* is a special type of deductive explanation; for a certain event or set of events can be said to have caused a specified "effect" only if there are general laws connecting the former with the latter in such a way that, given a description of the antecedent events, the occurrence of the effect can be deduced with the help of the laws. (Hempel 1965:300–301)

Archeology as Science

In Salmon's view, causal relations need not be conceived as deterministic, and he considers them to be "a species of statistical relevance relations" (Salmon 1977:165, n. 30). Salmon says that "a causal explanation of a statistical regularity is a description of how that statistical regularity arises out of causal connections among events (or types of events) in the world. Such an explanation is not an argument. . . . It is, instead, more like a model of the universe in which the causal nexus is displayed" (W. Salmon 1975a:168). Thus, "the explanation may provide the materials from which an argument can be constructed, but the argument itself is *not* an integral part of the explanation" (W. Salmon 1975b:119).

Although it may still be somewhat difficult to understand how statistical relevance can mean causal relevance and yet not be an argument from cause to effect, other features of Salmon's model do make it appealing to archeologists (and others who are concerned with statistical generalizations). One such feature is the important role played in actual scientific explanation by inductive logic. As indicated in the reference to Hume's problem of induction, although practicing scientists proceed in a generally hypothetico-deductive fashion to test speculations or hypotheses, acceptance of tested hypotheses as *confirmed* (and hence as most probably true of the world) requires further an inductive leap of faith from the observed and experienced to the unobserved and unexperienced. As Salmon reiterates: "There is no rule that tells one when to accept an hypothesis or when to reject it; instead there is a rule of practical behavior that prescribes that we so act as to maximize our expectation of utility" (Salmon 1971b:77).

To act on this rule of practical behavior one must know at least rough probabilities for explanandum events. For example, given the occurrence of event A, it either is a good bet or it is not a good bet that B will also occur because we know that x percent of the time in the past, in circumstances C (which pertain here), when A (a set or complex of events or processes) occurred, then so did B (a different set of events or complex of events or processes).

Salmon exhibits use of the practical rule with respect to the various reference classes to which the explanandum event (that is, the particular event to be explained) can be referred. One example he uses is that of determining the probability that a particular man will be alive ten years from now (Salmon 1971b:42). In working out the probability, one considers age, sex, occupation, and health to be relevant, but such variables as car license number are irrelevant (some detailed discussion of Salmon's model in general and of reference classes in particular is provided by Lehman 1972 and Salmon 1973). That is, the relative frequency of survival for the next ten years is expected to vary significantly among reference classes of the following kinds: humans, Americans, American males, 42-year-old American males, 42-year-old American male steeplejacks, and 42-year-old American male steeplejacks suffering from advanced cases of lung cancer. Each partition of the class of American males into subclasses according to age, occupation, and health is relevant to the problem of determining the probability of survival over the next ten years. Although one can imagine cases to the contrary, on the basis of present knowledge it is unlikely that partition into subclasses according to car license number would be relevant to the problem. That is, we would predict relative frequency of survival for the next ten years to be the same in the following three classes: 42-year-old American male steeplejacks with advanced cases of lung cancer; 42-year-old American male steeplejacks with advanced cases of lung cancer whose license plate digits end in an odd number; and 42-year-old American male steeplejacks with advanced cases of lung cancer whose license plate digits end in an even number.

An archeological example of the kind of reference classes Salmon is discussing can be generated by assessing the probability that the archeological deposits in a rockshelter in the hills of north central Tennessee will remain undisturbed for the next five years. Relevant factors for determining the probability are the ownership of the land where the shelter is situated (private or public land; if private, the attitude of the landowner); the stability of the ownership; the location of the shelter with respect to the ranges of local hunters, cave explorers, and relic collectors; and the conspicuousness of the shelter and of the archeological materials. An irrelevant factor is the composition of the rock forming the overhang. For example, preservation chances for the next five years would be approximately the same for the following classes: an open, dolomitic limestone rockshelter on public land with a scatter of chert flakes in and near it adjacent to a jeep trail in a region where two active relic collectors are known to be operating; an open, sandstone rockshelter on public land with a scatter of chert flakes in and near it adjacent to a jeep trail in a region where two active relic collectors are known to be operating; and an open, oolitic limestone rockshelter on public land with a scatter of chert flakes in and near it adjacent to a jeep trail in a region where two active relic collectors are known to be operating.

Merrilee Salmon (1975:463–464) stresses the compatibility of the S-R model with an emphasis on systems because she believes that systems proponents are trying to come to grips with relevance. To the extent that this is true, she is correct (but see Salmon 1978; and chapter 2 here). However, to the extent that systems proponents believe a systems approach to be alternative to concern with laws and lawlike generalizations (Tuggle, Townsend, and Riley 1972; Flannery 1973), those systems proponents part company with the S-R model. As already noted, Salmon's S-R model is nomological: S-R explanations make reference to laws. For that matter, a systems approach necessitates continual consideration of laws relating the elements of the system to one another, or relating one system to another system (Hempel 1965:297–330, 403–410; R. Watson 1976b; chapter 2 here), or relating the whole system at one time to the whole system at another time. Thus it is incorrect to present a systems approach as though it were an alternative to a nomological approach.

The Parity of Explanation and Prediction

Both Salmon's model and Hempel's model include specific reference to the *parity* or *symmetry* of explanation with prediction. Confirmed explanations of particular events and processes or of general regularities provide the bases for constructing theories that can be used to make reliable predictions about the future.

> It is this potential predictive force which gives scientific explanation its importance: only to the extent that we are able to explain empirical facts can we attain the major objective of scientific research, namely not merely to record the phenomena of our experience, but to learn from them, by basing upon them theoretical generalizations which enable us to antic-

ipate new occurrences and to control, at least to some extent, the changes in our environment. (Hempel and Oppenheim 1953:323)

> To explain an event is to provide the best possible grounds we could have had for making predictions concerning it. . . . To explain an event is to show to what degree it was to be expected, and this degree may be translated into practical predictive behavior such as wagering on it. In some cases the explanation will show that the explanandum event was not to be expected, but that does not destroy the symmetry of explanation and prediction. The symmetery consists in the fact that the explanatory facts constitute the fullest possible basis for making a prediction of whether or not the event would occur. To explain an event is not to predict it ex post facto, but a complete explanation does provide complete grounds for rational prediction concerning that event. Thus, the present account of explanation does sustain a thoroughgoing symmetry thesis, and this symmetry is not refuted by explanations having low probability weights (Salmon 1971b:79).

However, some philosophers of science do not agree that explanation and prediction are logically symmetrical, for example, Scriven (1962). Practically speaking, explanation may be possible only after an event, and thus prediction in such a case would be a *practical* impossibility. We believe Hempel has shown adequately that there is *logical* symmetry between explanation and prediction. We do not discuss the matter further here (but see Hempel 1963:116–120; 1965:364–376; and also Brodbeck 1962).

Systematization and Causation

Both Hempel and Salmon believe that systematization is essential to scientific knowledge. Hempel (1965:488) says that "all scientific explanation involves explicitly or by implication, a subsumption of its subject matter under general regularities; that it seeks to provide a systematic understanding of empirical phenomena by showing that they fit into a nomic nexus." The goal of scientists is to construct theories expressing the structure of this nomic nexus in the most effective, efficient, and precise manner possible. Thus Hempel says,

> Theories are usually introduced when previous study of a class of phenomena has revealed a system of uniformities that can be expressed in

the form of empirical laws. Theories then seek to explain those regularities and, generally, to afford a deeper and more accurate understanding of the phenomena in question. To this end, a theory construes those phenomena as manifestations of entities and processes that lie behind or beneath them, as it were. These are assumed to be governed by characteristic theoretical laws, or theoretical principles, by means of which the theory then explains the empirical uniformities that have been previously discovered, and usually also predicts "new" regularities of similar kinds. (Hempel 1966:70)

Salmon makes similar statements, although he emphasizes causal relations: "To give scientific explanations is to show how events and statistical regularities fit into the causal network of the world" (1977:162). But he also indicates elsewhere that there may be important differences between explanations of regularities and explanations of particulars. There may be

deep significance to the distinction between the attempt to explain particular events and the attempt to explain general regularities (even though the distinction itself may be very difficult to characterize). . . . Although explanation of particular events has its place (usually in applied science), scientific comprehension seems to demand theoretical explanations of general regularities in nature, and our intellectual curiosity cannot be satisfied without them. It appears that the most pressing philosophical problems concerning scientific explanation center upon the nature of theoretical explanation. (Salmon 1971a:109, 110)

Here Salmon is referring to the ultimate goal of science: construction of formal theories (see also W. Salmon 1975b). We discuss archeological theory in the following section and in the section on archeology as science as well as in chapter 5, but first we turn to one other relevant topic in the voluminous literature on explanation: explanation in history.

Explanation in History

Historical explanation is relevant to us because archeology is a study of the past in which the archeological record supplements and complements or takes the place of historical documents. Some scholars argue that explanations in history are sufficiently different from those in the natural sciences or even the social sciences so that historical explanation is logically distinct from scientific (or social scientific) explanation. Perhaps the most extreme is Michael Oakeshott, who stresses the uniqueness of historical events and defines historical explanation as "a full account of change" for which no reference to laws is necessary (Oakeshott 1933:143; and see below in the discussion of Dray). Another historian, Collingwood, states that historical explanations are the result of historians entering into states of mind similar to those of the people whose activities are to be explained (1946; see below).

Others believe that explanation in history has the same logical structure as explanation in the natural sciences (Hempel 1942; Nagel 1961; Popper 1959; Rescher 1970; Rudner 1966). In a classic paper, Hempel states that explanations in history are of the same logical form as explanations in the empirical sciences (Hempel 1942, reprinted in Hempel 1965:231–243). Dray disagrees with Hempel because Dray believes history is one of the humanities rather than one of the sciences and that historians are critics rather than scientists (Dray 1957, 1964: chs. 1–4). Dray says that philosophers of science who insist that history is or ought to be scientific ignore or underemphasize some crucial features of historical inquiry, which he summarizes as follows:

> Those features . . . are a mode of explanation which does not obviously proceed by subsumption under general laws; an approach to the construction of a history which includes a concern for "assessment" as well as mere "truth-telling"; and a concept of causal connection which involves moral as well as inductive considerations. (Dray 1964:59)

As to explanation without subsumption under general laws, Dray notes that Hempel's later discussions of models of explanation include a weak form of CL explanation based on probabilistic laws (the I-S model). Many historical explanations conform to the I-S model rather than the D-N (or D-S) model. Downplaying the fact that I-S explanations are still nomological, Dray criticizes Hempel for loosening the requirements of his original D-N model:

> A theory that begins by elaborating the essential meaning of explanation a priori, rather than trying to discover what the practitioners of the discipline concerned themselves call explanation, is surely on weak

ground when it relaxes its requirements in the face of difficulties of application (Dray 1964:7).

But in their original article Hempel and Oppenheim note the problems and difficulties involved in analyzing explanations that include statistical laws (Hempel and Oppenheim 1953:324). Hempel would deny that he revised his model because of difficulty of application by historians or others. As noted above, he utilizes his model to test knowledge claims and does not intend it to be a summary description of how scientists actually work.

Despite Dray's rejection of Hempel's formulations of the CL model, Dray does say that *"what* a historian explains (if he is clearheaded enough to ask a precise question) must be specifiable in general terms" (1964:9). The real question, he continues, is whether the historian—having specified the general issue that concerns him—can properly claim to have explained it without showing that it follows in accord with laws from other events also specified in general terms. Dray does not address adequately the issue of implicit as well as explicit reference to general laws. Dray refers to Michael Oakeshott, who, as noted, occupies an extremist anti-CL position and who claims, "The moment historical facts are regarded as instances of general laws, history is dismissed" (Oakeshott 1933:154). "The method of the historian is never to explain by means of generalization . . . [but] by means of greater and more complete detail" (Oakeshott 1933:143).

Oakeshott's alternative to the CL conception of explanation is referred to by Dray as a "continuous series" model. He defines this as giving an explanation by detailing the events intervening between the two events whose conjunction is to be explained, for example, the court policy of Louis XIV and the outbreak of the French Revolution. A historical explanation of these events, according to Oakeshott, consists simply of a detailed tracing of the relations between the classes in France at the time in question and makes no reference to laws.

The CL theorist's reply is that the explanatory events are "related" only insofar as they follow from each other in accordance with relevant general laws or lawlike generalizations. If the reference to laws is not explicit, then it is implicit. What other sense of continuity or relation between events is possible?

However, Dray denies that historians would accept the notion that what they are doing is applying the CL model at every stage in a continuous series explanation, i.e., he maintains that CL subsumption is not the historian's criterion of historical connectedness. He concludes that Oakeshott establishes at least the point that subsumption under law cannot constitute a *sufficient* condition for giving an explanation in history (that is, such subsumption must be supplemented in some way).

Other objections to the application of the CL model are raised by other historians, one of the most prominent and persuasive of whom is R. G. Collingwood (1946). Collingwood emphasizes that history is concerned with thinking human beings whose actions are affected by internal processes (their thoughts) to which the historian-observer has no immediate or easy access. Human actions can be explained only by reference to the thoughts of human agents because actions express thoughts. To explain an action by referring to an agent's thoughts does not necessitate subsumption under general laws. Instead, Collingwood says, to understand and hence to explain an action a historian must put himself in the place of the agent and try to recreate the agent's thought processes. The object of this endeavor is to clarify the purpose or the rationale of the agent's action, from the inside out as it were. "When the historian can see that the agent's beliefs, purposes, principles, etc., give him a reason for doing what he did, then he can claim to understand the action" (Dray 1964:12). Dray refers to this kind of explanation in history as "rational explanation"; it is also called the empathic or "Verstehen" model. (*Verstehen* is a German word meaning to understand or comprehend.)

Hempel discusses this empathic approach to explanation in history and concludes that it does not embody an alternative to the CL form of explanation, that it is not a method of explanation at all, but rather a means for generating explanatory hypotheses (Hempel 1965:239–240). Archeologists also often generate hypotheses by trying to put themselves mentally in the places of the ancient people they study to predict site locations, what local resources were exploited, and other past behavioral patterns. This is one way to derive hypotheses possibly explanatory of an archeological situation, but it is

Archeology as Science

usually less satisfactory than basing hypotheses on probability sampling of data from the region being studied.

Collingwood's defenders maintain that Hempel's discussion is irrelevant to what Collingwood means. Collingwood is attempting to draw attention to the historians' criterion of intelligibility or connectedness (referred to above in the discussion of Oakeshott): To explain an action, it is enough to show that it follows rationally from an agent's thoughts.

Hempelians reply to this that such explanation is not complete unless a further assumption is made that at the time in question the agent was a rational agent and was disposed to act appropriately (i.e., rationally) in the given situation. And this is an implicit assumption of a lawlike generalization about human behavior. So the explanation has a CL form, something like this: "A rational agent, when in a situation of kind C, will invariably (or with high probability) do X" (Dray 1964:14). And it is enough for nomological explanation if X means no more than "behave rationally."

Followers of Collingwood, however, deny that this additional assumption is necessary before historians can claim understanding of the agent's action. Perhaps their nomological assumptions are not explicit, but formal justification of their knowledge claims requires that they be made explicit. In describing what some historians do, Collingwood apparently believes that he has fully characterized historical explanation. Hempel goes further to uncover the implicit lawlike generalizations that justify the historians' knowledge claims. As mentioned above, this is a difference of interest in the logic of discovery (Collingwood) and the logic of justification (Hempel).

The second feature of historical inquiry listed by Dray has to do with objectivity, the issue here being whether historians can, or should, try to reconstruct the past "just as it was." Can historians' conclusions be true in a sense that is independent of the unique perspectives manifested by individual scholars? Is there any sense in which one can speak of historians' accounts as "objectively true"? This concern is often alluded to in discussions between idiographic (particularizing) and nomothetic (generalizing) archeologists, particularists accusing generalists of distorting the evidence to fit preconceived molds (explicit hypotheses), while the latter accuse the former of operating covertly with implicit but unacknowledged hypotheses so that their work cannot be adequately evaluated.

Dray presents various sides of the argument and concludes that history is different from science because value-free historical reconstruction is not possible. He takes this to mean that history cannot be objective as science is. Historians must select for study a period and a place (or a few comparative periods and places) they believe to be important or significant. Such selection certainly involves value judgments. Historians also must rely on standards (value judgments) about what is important within the selected study area. Even if one of the goals is to interpret historical events by means of the standards and beliefs held by the historical participants themselves, historians still must choose which participants (or classes of participants) to investigate: "In writing the history of the Roman invasion of Britain, do we adopt the standards of the Romans or the Britons?" (Dray 1964:39). The answer is that a fair historian tries to do justice to both.

Thus, Dray's opinion—which he takes to be in opposition to that of philosophers and others who believe historians should be more scientific—is that history is unavoidably a value-laden pursuit, whereas he believes science to be a value-free pursuit (see also the next section of this chapter). In fact, of course, science is just as value-laden in this sense as is history and all other fields of study (Rudner 1966:73–83).

The difference between scientists and historians is not nearly so distinct as Dray describes it. As discussed further in the next section, scientists choose what events or processes to study from many possibilities; they make value judgments about what is important or interesting; they decide what observations to make to answer their questions (chosen from a wide range of possible approaches); they must decide how many observations are sufficient to confirm or disconfirm their ideas about the specific subject, and whether possible alternative observations are necessary or desirable; and they must present their observational results and their conclusions in sufficient detail for their colleagues to evaluate their work. This is exactly parallel to what careful historians do (the last two steps correspond to the detailing of evidence from documents and inferences from doc-

Archeology as Science

uments to support the historian's conclusions about the relationship between two or more historical events).

We conclude that Dray's characterization of history does not show that the justification of historical knowledge is formally different from that of scientific knowledge. It is just that much historical work is not explicitly scientific. Claims to historical knowledge are justified in the same way as are claims to scientific knowledge, and thus history is just as objective as science. If history *were* confined to untestable knowledge claims, as Collingwood suggests (but implicitly denies as his faith in the regular operation of human rationality in the past shows), then historical accounts would indeed be no better than historical fiction. However, empirical study of human action gives us general criteria for distinguishing history from historical fiction, just as empirical study of physical phenomena gives us general criteria for distinguishing science from science fiction. No historical or scientific account is certain, but some are better than others, and we can find out which by checking their scope, accuracy, utility, and degree of confirmation.

Our comments on Dray's third feature of historical inquiry—causal explanation in history—are in many ways similar to those on objectivity in history. Because of the large number of possible significant variables in any given historical situation and because thinking human beings are always involved, Dray believes that the causal conclusions of historians contain not only inductive considerations (in Hempelian terms, the explanations are of the probability-based or I-S form) but also moral judgments about the behavior of the historical human participants. Historians do not use the term *cause* to mean sufficient condition, he says, but rather the historian's reason for singling out one or a few relevant conditions from a possible multitude of relevant conditions involves evaluation on moral grounds of the human actions in question.

Because our interest is in a generalized CL concept, not in just the D-N model, we see no problem with the assessment of causal historical explanations (including many archeological explanations) as being based on probability generalizations. Many scientific explanations are of the I-S form.

As for the moral judgments that Dray finds to be ingredients in causal explanation in history, he makes it quite clear that he is speaking of the actual behavior of some practicing historians in selecting among a variety of possible causal factors (Dray 1964:55). Moral grounds are probably difficult ones from which to seek laws and to construct a theory of history, and there is no a priori reason why this approach should lead to significant explanations. (Nevertheless, such explanations are, as indicated below, logically of the same form as any other CL explanation.) Neither is there an a priori reason why decisions about what were the most important or most significant events in a proposed causal array could not be made by examining sufficient causes that are, for example, in the realm of economics rather than morality. Dray and others assume without adequate defense that the causes of human action are more importantly moral than, say, economic. However, what is important to our point here is that the moral explanations he proposes make explicit or implicit reference to confirmed or suspected laws of human behavior that are part of a general, theoretical, nomological framework that encompasses the subject matter of history. In history and in many of the social sciences, there is no agreement on a single framework of laws for the various aspects of human behavior each studies. Therefore, some theorists deny that these fields are sciences or argue that they cannot be sciences until or unless they are comprehended under a unified theory. Others believe them to be partly scientific and partly not. Still others accept them as scientific as long as practitioners, while adhering to empirically based methods, seek to increase knowledge of their subject matter in a systematic manner. We think it obvious that all are scientific to the extent that their knowledge claims are explicitly or implicitly justified with reference to theories that exhibit a generalized CL form.

The most powerful sciences are those that have axiomatized unified theories. We believe that archeology is such a complex subject that it may be quite a long time (if ever) before anything resembling a unified or axiomatized theory is developed and accepted by a majority of practicing archeologists. There seems to be only one potential candidate at present (Dunnell 1980b, 1982b; see chapter 5 here), and it is too early to tell how that candidate will fare. However, we remain as convinced as we were ten years ago that progress toward

Archeology as Science 35

a grand theory—or a set of interlocking or complementary lesser theories—encompassing archeology depends on archeologists being explicit about their assumptions, research designs, and goals. In other words, we stress once more the importance of stating fully and clearly how archeological knowledge claims are supported by the laws and theories that subsume them. This requires both an understanding of the logic of justification as presented here and a recognition of the fact that procedures of discovery such as Collingwood's are only part of the full story of the acquisition and grounding of scientific knowledge.

We conclude our précis of some of Dray's writings on the philosophy of history with a sentence in which he seems to admit that no hard and fast conclusions can be drawn at the present time about the *structure* of history as a discipline, about the relationship of that structure to the behavior of historians, or about the relationship of the structure of history to that of other disciplines (such as the natural or social sciences):

> What critical philosophy of history must make clear is the extent, if any, to which such features can be represented as part of the *structure* of the inquiry—derivable, that is, from its "idea"—rather than just *facts*, interesting or otherwise, about the way most historians happen to operate. (Dray 1964:59)

Our own position with regard to history is the same as our position with regard to archeology: the documents of history (or, in the case of prehistory, the archeological record) can be used either primarily idiographically or primarily nomothetically depending on the goals of the investigator. Practical difficulties in retrieving and manipulating the data will be encountered that are probably greater for the archeologist than for the historian, but in neither case are these data *intrinsically* usable *only* idiographically (contrary to Oakeshott) any more than the data analyzed by natural scientists are intrinsically usable *only* nomothetically. Although many, perhaps most, historians are closer to the idiographic end of this spectrum than the nomothetic one, this does not mean that they work unscientifically. In the discussions of archeological theory during the 1960s and 1970s, there was often a tendency to equate an idiographic emphasis with a nonscientific approach and a nomothetic emphasis with a scientific approach. Such an equation is incorrect. A scientific approach simply necessitates a search for possible explanations (that is, hypothetical formulations) of seeming regularities, with the important provision that both the possible explanations and the seeming regularities must be empirically testable. That is, one's research and conclusions must be confirmable or disconfirmable by other investigators. However—as we stress repeatedly—although formulating and testing hypotheses is necessary to the advancing of knowledge in any field, the scope and content of possible explanations and regularities depend on the experience, interests, and skills of individual scientists. (For further discussion of these and related issues, see chapter 4 and the next section of this chapter on archeology as science).

Before concluding this portion of chapter 1, we need to consider one other aspect of science and the scientific method: What degree of congruence is possible and/or required between the idealized model of scientific procedure provided by philosophers and the actual behavior of practicing scientists?

Do Scientists Work Scientifically? Thomas Kuhn and the Sociology of Science

In 1962 Thomas Kuhn, a historian of science originally trained as a physicist, published *The Structure of Scientific Revolutions,* which created a considerable furor in the academic world, especially among social scientists and philosophers of science. The book is fascinating and stimulating for a number of reasons, but for our purposes here, we need consider only two of the points it raises: (1) whether scientists really work scientifically (that is, in accordance with the scientific method as traditionally defined); and (2) the significance for a scientific discipline or community of Kuhn's concept of the "paradigm."

(1) Many people who read Kuhn's original explication (Kuhn 1962) received the impression that he was characterizing science as being a basically irrational pursuit, dominated by fads. They took him to be showing that switches from old beliefs to new ones are achieved

Archeology as Science

not by rational evaluation of empirical results but by wholesale conversion—much like a religious experience—from one theoretical persuasion to another.

Kuhn himself denies this interpretation and has recently rebutted it specifically and at some length (Kuhn 1977: chap. 3). The point he was making, he says, is not that scientists ignore rational criteria for choosing one theory over another but rather that the evaluations and conclusions different scientists draw from consideration of the same basic criteria (accuracy, consistency, scope, etc.) may, and usually do, differ. Why? Kuhn answers,

> Perhaps they interpret simplicity differently or have different conclusions about the range of fields within which the consistency criterion must be met. Or perhaps they agree about these matters but differ about the relative weights to be accorded to these or to other criteria when several are deployed together. With respect to divergences of this sort, no set of choice criteria yet proposed is of any use. . . . One must deal with characteristics which vary from one scientist to another without thereby in the least jeopardizing their adherence to the canons that make science scientific. Though such canons do exist and should be discoverable, they are not by themselves sufficient to determine the decisions of individual scientists. (Kuhn 1977:324–325)

Kuhn says that the differences among the conclusions drawn by different scientists operating under the same general set of rules stem from each individual's unique experience within the scientific field, from factors in the cultural milieu outside the specific scientific field, and from personality differences. He concludes,

> Every individual choice between competing theories depends on a mixture of objective and subjective factors, or of shared and individual criteria. Since the latter have not ordinarily figured in the philosophy of science, my emphasis upon them has made my belief in the former hard for my critics to see. (Kuhn 1977:325)

Thus, Kuhn says, scientists *do* behave scientifically, but there is a strong subjective element in all their scientific behavior. He concludes that the criteria of choice (accuracy, consistency, etc.) do not actually function as *rules* to *determine* choice but rather as *values* that *influence* choice (Kuhn 1977:331); but then he admits that he cannot answer the question of how such a value-based enterprise can progress as we know a science does, producing more and more accurate predictions and better and better techniques and controls. Nevertheless, he insists that the inevitably present subjective behavior of practicing scientists has deep philosophical significance and must be taken into account by philosophers of science. "Essential aspects of the process generally known as verification will be understood only by recourse to the features with respect to which men may differ while still remaining scientists" (Kuhn 1977:334).

Kuhn thus deliberately throws the subjective element into the center of philosophical discussion about verification or justification procedures in science. He questions the validity of the long-recognized distinction between the context of discovery and the context of justification (Kuhn 1977:327).

As indicated several times above, we believe that this traditional dichotomy is valuable and important. We discuss Kuhn's opposing view briefly here because it has been adopted by many social scientists.

First, Kuhn is *not* saying that scientists (physicists, for example) are actually unscientific in their professional work. Yet this is what many people apparently do understand as one of the major points, if not *the* main point of his book (Kuhn 1977:320–321). From the supposed revelation that working scientists do not actually behave in a scientific way, many social scientists have gone on to debunk the elite "hard sciences," and they express relief at therefore being released from any necessity to emulate their methods. Even the abbreviated discussion above shows that such an inference is wrong; Kuhn does not say that scientists are unscientific. Although insisting that there are inescapable subjective factors in all scientific behavior, Kuhn notes that all the scientists he has observed continually refer to a common set of verification criteria. The subjectivity arises in their interpretation of the given criteria.

(2) We argue in this book that archeologists are just beginning to develop such widely recognized ceriteria or standards of verification or justification of knowledge claims, and that the best way to further the development of these standards is to apply techniques that are

successful in other fields of empirical inquiry. These are the techniques discussed in the first part of this chapter and referred to as the scientific method: explicit formulation of hypotheses, laws, and theories; explicit testing of hypotheses; and explicit evaluation of results. Public evaluation of the results by oneself and by one's peers is crucial and brings us to the second topic listed above, the notion of a "paradigm" as many readers understood it from Kuhn's 1962 book. Although Kuhn has repeatedly admitted that his use of the word *paradigm* in the 1962 edition of his book is vague (Kuhn 1970c, 1974; and see also Shapere 1971), most readers seem to believe that by paradigm he means the consensus among practitioners about problem definition, problem-solving techniques, and the recognition of successful solutions that characterizes a mature science. Kuhn now prefers to call this complex the "disciplinary matrix" of a science rather than its paradigm and would reserve the word *paradigm* to mean the exemplars or standard examples used in textbooks and classrooms to impart methodological essentials to students. (However, he is pessimistic about the situation: "I see little chance of recapturing 'paradigm' for its original use, the only one that is philologically at all appropriate" [Kuhn 1977:307]).

So our first point with respect to the currently popular notion of a paradigm is that the word *paradigm* is used with several different meanings in *The Structure of Scientific Revolutions*, that the meaning most people grasp and use is one that refers to those common understandings within a scientific field about how to define problems and attack them and how to distinguish a successful from an unsuccessful solution. It is these common understandings, the disciplinary matrices as Kuhn would now have it, that define progress in a field by distinguishing good research from bad and success from failure. In a well-developed science with an axiomatized, partly axiomatized, or at least robust theory, the disciplinary matrix is delimited by this theory. The theory provides criteria for evaluation and provides the justification for decisions about what is good or bad research, or successful or unsuccessful solutions of problems.

We believe that a disciplinary matrix for archeology—like that for many social sciences—is not very well defined because high-level archeological theory is not well defined. However, progress will be facilitated by the inclusion in archeological reports of discussions of the grounds on which the research results are justified. Only with the aid of such information can broad theoretical formulations be developed.

In concluding this brief discussion of Kuhn's writings, we note that the dissatisfaction he expresses with the logical models and other formulations of philosophers of science (Kuhn 1970a; 1977:121, ch. 13) arises from the fact that as a historian of science he is struck by the way scientists actually work. Scientific practice seems to contradict the traditional model of scientific method constructed by philosophers. One major contradiction seems to derive from claims to objectivity in the face of ubiquitous subjective factors in scientific research. Kuhn might be seen as playing the role of an ethnographer in pointing out to philosophers of science that—according to his observations—the actual behavior of scientists and the development of scientific knowledge differ significantly from their idealized models of scientific method. How can science be objective when there are ineluctable subjective elements in the verification procedures used by scientists, just as there is a strong subjective element in scientific discovery? We believe the answer given above is adequate. Whatever subjective grounds are used for choice of problems, data, and criteria for justifying conclusions, scientific work is still objective in the sense of being open to public test and criticism of both these procedures and the grounds on which they are based. As remarked above in the discussion of Dray, there is always a third viewpoint from which to evaluate competing claims (for example, about the causal roles of moral vis-à-vis economic factors), and out of this general scientific method of forming and testing explanatory hypotheses, science *does* progress. It is just this progression that the popular "irrationalist" interpretation of Kuhn's position cannot explain.

As practicing archeologists, we recognize both the usefulness and the dangers of the subjective element in archeological inference. Of course, it is not possible to remove it. What is important is to recognize it and allow for it. Unrecognized and uncontrolled subjective elements have often played far too large a role in archeological research and reporting. Thus we argue that archeologists should be familiar with the general CL model of scientific method because awareness of the matters emphasized by the model (especially what knowledge claims are and how they are justified) will result in improved archeological research designs, fieldwork, analyses, and results. We stress, however, that simply going through the motions of a hypothetico-deductive approach will not guarantee significant research results. Attention to the CL model must be combined with concerted efforts to advance theoretical understanding of archeological materials. And one's choice of where to direct one's efforts will inevitably be determined in part by subjective factors.

Conclusion

Philosophers do not agree on the correct or best model of explanation, but variations of the CL model continue to be basic and prominent. We stress the reasonableness and usefulness of the generalized CL conception of explanation. Our view of the broad scope of the generalized CL model is presented in tables 1.1 and 1.2, together with a summary of the models of explanation discussed in this chapter. In conclusion, we reiterate our belief that the generalized CL model is important because it illustrates crucial aspects of archeological method. The generalized CL conception of explanation shows that explanations of particulars must derive from theories, or at least from sets of general relationships (possible laws), that archeologists have good empirical reasons to believe are confirmed. Then it is incumbent upon archeologists to make explicit the general relationships from which explanations derive and to undertake investigation of these relationships should their status—adequately confirmed or not—be unclear. As already noted, explanation of the general relationships themselves is most important of all and is possible only if a general theory or at least a series of minitheories (Wasserman 1981; and see below in the section Hypotheses, Explanations, Laws, and Theories) can be constructed from which these and other laws are derivable. The explicit construction of archeological theory is only beginning (Hanen and Kelley in press; Salmon 1982; Wylie in press).

Archeology as Science

To relate the topics just discussed to the practice of scientific archeology, we begin with the three aspects of epistemology discussed earlier in this chapter that are especially crucial to scientific archeologists: (1) Knowledge of the World; (2) Truth; and (3) Hypotheses, Explanations, General Laws, and Theories.

Knowledge of the World

Lewis Binford summarizes the attitude of scientific archeologists to the aspect of reality—the past—that they investigate: "We assume that the past is knowable; that with enough methodological ingenuity, propositions about the past are testable; and that there are valid scientific criteria for judging the probability of a statement about the past" (Binford 1968a:26).

Although much of the data with which archeologists work derives from objects of "material culture," this does not mean that the archeological record is devoid of information about nonmaterial features of past societies. On the contrary, as Binford insists, data relating to entire past cultural systems are present in the archeological record (Taylor 1948: chaps. 5, 6 also states this view). Binford adds, "It is virtually impossible to imagine that any given cultural item functioned in a sociocultural system independent of the operation of 'nonmaterial' variables" (Binford 1968a:21). He goes on to say, in devising means to extract this information about nonmaterial variables, we cannot restrict ourselves to knowledge of material culture. In order to provide explanations of whatever portion of the archeological record is under investigation, we must be aware of "the full range of determinants which operate within any sociocultural system, extant or extinct." Thus, Binford claims that the limitations on our knowledge of the past lie in the inadequacy of our knowledge of sociocultural systems in general and the resulting inadequacy of our archeological research designs and methods; the limitations are not in the archeological record itself.

This is somewhat overstated. That is, even if all the material items of a culture are related to its nonmaterial aspects in ways that archeologists know and can recognize, the archeological remains may still be so limited, altered, or sparse (and many may even have been destroyed) that a comprehensive description of the past cannot be derived from them, not just because our general knowledge, techniques, or intelligence are limited, but because the material that is left simply does not reflect the complete past (see Schiffer 1972, 1976:ch. 3; Wood and Johnson 1978; Gifford 1981). Thus, the possibility of the material's being so limited that little knowledge can be gained from it is certainly real. However, one should not allow this possibility to curb one's attempts to investigate those aspects of past human behavior that one wishes to understand.

The position defined by Binford is precisely that described in our first chapter: archeologists operating as scientists assume that there is a real, knowable (empirically observable), orderly world. What they want to know about this world is past human events and behavior patterns. Although the humans themselves are long dead and their patterned behavior itself is no longer observable, these can be studied systematically because archeological remains and their spatial interrelationships exist today as empirically observable records of them. Some of the methods and techniques used to make inferences about prehistoric human groups are described in succeeding chapters.

Truth

Our position with respect to the truth of statements derived from archeological studies is that of other scientists: one does not expect to attain certainty, but those hypotheses that are most adequately confirmed in the sense that they fit best with what is already known and lead to accurate predictions about what is not well known (see next section, and also chapter 4) at any given time are regarded as provisionally true. Flannery expresses this view by saying,

> The process theorists assume that "truth" is just the best current hypothesis, and that *whatever* they believe now will ultimately be proved wrong, either within their lifetime or afterward. Their "theories" [hypotheses] are not like children to them, and they suffer less trauma when the theories [hypotheses] prove "wrong" (Flannery 1967:122).

By "process theorists," Flannery means archeologists who are more interested in the general characteristics of cultural processes ("cultural process" or "culture process" means the way a culture works—the interrelations of its systems and subsystems—at any one time and/or through time) than in the specifics of cultural history ("cultural history" or "culture history" means the chronological and geographic particulars distinguishing cultures and their relationships across space and time). In the quoted statement, Flannery is expressing the view that the most adequately confirmed hypothesis available at the moment is the best approximation to truth.

Julian H. Steward made the same point some thirty years ago in a well-known paper published in the *American Anthropologist*, "Cultural Causality and Law: A Trial Formulation of the Development of Early Civilizations." (Steward uses the words *formulation* and *theory* where we would use *hypothesis*.) Steward says,

> It is obvious that the minutiae of culture history will never be completely known and that there is no need to defer formulations until all archeologists have laid down their shovels and all ethnologists have put away their notebooks. Unless anthropology is to interest itself in the unique, exotic, and nonrecurrent particulars, it is necessary that formulations be attempted no matter how tentative they may be. It is formulations that will enable us to state new kinds of problems and to direct attention to new kinds of data which have been slighted in the past. Fact-collecting of itself is insufficient scientific procedure; facts exist only as they are related to theories, and theories are not destroyed by facts—they are replaced by new theories which better explain the facts. Therefore, criticisms of this paper which concern facts alone and which fail to offer better formulations are of no interest. (Steward 1949:24–25)

In this statement Steward makes some of the same points stressed in the present chapter, especially that hypotheses ("trial formulations") are needed to give direction to research.

Hypotheses, Explanations, Laws, and Theories

Archeological hypotheses, like those of any other discipline, are the results of attempts to explain particular observations or classes of observations, or they are descriptions of possible lawlike regularities, relationships, or patterns. As already noted, many philosophers of science deliberately omit consideration of the *origins* of hypotheses and of possible processes of hypothesis formulation. However hypotheses are generated, these philosophers take the crux of scientific procedure to be the testing and confirmation or disconfirmation of hypotheses. We do not intend to dispute this traditional emphasis here (although some philosophers do; see Caws 1965: ch. 32; Caws 1969; Hanson 1958; and Wylie 1981). However, how hypotheses are generated is of importance to working archeologists, so we begin this section with a discussion of hypothesis formulation in archeology.

In a fully axiomatized science, all hypotheses would be inferred from the basic axioms; in sciences that are not axiomatized but do have extensive theories, explanatory hypotheses would derive from these theories. In archeology, which has no comprehensive theory but often depends on the theories of other sciences such as biology, geology, chemistry, and physics, some hypotheses derive from archeologists' knowledge of theories in these and other fields.

Lack of a comprehensive theory is common to most of the social sciences. This is partly because of the comparative youthfulness of these fields as formal disciplines and the extreme complexity of their subject matter. Also some anthropologists and archeologists are uncertain as to whether human behavior can or should be studied using the same basic methodology as is employed in chemistry and biology. Even among those archeologists like ourselves who believe it can and should be, there is disagreement about the need for and form of an archeological theory (Dunnell 1980a:477–478; 1982b). We believe archeology to be very similar to geology in that there is no single theory that encompasses the whole field. Nevertheless, much of what archeologists do (for example, dating materials, analyzing artifacts to determine source areas, and assessing the nature and degree of geological and biological activity affecting a site) depends directly and indirectly on the theories of fields such as biology, chemistry, and physics. Where these theories do not apply (for example, in trying to understand how ranking and stratification arise in human societies and how these forms of sociopolitical organization are reflected in the archeological record), archeologists rely on a wide variety of other theories and data about human behavior to help them devise hypotheses. Hence archeologists, like other social scientists, often try new approaches. In general they are open to all promising techniques, methods, and concepts regardless of their sources. This is a clear indication of lack of a unitary theory in a field of study. Although it has the advantages of any "shotgun" approach, it has the distinct disadvantage that progress is difficult to measure, and there is considerable confusion even about basic issues. Because such confusion still characterizes Americanist archeology, we believe it highly desirable that archeologists study the essentials of scientific procedure. If they understand what is meant by the concepts of empirical observation, hypothesis, test, law, theory, and explanation, they will be able to evaluate their own work and that of others with respect to the possible goals of archeological research.

Some archeologists believe no further progress is possible until we construct a comprehensive theory (a grand theory, hypertheory, or macrotheory; Dunnell 1980a and b, 1981, 1982b). The development of an archeological macrotheory would require, at least in the long run, a significant degree of axiomatization of archeology. But axiomatization is a condition only incompletely attained at present even by the most advanced of the natural sciences (physics and chemistry). The subject matter of these sciences, complex though it is, is many orders of magnitude simpler than the subject matter studied by archeologists, who try to understand the functioning of past human groups through a time span of two to three million years. Hence, although we are sympathetic with those who seek a macrotheory for archeology, we believe it may be a long time before such a theory is constructed and widely accepted. We believe that systematization of archeological knowledge in a series of minitheories (Wasserman 1981) is the only practical procedure, and that it is a necessary alternative to the traditional laissez-faire mode of interpreting the archeological record. By archeological minitheories we mean those David Clarke discusses (Clarke 1973; Hodder, Isaac, and Hammond 1981:2–5), some of which we examine in the rest of this book. These include predepositional theory (explanations for patterns of discard in various social and cultural contexts) and postdepositional theory (explanations for patterns in the decay, disturbance, and destruction of archeological materials). Patterns of discard, decay, and disturbance are known to Americanist archeologists as site-formation processes (Schiffer 1972). These minitheories at least partly comprise what many archeologists now call middle-range theory (see the discussion of middle-range theory in chapter 5).

Given that there is no macrotheory from which to derive explanatory hypotheses, where *do* archeologists obtain their hypotheses?

Archeological hypotheses range from such things as the tentative identification of a floor level (which the student must learn to detect by the color, texture, composition, and so on of the deposit being excavated) to tentative explanations (drawn from the archeologist's understanding of relevant portions of anthropology, demography, economics, political science, sociology) for major shifts in site sizes and locations over an entire region, to relatively complex models (constructed with the aid of data drawn from all the previously listed fields plus several others such as biology and the medical sciences, history, and psychology) meant to help explain major human evolutionary trends.

Ethnographic studies have long been sources of hypotheses useful to archeologists. Today many prehistorians engage in their own ethnographic studies (Binford 1978b; David 1972; Gifford 1981; Gould 1980; Kramer 1982; Watson 1979a). The kind of information sought varies widely, as indicated by the publications cited. Other archeologists have undertaken detailed experiments that not only furnish them with hypotheses about ancient techniques and procedures but also produce data on regularities (for example, rates of land clearing, or monument construction, of artifact manufacture, yields of food resources when specific techniques are applied in particular environments, and size and other characteristics of living space as reflections of size and organization of the group using that space) that are directly applicable to interpreting archeological records (Callahan 1976; Coles 1979; LeBlanc 1971; Kramer 1980; Schacht 1981).

Historical and classical archeology offer invaluable opportunities for the study of entire complex societies by combining information from documents with that from excavations. Documents are excellent sources of detailed hypotheses about past societies. Some of the most fascinating of these hypotheses involve comparison of what people say they do and what they actually do (Ascher and Fairbanks 1971; Rathje 1978; South 1977:326).

In chapter 3 we consider the general topic of systems theory and a systems approach to archeology. One of the points made in that chapter concerns the role of a systems approach in hypothesis formulation. In chapters 4 and 5 we discuss computer simulation of prehistoric cultural subsystems. This is a way of combining data from ethnography and other sources in a relatively complex hypothetical formulation (usually called a model) that is a rich source of detailed hypotheses about the past culture being investigated.

Hypotheses vary a great deal in scope. Some are highly restricted ("This is a hearth," "This is a projectile point," "This is a store room"), while others are wide in scope ("In no hunting-gathering society dependent on dispersed resources do local groups exceed fifty persons in size," "For any two or more communities in which people make painted pottery, similarity and dissimilarity of the designs on the pottery directly reflect the intensity of interaction between the communities").

Similarly, some archeological hypotheses rest on only a few basic assumptions. For example, "These rocks are ancient tools," is an assertion depending on recognition of a combination of characteristics known to result only from human workmanship (kind of material from which the objects are made, their context, their overall condition, edge angles of flaked surfaces, presence or absence of striking platform, and nature of striking platform if present). The ability to evaluate these characteristics is an integral part of the expertise of trained archeologists. Many such hypotheses possibly explanatory of some parts of the archeological record are based on the assumption of large bodies of information obtained from a wide variety of disciplines besides archeology. For example, "Unequal access to vital economic resources is a necessary if not sufficient cause of the rise of complex, state-based societies" is a proposition that could help explain portions of the archeological record in many areas and that could be tested by use of information from economics and political science as well as from history, social anthropology, sociology, and psychology.

Archeology as Science

Regardless of the origin, scope, or nature of a hypothesis, the archeologist who states it always—with or without justification—takes information and some relationships as given and postulates other relationships as possible, significant, and testable. Hypothetical formulations intended to explain some portion of the archeological record range from the potentially valuable and the highly useful to the trivial. Decisions as to which are valuable or useful and which are not must be made by archeologists and their colleagues in closely related fields. However, hypotheses broad in scope and postulated to explain *classes* of phenomena are of more scientific interest in archeology, as in any other field, than those serving to explain particulars. As Wesley Salmon says,

> Explanations of particular events seldom, if ever, have genuine scientific import (as opposed to practical value), and . . . explanations which are scientifically interesting are almost always explanations of classes of events . . . the goodness or utility of a scientific explanation should be assessed with respect to its ability to account for entire classes of phenomena, rather than by its ability to deal with any particular event in isolation (W. Salmon 1975b:119–120).

Whatever the scope or usefulness of any hypothesis, the method of testing is that described earlier in this chapter: implications inferred from the hypothesis are checked empirically.

An important conclusion to be drawn from all this is the following: Faithful adherence to the procedures described above (problem definition, formulation and testing of alternative hypotheses, evaluation of results with respect to level of confirmation and achievement of stated goals) is vital but *will not ensure significant, creative, or useful research*. Accomplishing significant, creative, and useful research depends upon the ability of the investigator to design the work so that it builds on previous research while advancing knowledge of the subject matter in question. Such an ability is one part aptitude and many parts hard work assimilating what is already known and devising alternative ways to find out more.

An example of the testing of very limited particularistic archeological hypotheses (but ones essential to understanding the specific archeological situation under investigation) is the manufacture and trial burning of various kinds of torches inferred to have been used by the aboriginal explorers of Salts Cave and Mammoth Cave, Mammoth Cave National Park, Kentucky (Watson et al. 1969:33–36). Experimentation—testing of a variety of hypotheses about the composition and size of such torches—resulted in much very particularistic information about aboriginal caving techniques of interest to a few archeologists, to the chief interpreter and the guides of Mammoth Cave National Park, and to tourists visiting Mammoth Cave, but of minor significance to anthropological archeology as a whole.

James Hill's study (Hill 1968) of the prehistoric site of Broken K in Arizona, which we discussed in some detail in *Explanation in Archeology*, illustrates testing of a particularistic hypothesis concerning prehistoric room functions at the pueblo. The hypothesis can be stated as follows: The forms of rooms in the prehistoric pueblo are similar to those in contemporary pueblos, therefore the prehistoric functions (storage, living, ceremonial) of the rooms at Broken K were similar to those of contemporary pueblos.

Examples of tests of hypotheses of wide scope and of considerable general interest are found in the work of archeologists and others investigating the origins of state-based, complex society. Wittfogel (1957) suggests that the special requirements of irrigation-based technology are critical in centralizing power and in stimulating the rise of bureaucratically dominated, state-based societies in various parts of the Old World. Julian Steward (1949) is also impressed with the causal role of irrigation in the evolution of archaic states. However, Robert McC. Adams (1965) in his investigation of the beginnings of civilization in southern Mesopotamia does not find the Wittfogel hydraulic hypothesis to be upheld. The origins of Mesopotamian civilization long antedate the development of elaborate irrigation works and water-regulating bureaucracies, and a complex series of causal factors is apparently crucial in its evolution (Adams 1960a and b, 1965, 1981; Adams and Nissen 1972). One of Adams's students (Henry Wright) together with one of *his* students (Gregory Johnson) have undertaken tests of other hypotheses (centering on trade and exchange patterns) concerning the origins of the state in Mesopotamia (Wright and Johnson 1975; Wright 1977). They are working in an area (ancient Elam) near to but distinct from that of

Adams in Sumerian Mesopotamia; hence their results constitute a test case separate from that of Adams, and their findings amplify and refine his conclusions about the development of complex, state-based society.

Such archeological investigations involving long-term cultural historical sequences are fundamental to the derivation and testing of possible theories and laws about human cultural development. We note in *Explanation in Archeology* (1971:50–51, 164; and see chapter 5 here) as do others (Braidwood 1967; R. Watson 1976a), that such a body of archeologically derived laws is an important contribution that archeologists can make to the social sciences. However, the establishment of these laws requires persistent work by archeologists to formulate, test, and confirm hypotheses relating presently observable archeological remains to events and conditions no longer extant. Thus, using the assumption (which is really a hypothesis confirmed in other tests) that archeological remains are systematic and adequate keys to ancient human behavioral patterns and events, we can derive and test laws about these human activities. Given that some of these activities may no longer be engaged in by living peoples, archeologists are then in a position to provide general information about the human potential (by describing past human actualities) that could be attained, tested, and confirmed in no other way.

The archeological examples referred to above embody attempts to provide laws about cultural processes. However, only very recently have archeologists begun to discuss and to work systematically at formulating and testing hypotheses about how human activities result in patterned archeological remains that reflect these activities and about how natural and cultural forces alter, diminish, and destroy those remains (Schiffer 1972, 1976; Gifford 1981; Stein 1983; Wood and Johnson 1978). Theories of site formation must be delineated and evaluated before the derivation of detailed information about prehistoric human behavior from the archeological record can be fully justified.

As stressed earlier in this chapter, we believe that the general CL conception of explanation is useful and valuable because it directs attention (1) to the importance of problem-oriented research, i.e., of explicitly formulating and testing explanatory hypotheses; (2) to the role played by laws and possible laws in archeological explanations; and (3) to the necessity for justifying knowledge claims in a systematic way by demonstrating how explanatory hypotheses are dependent on specific laws (possible or established) that are subsumed by a particular theory. This procedure is necessary for establishing publicly accessible archeological knowledge. We have said that archeologists can learn some valuable lessons about such procedures from philosophers of science, but we cannot stress too strongly that the *content* of that procedural framework, the actual substance of archeological hypotheses and explanations, must be provided by working archeologists themselves. Archeologists also make the final judgments about their confirmations. The hypotheses and their tests must be firmly grounded in archeological data.

In summary, familiarity with some philosophy of science does not ensure that an archeologist can produce significant hypotheses, or that he or she will devise ingenious and appropriate tests, or carry out these tests skillfully, honestly, and completely and then promptly report them (for an expanded consideration of this and related topics see Read and LeBlanc 1978; and Wylie 1981: ch. 5). Nor will familiarity with philosophy of science enable archeologists to decide when their own specific hypotheses or those of others have been sufficiently tested. That is, archeologists themselves must decide— implicitly or explicitly—how much of what kind of testing is enough, whether or not specific archeological knowledge claims should be considered to have been justified, what kinds of further tests are required or desirable, and which lawlike generalizations invoked by archeological explanations are sufficiently strongly confirmed so that they can be considered established and which are not (see chapter 4). It is important to make specific reference to the crucial lawlike generalizations that subsume all major explanatory formulations offered, together with some evaluation of the confirmatory status of those generalizations.

Finally, we stress again the crucial role of theory in structuring the specific studies archeologists make and in providing the ultimate criteria for evaluating archeological procedures and results. As already noted, there is as yet no macrotheory for archeology, but there are several potential and developing bodies of minitheory. Besides the degree of its success in solving immediate problems, all archeological work can be evaluated according to its contribution to the construction of theory, either minitheory or macrotheory. Therefore, primary consideration must be given to theoretical issues throughout the entire process of designing, carrying out, and publishing an archeological investigation. Uncertainty among archeologists about justification of their results would be lessened if they would include in their reports discussions of what they consider to be adequate grounds for the confirmation of their hypotheses.

Hypothesis Testing in Archeological Fieldwork

Some specific examples of testing archeological hypotheses have been provided in the previous section, and there are further illustrations in succeeding chapters (see especially chapter 4). In concluding the present chapter, we turn to some other practical matters that always come up in discussions about problem-oriented fieldwork and hypothesis testing in archeology.

A common misconception is that a definite excavation program consisting of problems to be solved and hypotheses to be tested constitutes a framework so restrictive that the practicing archeologist can alter neither problems, hypotheses, goals, nor procedures in the course of actual excavation. On the one hand, it is inefficient to excavate with no plan or problem in mind to which the data might contribute a solution, but on the other hand, if one knew before excavation exactly what the data would show, there would be no reason to dig. The usual situation is that we know enough to pose hypotheses for which digging can in principle provide tests but are open to altering hypotheses, problems, and procedures if the excavation does not provide data for the precise testing of just those hypotheses with which we began.

Practically speaking, an archeologist who has committed a considerable amount of time and money in preparation, who has obtained permissions and transported personnel, and who has begun digging at a given site need not pull up stakes because the data being turned out of the ground appear to be less significant for solving the original problems than he or she had hoped. What is demanded by scientific archeological procedure is that archeologists take into consideration whatever data result from their excavations, altering hypotheses if necessary and adjusting tests in the light of these data. In extreme cases, as a result of particular combinations of circumstances, archeologists may have to abandon some portion or—rarely—all of the entire original plan in order to do justice to the material at hand. This might be unfortunate given their desire to solve certain problems, but it is not unscientific. Hypotheses nearly always must be modified as data accumulate; some hypotheses may even be discarded and replaced by others.

Because it is impossible to collect *all* the potential data in any archeological situation, archeologists must constantly decide whether the information they are collecting justifies the necessary destruction of materials from which other information could be extracted. Different archeologists excavating the same site would make different choices, but it would be unrealistic and wrong to suggest that an archeologist ignore everything in the excavation except what bears directly on the hypotheses being tested. For example, one may begin an excavation having planned for and anticipated recovering detailed data on subsistence. If it becomes apparent as work progresses that the site also contains a series of subfloor burials accompanied by grave goods reflecting status or rank, then one must decide whether or not to shift the focus of the study to make the most of these newly disclosed data, or to ignore them, or to come to some compromise objective.

Situations of this sort arise frequently, but there is less and less excuse for archeologists to be surprised by major blocks of totally unanticipated data (such as an unsuspected Roman occupation horizon obscuring a part of the Early Bronze Age community an archeologist wishes to investigate) that necessitate drastic modification of one's plan of attack. If an archeologist has considered the entire range of related problems to be solved and hypotheses to be tested, has studied the available literature thoroughly, and has examined the site and its environmental context carefully by using systematic surface surveys and test excavations, then major surprises of the sort just described will be the exception rather than the rule. Although an archeologist is not bound to the original excavation plan or hypotheses, he or she *is* required to be explicit about what problems are finally chosen to be solved, what hypotheses are finally formulated to be tested, and what their theoretical significance is. Seldom will a site be excavated for which an archeologist has set out hypotheses that do not need modification in the light of the emerging data. Nevertheless, this procedure does result in a steady increase in publicly accessible archeological knowledge.

An example of how empirical data from the archeological record can cause major alterations in hypotheses yet also cause an increase in knowledge of the past is provided by some recent research in western Kentucky (Chomko and Crawford 1978). Flotation of sediments from the entry chamber of Salts Cave, Mammoth Cave National Park, Kentucky, together with analysis of botanical remains from the cave interior resulted in the suggestion that a series of native North American cultigens (sunflower, sumpweed, chenopod) were probably domesticated *prior* to local adoption of the tropical cultigens (squash, gourd, maize, beans) widely used at the time of European penetration of the eastern United States (Yarnell 1974, 1978). A research project was designed to locate and define the postulated Late Archaic native North American horticultural complex by applying flotation/water separation techniques to well-known, rich midden sites of the relevant time period on the Green River (a major tributary of the Ohio River) in western Kentucky some forty to fifty miles downstream from Salts Cave (Marquardt and Watson 1979, 1983). Analysis of the botanical remains from two of the midden sites resulted in forceful disconfirmation of the hypothesis: fragments of charred squash rind were found in surprisingly early context (radiocarbon determinations—uncorrected—indicated mid-third millennium B.C. to late second millennium B.C.), but no trace of cultivated sunflower, sumpweed, or chenopod was recovered (Crawford 1982; Wagner 1982). Since this discovery was made, corroborating instances have been documented at several other sites in the Midwest and Midsouth (Watson 1980; Kay, King, and Robinson 1980; Chapman and Shea 1981; Cowan 1981; Asch and Asch 1980). It is now clear that most of our ideas up to 1976 about the origins of food production in the Eastern Woodlands were quite wrong and that the entire process (especially when compared with the beginnings of horticulture in the Southwest) was much more complex than previously suspected.

Such examples—by no means rare—exemplify the fact that, although archeological theories are often somewhat *under*determined empirically (that is, because of the complexity and difficulty of archeological research, archeological tests of the implications of theories or hypotheses are often delayed or inconclusive), they are not *un*determined. As shown, the archeological record can provide decisive answers to some important questions. Archeologists should design their research to maximize the information potential of archeological remains by careful and ingenious application of available techniques and by devising new techniques to answer specific questions about specific portions of the human past. It is a serious mistake to think that archeologists are bound to rigid research plans during this process.

Another kind of misunderstanding about how problems and hypotheses are formulated and modified in the light of data may lead to another kind of criticism. That is, some critics object to the fact that explicit hypotheses are sometimes formulated only *after* archeologists have seen the data. However, this procedure is not necessarily objectionable for, in logical terms, the order of genesis of problems, hypotheses, and the data pertinent to them is immaterial. But for clear exposition of results, the problems, hypotheses, and pertinent data are carefully set out to show their logical relations. This often gives the impression that the scientific work that obtained these results also proceeded in a straightforward, unproblematic way, from theory to problem definition to hypothesis formulation to research design, and finally to implementation, analysis, and publication. But of course scientific work does not typically proceed as neatly as does a scientific report; it is the misconception that it does, or the even greater misconception that it must, that gives rise to the criticism that *post hoc* problems and hypotheses and their solutions and tests with pregathered data are not legitimate. Which actually comes first is logically immaterial because, logically, problems, hypotheses, solutions, and tests are atemporal; what is important is not the temporal order of their generation or presentation but their conceptual relations that show how the results are justified or confirmed.

It must be stressed that in any circumstances in which one's work constitutes a test of a hypothesis, the form of the general hypothetico-deductive method is preserved. In whatever way the hypotheses are generated, one's data must stand in the logical relation of being a test of the hypotheses, contributing to their confirmation or disconfirmation and hence to greater understanding of the theoretical issues they were designed to investigate.

Thus, there is good epistemological reason for ordering *reports* with problems and hypotheses clearly stated before supporting data are given. But it is misleading to infer that this is or should invariably be the sequence by which scientific *research* actually proceeds, because this may suggest to potential critics and young scientists an ideal that is seldom exemplified in practice. James D. Watson's *The Double Helix* (1968) and Donald Johanson and Maitland Edey's *Lucy* (1981) provide an abundance of dramatic, behind-the-scenes detail about how contemporary scientific research is carried out as distinct from the manner in which the results are reported in technical accounts. This is indicated even more strikingly by the fact that different participants in the same research may have strongly differing perceptions of these same events, while agreeing about how the data support the conclusions.

The logical form of scientific knowledge—that is, the relations among hypotheses, data, and conclusions—suggests only the general order of procedure for scientific investigations. *Logically* the order of this procedure is not important, but *practically* there is a world of difference between—on the one hand—finishing an excavation and then deriving one or more *post hoc* hypotheses and—on the other hand—positing a new hypothesis and deriving its implications for testing while excavation is in progress. Completely *post hoc* hypotheses can be tested only by data that happen to be relevant to them. If, on the other hand, hypotheses are defined before work begins or while it is still in progress, data relevant for testing implications can be deliberately collected, thus greatly increasing the likelihood that the hypotheses can be properly tested and—as is so often necessary—modified and retested. Thus, while not discounting the scientific value of *post hoc* hypotheses, we believe that archeological research proceeds much more efficiently if one formulates research problems and hypotheses before beginning work. Therefore, *because* we are experienced in the practical difficulties of excavation, we continue to stress the necessary priority of careful research design. Too much work and too many resources can be wasted otherwise. Closely controlled, problem-oriented archeology can be done on the basis of present knowledge. We believe that as archeologists realize the advantages of explicit, a priori research designs, closely controlled, problem-oriented archeology will become the rule.

New Archeology as Narrow Deductivism

In a detailed consideration of the development of archeological theory since the 1930s, philosopher Alison Wylie has recently advocated what she refers to as a "realist approach" to the archeological record (Wylie 1981:195–197, 284–285, 375–381). She defines a *realist* as one who believes that the entities and processes postulated in a theory exist even though they cannot be directly perceived. She contrasts such a person to an *empiricist*, who—according to her definition—refuses to consider any mechanisms, entities, or processes that cannot be directly perceived empirically. (Here Wylie is referring to *ontological* matters—"What is there?"—rather than epistemological ones—"How do you know?") A large part of her dissertation (Wylie 1981) consists of analyses to expose empiricist versus realist themes in anthropological and archeological literature from Kluckhohn (1939, 1940) to Taylor (1948); Binford's 1960s' publications; and those of Fritz and Plog; Hill; Watson, LeBlanc, and Redman; and others. Predictably, she finds many of the sources somewhat confused but does document what she believes to be a deleterious or at least disadvantageous conflict between the two approaches. In brief, she believes that the 1960s–1970s insistence on a model of science in the positivist mode—beginning with Binford's references in his early papers to the Hempelian D-N model of explanation in science and further developed in various writings on the new archeology, *Explanation in Archeology* included—is not only contrary to the goals of the new archeology program but also is contrary to the practice of the new archeologists. She finds that these archeologists whom she takes to be advocating a slightly modified form of the basic narrow empiricism they label and reject as traditional or old archeology actually *do* archeology as realists. That is, they do not themselves operate like narrow empiricists as she would have predicted from some of the things they say. Hence, she suggests that these archeologists should align their preaching with their practice and advocate an explicitly *realist* approach to archeology rather than an implicitly narrow-empiricist approach.

We agree that preaching should be aligned with practice, but we also believe that Wylie's characterization of the contrast or conflict between empiricism and realism, as she defines them, in archeological writings is much too sharply drawn. It is unlikely that any archeologist—old or new—wholly fits her definition of a narrow empiricist (one who refuses to consider any mechanisms, entities, or processes that cannot be directly perceived empirically). The emphasis on a deductive (or hypothetico-deductive) approach that was so prevalent in the 1960s and 1970s literature on new archeology was understood by its proponents (including Watson, LeBlanc, and Redman 1971) to mean *beginning* an archeological investigation with a general problem or proposition in the form of a hypothesis or model (a model being a complex hypothesis or set of hypotheses). One then *deduced* implications for the archeological record from the general proposition (hypothesis or model) and examined the record to see whether one's predictions about it as drawn from the hypothesis or model were accurate. Wylie is concerned that heavy emphasis on a strictly deductive approach as the ideal of scientific archeology misrepresents the actual complexity and basically inductive nature of test procedures involving the archeological record (Salmon 1976).

Many archeologists who were dubious of or actively resisted the new archeology platform shared this same concern that dogmatic narrow deductivism was being imposed as an antidote to the atheoretical narrow inductivism ("let the facts speak for themselves") that so distressed Walter Taylor in the 1940s and the new archeologists in the 1960s. Narrow deductivism seemed as undesirable as narrow inductivism. Indeed, were it possible to isolate pure specimens of either, one would probably be hard-pressed to say which was the lesser evil. But pure specimens do not exist among practicing archeologists. What the new archeologists thought they were advocating (see Watson, LeBlanc, and Redman 1971:12–16, 114–121, for example) is an iterative (to-and-fro) approach that begins with a general question (hypothesis or model) and a suspected answer or set of entailments (test implications) that direct one's attention to specific data sets relevant to the matter being investigated. As these data are collected and analyzed, one's understanding of the original question, hypothesis, or model inevitably changes so that one refines it to make it more precise, or drastically reformulates it, or discards it. But some of the literature of new archeology (including parts of *Explanation in Archeology*) is not very clear in setting this out and is incomplete, misleading, or simply wrong in its references to deduction and its characterization of the contrast between inductivist and deductivist approaches. Moreover, the deductivist approach—even as conceptualized by the early new archeologists—cannot be completely disentangled from a narrowly inductivist one in which particular data are described in detail to serve no explicit purpose. Nevertheless, there *is* an important difference in emphasis between starting with an overt question, hypothesis, or model on the one hand (which is what the new archeologists were advocating) and just collecting information because it's there without the explicit guidance of such hypotheses and models on the other (which characterized much of pre-1960s archeology).

To return to the ontological issue raised by Wylie, we believe that one of the most fundamental concerns of new archeologists *was* with the processes and events that had created the record, and certainly they would not have been willing to accept what she claims are the consequences of following a strict positivism (i.e., restrictive observation of the record in and of itself), and Wylie agrees with this. We believe that some of the strain Wylie perceives in the literature is simply the result of faulty rhetoric or naiveté on the part of the authors (ourselves included), but we agree that there is potential danger of dissension and of increasing confusion about disciplinary goals if archeologists continue to be naive, thoughtless, or poorly informed (see the discussion in the preceding section). Insofar as this potential danger is realized, the tension that Wylie defines (between narrowly conceived empiricist systematization of archeological data and deep concern about the entities and processes that created those data) is introduced into the discipline.

This tension must be resolved in some way by each individual archeologist because, insofar as it remains implicit or unrecognized, it does compromise the effectiveness of the archeological endeavor. The crucial task now is to fit to the exigencies of archeological practice the methodological principles that have emerged or are emerging from this adjustment of goals between empiricist systematization of archeological data, on the one hand, and concern about the entities and processes that created those data, on the other. We believe that archeologists can make justifiable decisions about how to use the archeological record only if they understand the general problems of scientific explanation, confirmation, and theory formation. Our presentation of these problems is elementary and heuristic and derives from a viewpoint of fieldwork, materials analysis, and data interpretation because responsible *practice* of archeology in the field depends on understanding these theoretical issues. Archeology can be neither solely practical nor solely theoretical; it is necessarily, pragmatically, both.

Socrates claimed that an unexamined life was not worth living. Unexamined archeology is not only not worth doing but also it is dangerous because it diminishes the archeological record without utilizing its information potential to the fullest. Wylie's goal in her dissertation, and one of our major purposes in this book, is to aid archeologists in examining the conceptual basis of their work so that results can more closely approximate the maximum potential of the archeological record.

Wylie's critique is an impressive analysis of the literature on archeological theory, even though we think she makes the empiricist–realist division between archeologists sharper than it really is. We stress again that those who wish to understand and to evaluate what she and other analysts have to say about archeology must familiarize themselves with the issues and discussions outlined in this chapter.

The Generalized Covering Law Model in Archeology

In this chapter we describe, discuss, and provide examples of the use of a very generalized covering law model of explanation in archeology. We join with many philosophers of science who argue that all knowledge claims are based on implicit or explicit reference to lawlike generalizations. Our concern in *Explanation in Archeology* (1971) and our concern now is to recommend the explicit adaptation of this model to justify and advance archeological knowledge. We stress that the model is general and that it can be used in a variety of formal and informal applications. And we stress that our approach is not that of philosophers studying the model itself but that of working archeologists utilizing the model heuristically.

Despite our statements to this effect in *Explanation in Archeology*, some critics took us to be trying to impose a formal hypothetico-deductive model of the strict deductive-nomological form on archeology. We were even taken by some to forbid the use of deductive-statistical and inductive-statistical models. Certain of these critics recommended a statistical relevance model to avoid some of the formal problems of the strict deductive-nomological model. But as the present text should make clear, we take all of these—the D-N model, the D-S model, the I-S model, the S-R model, systems theory, and even the Collingwood/Dray *Verstehen* model—to be more or less formalized and specialized applications of the generalized covering law model.

Just how do we conceive of this model? First, we are scientists, not philosophers. We assume that there is a real world that has existed in the past, exists now, and will exist in the future. This real world provides us with the objects of our study. This world is knowable, and we are capable of understanding it. The world is knowable because the elements of which its objects and events consist, and the objects and events themselves, are related to one another in orderly patterns. We can know the world because we are capable of abstracting and comprehending the patterns and regularities exhibited by the objects and events in the world. And most importantly, this knowledge is public in the sense that any human being can perceive the world, understand it, and improve knowledge of it through critical discussion and critical comparison with the knowledge accumulated by other human beings. Our knowledge of the world is thus empirical, and the world we know is objective. As scientists, we begin with these assumptions.

Our knowledge of the world is hierarchical, as is the generalized covering law model of knowledge that we recommend for heuristic

Archeology as Science

use. The model consists of hierarchically related statements on three levels: knowledge claims about particular objects and events, knowledge claims about lawlike generalizations, and knowledge claims about theories. Knowledge claims about particulars are justified with reference to lawlike generalizations, and lawlike generalizations are confirmed in part by the truth of statements about particulars. Theories comprehend or unify sets of lawlike generalizations and thereby provide some confirmation for these lawlike generalizations. But the ground-level justification of theories and lawlike generalizations is and must be true statements about empirical, observable, particular objects and events.

We suggest that archeologists approach their work with specific problems in mind. We suggest that they state tentative solutions to these problems as hypotheses and then devise publicly repeatable ways of testing these hypotheses. Only when these knowledge claims are clearly stated and confirmed can they be considered to be justified parts of archeological knowledge.

In practice, some archeologists are more interested in finding out about particular objects and events than in discovering general relations that pertain among them. Primarily particularist archeologists (and historians and other social scientists) may then take for granted a large number of lawlike generalizations from all the sciences and use these generalizations to justify their knowledge claims about particulars. For example, if an exotic marine shell is found in conjunction with a flexed human skeleton buried in a pocket of disturbed deposit surrounded by an undisturbed matrix, one might claim that the shell had been the possession of a living human being who treasured it for its unusual qualities and that it may also have been thought to have magic or religious significance for it was buried with the body. Whether these remarks are presented as hypotheses or as statements of fact, they depend both for their comprehension and for their justification on many lawlike generalizations from at least the following fields: geology, psychology, sociology, and history. Some of these generalizations are compressed into the assumption that the objects under consideration are the remains of a dead body buried by other, living human beings. (The hierarchical relations of such assumptions are delineated by R. Watson, 1976a).

Other archeologists are primarily interested in discovering lawlike generalizations about sociocultural processes and human behavior that resulted in such social manifestations as, for example, the origin of agriculture or the origin of the state. This work requires them to coordinate particularistic data with lawlike generalizations and to integrate sets of the generalizations.

In actual practice, all archeologists (like all scientists) depend in all their work on the interrelations of statements about particulars, lawlike generalizations, and theories. In the advance of knowledge, the generalized covering law model operates as follows: Tentative knowledge claims about particulars are made on the basis of interpretations derived from general knowledge about human behavior and human societies. Particularistic data are then used to test lawlike generalizations. Hypotheses about particulars are suggested by the generalizations, and hypothetical lawlike generalizations are suggested by the particulars. Anyone trying to interpret and to understand the archeological record must work back and forth from particulars to generalizations, getting ideas and insights and testing knowledge claims in a to-and-fro, stepwise manner. Lawlike generalizations suggest ways to test hypotheses about particulars. And the particulars suggest ways to test lawlike generalizations. Then when lawlike generalizations themselves are comprehended in theories, their interrelationships may suggest further lawlike generalizations that can be tested, and their integration may provide additional confirmation for the lawlike generalizations themselves and may suggest further ways of testing and confirming claims about particulars.

Some critics argue that this process is invalid because it is circular. Obviously a circle is involved if particular data are interpreted on the basis of a lawlike generalization that in turn is confirmed by reference to these same data. But it is not a vicious circle for many reasons. First, the formulations of both the particular interpretation and the generalization are made together, each informing and influencing the content of the other. It is a process of mutually interacting modification and development. Second, both the formulation and the testing of each particular statement and generalization are influenced also by interaction with myriad other particular statements and generalizations. In particular, lawlike generalizations themselves are tested not only in the light of particularistic data but also with respect to their relations to other lawlike generalizations. It is in the description of these interacting interpretations and tests on all three levels of particulars, generalizations, and theories that one can speak of the generalized covering law model as incorporating or exemplifying what is known as systems theory.

But are we claiming that scientists actually work this way, keeping all these interrelations in mind? Of course not. Nor are we claiming that scientists *should* always work this way. What we do advocate is that archeologists should keep in mind the systematic interrelations among statements about particulars, lawlike generalizations, and theories. Archeologists should be prepared to set up their own tests of their knowledge claims on any level. They should be prepared to state the grounds on which they claim that their statements about particulars, laws, and theories are true.

We believe that archeology is best done with explicitly scientific methods. This is to state clearly what problems one wants to solve, and to emphasize problems with broad significance over those that are very narrow in scope. Then one should recognize that interpretations are based on assumed general knowledge about human behavior and culture and on lawlike generalizations from all the sciences from physics to history. Solutions to one's problems should be stated tentatively and in such a way that they can be tested (that is, formulated as hypotheses). Knowledge claims—particular or general—should be stated as fact only after they have been confirmed.

In conclusion, our concern here is largely with heuristics and the logic of justification in archeology. In one sense, it does not matter how one originates one's hypothetical explanations. They could come as brilliant insights in the shower. And be true. But to convince others of their truth, one must test them and show their relationships to confirmed lawlike generalizations and theory. Very often descriptions of the actual courses of actual discoveries (or the various logics of discovery) are not adequate for the justification of the true knowledge claims that result from those discoveries. In any case, we are not providing a cookbook of recipes for instant success in archeological research. But while we make the standard protests that we are *not* advocating *the* way to proceed in science, we do advocate that a *good* way to proceed in archeology is by stating problems, formulating hypotheses, and testing them empirically in the light of and for the purpose of establishing lawlike generalizations. This generalized covering law procedure is in fact the *only* successful systematic way of justifying empirical knowledge claims that has so far been devised.

In this first chapter we have outlined and discussed briefly some topics drawn from the philosophy of science that are relevant to archeologists operating as scientists. The archeological record, like any empirical subject matter, can be studied scientifically to provide information about the processes that resulted in that record. Archeologists can construct theories and derive laws about development and change in human society and culture from the archeological record.

We conclude the first chapter by specific reference to archeology and to the work of archeologists operating as scientists. We emphasize that, although consideration of the philosophy of science and discussions with philosophers of science are helpful and sometimes crucial, as practicing archeologists we are on our own when it comes to constructing archeological theories, evaluating the content of archeological knowledge claims, and assessing the adequacy of tests and confirmation.

In chapters 2 and 3 we examine two special topics relevant to the kinds of explanations archeologists offer: systems theory and ecological approaches. These topics are closely related because by definition ecology is systemic. Both have enjoyed considerable popularity among archeologists over the past several years; in fact, both are so well integrated into the contemporary practice of prehistoric archeology that they are virtually synonymous with it. However, to carry out our examination of basic aspects of archeological theory and method, we consider these approaches separately before relating them to the framework established in chapter 1.

In chapter 3 we discuss methods and techniques that archeologists can use to derive and test hypotheses about the past (chapters 4 and 5), and we conclude the volume with discussions of archeological publication, archeological theory, and the aims of archeology (chapter 6).

CHAPTER TWO
Systems Theory and Archeology

In chapters 2 through 6, we describe, analyze, and discuss several aspects of contemporary anthropological archeology. Hence the rest of this book contrasts with chapter 1 in being less abstract and less overtly theoretical, but our goal in these chapters remains the same as our goal in chapter 1: to summarize and integrate as clearly as we can crucial theoretical issues with the practice of archeology.

Systems Explanations in Archeology

During the last ten years, archeologists have talked about "general systems theory," "systems theory," and "the systemic approach" a great deal, and there is an important body of systems-oriented archeological literature. Advocates of systems theory in archeology are far too numerous to list exhaustively but include Binford (1965); Clarke (1968); Flannery (1968); Hole and Heizer (1969, 1973); Plog (1975); Renfrew and Cooke (1979); Sabloff (1981); Struever (1971); Tuggle, Townsend, and Riley (1972); Watson, LeBlanc, and Redman (1971: ch. 3). However, several detailed analyses by a number of critics have reached strongly negative conclusions about the validity and usefulness of systems theory in such varied fields as biology, library science, political science, sociology, and anthropology (Berlinski 1976: 2–19; Buck 1956; Hempel 1959; Hoos 1972:16–17). These critics find that the definition of key terms and concepts used by systems theorists are neither agreed upon nor adequately defined. It is probably fair to add that, similarly, there is no widespread, detailed or precise understanding of just what a systemic approach to the archeological record entails (Salmon 1978).

General systems theory, systems theory, and the systemic approach are not necessarily synonymous phrases; in fact, their connotations are often quite distinct. But almost all archeologists who espouse systems concepts are really concerned with the systemic approach. We believe the major reason for the attractiveness of this approach is the emphasis upon *interrelationships*. Whatever else may be meant by "systems theory" or "systemic approach," there is the clear implication of interrelatedness among components.

> A *system* is a set of objects together with *relationships* between the objects and between their *attributes*. (Hall and Fagen 1956:18)
>
> [A system is] an intercommunicating network of attributes or entities forming a complex whole. (Clarke 1968:669)
>
> Human ecosystems are characterized by exchanges of *matter, energy,* and *information* among their components. (Flannery and Marcus 1976:374–375)

Thus, the focusing of concern on relations among elements, among elements and groups, and among groups is the positive contribution of a systemic approach.

The concept of an integrated set of phenomena, analyzable as a unit called a system, in which a component is understandable only if its relationships and context are known, and for which relational changes in one component are likely to produce or be integrated with changes in another, is very similar to what is sometimes called functionalism in anthropology and sociology. In anthropology, emphasis on function as an explicit theoretical orientation is at least as old as the original formal exposition of functionalism by Malinowski, Radcliffe-Brown, and others. In archeology, the essence of Taylor's (1948) conjunctive approach is self-conscious concern with relationships and context. It was not until the early 1960s, however, that systems theory in its modern guise made its first appearance in the Americanist archeological literature, which it has dominated ever since. Although its recent popularity in archeology may have begun in North America, some of the strongest and most outspoken proponents were and are British archeologists following the trails blazed by David Clarke (1968, 1972).

Discussion of systems theory by Americanist archeologists in the 1960s was initiated—as were so many other inquiries—by Lewis Binford. His most influential exposition of a generalized systemic approach is his 1965 article in *American Antiquity:* "Archaeological Systematics and the Study of Cultural Processes." Binford's advocacy of a systems approach was in large part a reaction against the then prevailing view that culture comprises sets of shared ideas or values (norms). This definition of culture is usually referred to as the normative view, and—in archeology—it led to fixation on the characteristic, diagnostic, or typical pot, arrowhead, or site with accompanying neglect of the ranges of variation of these materials. On the other hand,

> From a systemic view . . . one excavated site represents a single example of one settlement type and does not reflect the whole settlement system. . . . A systemic definition of culture, therefore, imposes a number of data-collecting requirements on the archeologist. If his aim is to describe prehistoric lifeways, his frame of reference must be regional and not the boundaries of a single site. (Struever 1971:11)

Thus, a systemic approach was thought to be an effective antidote to a fixation on "typical" entities because it necessitates a shift from exclusive concern with entities to interest in the relations between and among groups and entities. An archeologist interested in such relations as possible laws of cultural process cannot search for the "typical" site and stop there; he or she must attempt to discover ranges of variation in the prehistoric record and to interrelate the causal variables that determined its present form.

As just described, the "systemic approach" is not a methodological or pragmatic statement about how to do analysis but is instead a fundamental statement about the nature of culture and how it can most profitably be studied. Such an approach requires a distinctive focus for one's questions and one's research designs (see chapter 3), but espousing this general approach does not necessitate adoption of new terminology or any particular procedures. However, people who have studied systems of various kinds have developed terminology, concepts, and methods of analysis that are useful in describing and analyzing cultural systems.

If we grant that the systemic approach is a useful way of looking at cultures, does that mean that it also is a viable alternative to a CL model as a means of explaining cultural systems? No. We remark on this in chapter 1, and we discuss the relation of CL models to systems theory below.

Meehan (1968) and Tuggle, Townsend, and Riley (1972) propose that systems explanations are highly desirable alternatives to CL explanations. Systems explanations are said to allow more complexity and more flexibility than CL explanations, and thus to be more "adequate." Flannery (1973) also suggests that there is a difference between the CL and systemic approaches to explanation. He correctly points out that those who accept the need for scientific archeology and who are interested in explanation as an archeological goal can be divided into two groups. On the one hand are those seeking the formulation of covering or general laws in isolation from any particular system under study. Such laws might range from "All hunters and gatherers are patrilocal" to "Storage facilities will increase with increasing population size." He contrasts this approach to the systemic approach as discussed here. With several years of hindsight, we can see that this split has not attained the proportions feared (possibly as a result of concern by Flannery and others). Currently, there seem to be very few attempts to generate covering laws in isolation, nor has anyone been able to "explain" a cultural system in any very comprehensive manner.

With respect to this last point, a systemic *flow chart* (as illustrated in figure 2.5) is not an explanation but rather a descriptive model of a system (and, nearly always, only part of a system). Not only does an arrow not fully describe the relationship between the two components (the boxes) it joins, but also it does not show why or under what conditions such a relationship exists. While such a flow chart can be heuristically very useful, it does not constitute an explanation of the system it depicts.

Systems explanations and CL explanations are not mutually exclusive. Systems explanations are of a logical form that can be incorporated under the logical form of CL explanations. Any systems ex-

Systems Theory and Archaeology

planation necessarily involves covering laws and can itself be written in a form that employs a complex, integrated, covering law. This point has been clearly established in the archeological literature by LeBlanc (1973:208) and Salmon (1978).

Nor is there an inherent difference in the "adequacy" of explanation between simple CL and systems explanations. Each is capable of providing an intuitively satisfying explanation, but neither approach guarantees such explanation (see tables 1.1, 1.2; also R. Watson 1976b, Read and LeBlanc 1978). Thus, the systemic approach is not so different from all others as some might suspect or wish, nor is it a panacea for solving all archaeological problems. It is, however, very important.

Systems Terminology

An introduction to the terms and concepts most commonly used by systems theorists is necessary if one is to follow the recent and current archeological literature. An important part of systems terminology refers to the interdependence of a system's components and the ability of the system to react to its environment and to regulate its processes.

One of the most useful systems concepts has to do with this regulating process. This is the idea of *feedback*. Feedback occurs when some portion of a system's *output*, or behavior, alters the *input* into the system (or part of the system) in such a way as to affect succeeding outputs (see figure 2.1). In other words, feedback occurs when some "result" of a system, for example, heat from a furnace or population growth from a human society, affects the working of the sys-

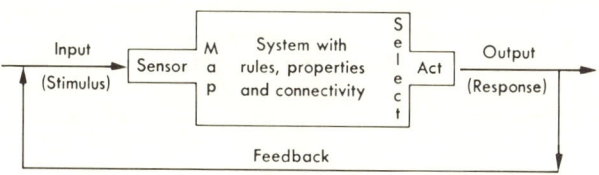

Figure 2.1. Simple System with Feedback

tem itself. Description of such feedback does not imply anything about why it exists; it may be a result of the laws of physics, or it may simply be built into the dynamics of a carefully engineered mechanism.

The study of feedback systems is known as *cybernetics*. Cyberneticists examine patterns of signals that transmit information within a system and from one system to another (Rapoport 1968:xix). Maruyama (1963) differentiates between two divisions of cybernetics on the basis of negative versus positive types of feedback. *Negative feedback* systems represent his first division. Such systems have negative feedback cycles to keep their *states* stable and within certain bounds. The state of any system can be viewed as its overall dynamic condition, which consists both of its current output and of the nature of the "setting" of its feedback loop. A furnace that is still emitting heat but whose regulatory device has turned off future heat generation is in a different state from one producing heat and programmed to produce even more heat.

Figure 2.2 illustrates a simple negative feedback system. An input or stimulus is received from the environment and affects the system. The system responds to the input in some regular fashion, resulting in a new state or status for all or part of the system and therefore in an altered output. The nature and magnitude of this output is sensed

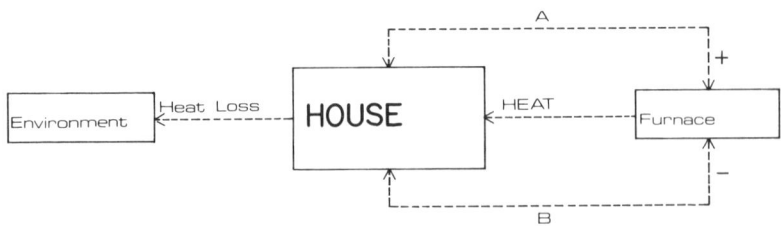

Figure 2.2. Diagram Depicting Heat Regulation in a House
Two feedback systems (A + B) or loops are needed. When the house reaches a chosen cold level, the thermostat (via loop A) reacts and turns on the furnace. When the house reaches a chosen heat level, the thermostat (via loop B) reacts and turns off the furnace. Note that no prior knowledge of how much heat will be lost is necessary for the system to work. Output from the house, in the form of house temperature, is all the information that is needed to regulate the system.

by the receptor part of the system, and its regulating devices modify the system's treatment of future input to produce output close to the original state. The method of regulation varies according to the type of system. Examples besides the centrally heated house shown in figure 2.2 include the genes of a cell and the preconceived specifications of a machine's inventor.

A negative feedback, or deviation-counteracting, system is thus one in which change in the system is reduced so that the system tends to return to its original state. A classic cultural example is the custom of *cargo* in some traditional Latin American societies. Due to the vagaries of luck, skill, family demography, and so on, certain families accumulate wealth disproportionately to the community as a whole. The greater the wealth differential, the greater the social pressure on such families to perform expensive community services (usually in the form of holding public office or financing religious functions). These services reduce the family wealth, thereby maintaining the status quo.

The actual forms taken by positive and negative feedback loops may be simple or quite complex. If the temperature exceeds 68°F, then the furnace will be turned off. This is a simple negative mechanism. However, we may have a situation where the feedback loop regulates the system in different ways depending on the output or state of the system. For example, the human energy expended on hunting small game may be low when the human population is low, regardless of the density of small game, large game being taken instead. When the human population increases, a new level of energy expenditure is attained. As the population increases and large game becomes scarce, there will be relatively more human energy expended on hunting small game. Then, if—in response to increased human predation—the density of small game falls below a certain level, a further response will be reduction of human energy expended on small game hunting regardless of the human population size. That is, the human population reaches a point of diminishing returns with respect to small game hunting and concentrates on other resources. Two instances of *threshold* phenomena are illustrated here: population increases until small game is hunted intensively; and then small game density is reduced to the point that the intensive hunting of it is curtailed. Such complex relationships are typical of the kinds of feedback loops in cultural systems.

The second division of cybernetics is the study of positive feedback, *deviation-amplifying* relationships (Maruyama 1963). Here, changes in part of the system result in more changes so that the system moves farther and farther from its original state. This concept has long been used in economic literature in discussions of increases in wages and prices during inflationary periods. (It is also illustrated by the well-known dictum, "the rich get richer.") In contrast to the stabilizing effect of negative feedback, positive feedback mechanisms may induce changes of state or structure.

An example of positive feedback is a series of small, unfortified, and reasonably peaceful neighboring villages. Their relationships with each other and with their physical environment are in a state of equilibrium that is only slightly unstable because of some pressure on available resources. One night in one of the villages, a house is burned and food stores are stolen. It is not known who is guilty, but the people of the affected village gain the support of one of the neighboring villages and raid the village they distrust the most. Integrating or homeostatic mechanisms such as treaties, ritual cooperation, and kin relations are not strong enough to keep the system within its former bounds. Retaliatory raids occur that force the many villages to combine into large centers that can be fortified and can support temporary armies. The amalgamation into larger settlements causes a localization of greater wealth, which leads to greater temptation to attack and loot. This situation leads to the necessity for a permanent defense force, which results in further temptation to use this army offensively to attack other communities. Thus, a cycle of warfare is started and propagates itself in a vicious spiral. Progressive changes lead to increasing amounts of warfare. An initial perturbation or change causes a large enough deviation from the normal state so that, instead of a return to the norm of no warfare, there is a change to ever-increasing warfare.

Detailed knowledge concerning the first warlike act (where and when it occurred, who did it, and so on) is irrelevant to the understanding of the amalgamation of the villages into cities and the state of increasing warfare. To gain a general understanding of the process and the state of affairs at any time in this system, one needs rather to understand the deviation-amplifying mechanisms that affect it.

These examples of positive and negative feedback systems are too simple to represent actual situations in any cultural system. Complex cultural systems are composed of many feedback loops, both positive and negative, of differing magnitudes. By means of these feedback loops, the components of the system interpret and respond to various inputs from other systems, from the environment, and from other components of the system.

One type of system characterized by complex feedback mechanisms is a *homeostatic,* or self-regulating, system. Obviously, such systems are characterized by negative feedback loops, but less obviously they may contain positive loops as well. For example, population size may be regulated by a variety of feedback loops. Under most conditions, increasing population sets into motion forces that tend to reduce population (negative feedback). But there may well be situations—such as a sudden large drop in population caused by warfare or plague, for example—when initial increases in population are followed by still larger increases (deviation amplification). A homeostatic system is one in which the overall result of all the feedback loops is to keep the outputs within certain bounds.

Another important concept is that of *equilibrium,* and related to it is the concept of *perturbation,* or change in the state of a system. A system is in equilibrium when feedback mechanisms keep its output within tight bounds. But there are two fundamental types of equilibrium: stable and unstable. A homeostatic system is in stable equilibrium when the system will return to its original state no matter how large the perturbation. A system in unstable equilibrium may be able to cope with small perturbations, but if any perturbation beyond a certain magnitude sets in motion a series of deviation-amplifying (positive feedback) mechanisms, operation of these mechanisms may make the situation irreversible, resulting in a state extremely different from the original one.

A pendulum is a simple example of stable equilibrium. Any movement away from the vertical position is counteracted by gravity: the farther the pendulum moves from the vertical, the greater the force returning it to the original position. In contrast, a gyroscope on a horizontal string is in an unstable situation: slight perturbations are counteracted, but if the perturbation is too great, the force of gravity amplifies the deviation, and the gyroscope falls off the string. In our previous example the villages were initially in a state of unstable equilibrium, and the initial raid was sufficient to upset the system. One can imagine other situations in which very stable systems exist whose deviation-countering mechanisms (for example, religious beliefs) are so strong that no raid can lead to endemic warfare.

Archeologists have adopted numerous other systems concepts and their associated terminology. For example, Kent Flannery (1972) offers an explanation of the rise of civilization by examining the processes of increasing segregation and centralization within society. He focuses on the emergence of *higher order controls* as an essential characteristic of state society and utilizes two mechanisms discussed by systems theorists to describe some of the crucial changes that take place during the rise of the state. The first is *promotion,* by means of which a low-level, special purpose institution becomes a higher-level institution serving a general purpose during a time of stress. A military coup in which a military leader takes control of the state government and becomes a political, economic, and perhaps even a religious leader, is an example of promotion. The second mechanism is *linearization,* by means of which low-level controls are permanently bypassed by higher-level controls. The takeover of local irrigation management by the state government is an example of linearization. Various forms of both promotion and linearization seem to have contributed to the rise of early civilizations. By focusing on these mechanisms of change rather than on the specific institutions themselves, Flannery isolates or defines the structural changes in the system so that they can be compared with structural changes in other systems.

A final set of systems concepts and terminology must be considered. First is the distinction between *open* and *closed* systems. A closed system receives no input from outside its defined boundaries, while an open system does. These concepts should be distinguished from those of environment and background environment. The background environment is sometimes viewed as something that can affect the system but that the system cannot in turn affect, whereas a system is a reciprocal part of its environment. The vegetation, climate, and geomorphology of a region are thus sometimes considered to be an effective but unaffected environmental background for cultural systems. But obviously cultural systems do often alter these environmental factors. Hence one must be very careful in using and interpreting these concepts.

Strictly speaking, the universe is the only closed system because every system within it is affected to some degree, however infinitesimal, by everything else it includes. However, for practical, analytical purposes we may restrict the number of relationships we are considering so that we can model essentially closed systems. What is considered to be background environment or outside an—analytically speaking—closed system is a function of the system, of our interests, and of our knowledge. Thus, many traditional studies of cultural systems are of analytically closed systems with background social and physical environments surrounding, but outside, them. However, as indicated in our discussion of environmental archeology (chapter 3), the understanding of cultural stability and change is greatly enhanced by considering the social and physical environment to be an integral part of the system. Indeed, we believe that culture can be understood only in mutual interaction with its "background" environment.

Describing Systems

The *state* of a system is its current structure in terms of attributes of its components and the nature of its relationships. This means that, given an initial state and assuming no environmental changes, the trajectory the system takes is uniquely determined, regardless of the path along which the system arrived at the initial state. Catastrophe theory (discussed in the Conclusion to the simulation section below) is based on the assumption that in some instances this path is important in determining the subsequent trajectory of a system. The effects of a system's history are, of course, manifest in some form in its current state. The question is about the extent of influence of these manifestations. Obviously it will differ in different cases.

A system can be most completely defined as a set of equations. However, a simpler way to represent the state of a system is by means of graphs (Harary, Norman, and Cartwright 1965). We use graphs to illustrate the example of the warring communities and to introduce some other aspects of a systemic approach. Let us assume that the only variables relevant to the warring communities system are the number of people per community and the percentage of each community under arms (soldiers). (Obviously this is a considerable simplification of the possibly relevant variables.) Figure 2.3 is a diagram of the states of the system.

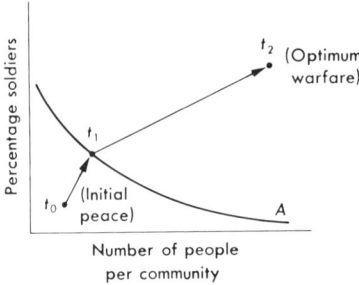

Figure 2.3. Graph of Possible States of Peace and War in the System

Each point on this diagram represents a possible state of the system in terms of these two variables. If the state of the system changes over time (t_0 to t_1), then the vector that connects these two points is the *trajectory* of this system during the specified time. The state of a system is specified by its position on the graph, and the change in its state is described by the trajectory. The graph can be divided into a number of different sections or regions, each representing a different type of situation (for example, peace or war). Within each of these regions there is usually one optimum point or state. Each of these regions can be thought of as a *basin of attraction*, and the lines between them as *boundaries*. Once the trajectory brings a system within a region, there is a tendency for that state to move toward this optimum point. The change of a system within one region is usually gradual and not discontinuous, but once it approaches—and as it crosses—a boundary between two regions, change is normally accelerated and may seem discontinuous.

This model is highly abstract. In reality, what happens is that the various feedback loops have different overall effects depending on the current output of the system. That is, when the state falls well within a region, a number of negative feedback loops keep it there. If, for whatever reason, the system's output places it near a boundary, the effects of the feedback loops are changed and there is a greater likelihood that positive feedback loops will produce effects, thereby rapidly changing the system states.

The variables of a system can also be expressed in graph form (figure 2.4). In this example the variables are the relative peace in a region and the relative concentration of wealth in each community. The graph represents three types of states for the system: stable, oscillatory, and unstable. The boundary lines must be defined on the basis of empirical investigations. At any time the behavior of the system can be shown by plotting the values of relative peace and concentration of wealth.

Point A represents a stable state of the system that has high relative peace and low concentration of wealth. The stable state would be characterized by stable conditions in *all* aspects (subsystems) of the system, not only in those involving peace and wealth. In other words, strong negative feedback cycles make it unlikely that the system will change significantly.

Point B represents an oscillatory or variable state of the system. In this case the system has less relative peace and more concentration

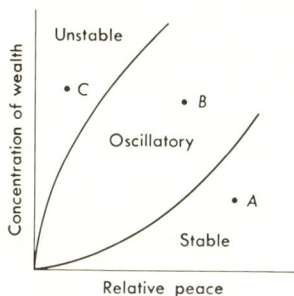

Figure 2.4. Graph of Potential Behavior of the System

of wealth than when in the state represented by point A. The system in state B is characterized by significant changes in comparison with the system in state A, but negative feedback cycles still tend to keep change from being so great as to destroy the system.

Point O represents an unstable state. In this case the system is characterized by little peace and much concentration of wealth. Negative feedback is weak and one could expect the system to change by moving to other unstable states, into an oscillatory state, or even through changes that destroy the system altogether.

A change in value of one of the variables can result in a change in the nature of the system's behavior. The relations in this diagram are an expression in structural terms of the possible range of behavior of the system.

Figure 2.3 represents the two alternate states this system can assume and, hence, the trajectory of possible changes available to it. It is useful, especially for more complex cases (i.e., where more than two alternate states are possible), to construct a diagram that shows all the possible trajectories the system might pass through in order to summarize all possible transitions. However, it must be made clear that a *description* of the trajectory of a system is not to be equated with an *explanation* of the processes involved. The products of an evolutionary or developmental sequence must not be confused with the processes that cause and govern the sequence. At any point along this trajectory, the interrelationships of variables within a system are what determine the current state of the system and its future course. This kind of graph is a useful way to describe a system, but as already noted, it is not the only way. We could generate an equation that shows the same relationships. In either case, however, full understanding requires knowledge of all the underlying relationships, not just of the form of the first trajectory.

One of the most useful tools in describing and understanding systems is a *flow diagram* (also called a flow chart, a directed graph, or a diagraph) showing the interrelationships of the main components in the system. Constructing the flow diagram forces the researcher to make explicit what types of data and which relationships must be studied. It also forces one to specify what components influence which other components and in what ways (figure 2.5) and makes clear other

Systems Theory and Archaeology

relationships that could potentially exist and must therefore be considered. The direction and future behavior of a system can be calculated from detailed analyses of the directions of influences between components and of the nature of the feedback loops. If a system is portrayed correctly, one can predict its future states and thus test one's understanding of its functioning. The complicating factors of random or stochastic effects are discussed below in the section on simulation.

Figure 2.5 is a flow diagram of the simplified warring communities situation discussed above. The logic and structure of this three-component system are straightforward. The three components are: the relative concentration of people and wealth per community; the relative agricultural efficiency of the people of the geographical region; and the frequency of warfare in this region.

According to this flow diagram, an increase in the concentration of people and wealth in large communities will increase the frequency of warfare, and in turn, an increase in the frequency of warfare will force more people to live in the concentrated and defendable centers. The two components influence each other positively, and the feedback loop between them (loop A) shows this deviation-amplifying relationship. If this were the only loop, or the dominant loop, involved in the system, then instability would continuously increase until the system breaks apart. Feedback loop B represents an increase in agricultural efficiency that makes possible a greater concentration of people in the city, but this in turn decreases the general agricultural efficiency because farmers are separated from their land.

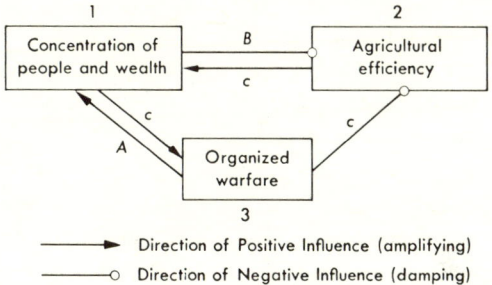

Figure 2.5. Diagraph of a Cultural System Model

Thus, the total effect of loop B is negative and equilibrating; left alone it would result in a state of high stability. Loop C in the system depicts a positive influence of agricultural efficiency on concentration of people and wealth, which has a positive influence on the growth of warfare, but increasing warfare in turn decreases agricultural efficiency. Consequently, the total effect of loop C, like that of loop B, is negative or equilibrating.

By examining the three components and loops, we can predict by inspection future behavior of the system. A real society—even one small part of a simple society—or an organism must be represented by many deviation-amplifying loops, as well as deviation-counteracting loops, and an understanding of a societal subsystem cannot be attained without studying both types of loops and the relationships among them. But in this simple example, the system can either expand and explode or it can oscillate between increasing and decreasing frequency of warfare. There are many examples of both types of results in the cultural-historical record of systems. It should be possible by a comparative study of the relevant variables in these societies to determine the values for each relationship that result in different types of behavior (that is, different trajectories) for these systems. The expression of the situation in the form of graphs and equations focuses the researcher's attention on crucial relations to be examined in future work and facilitates quantitative treatment of models of cultural change.

The example raises the important point that one can elaborate a flow diagram almost indefinitely. That is, one can usually take any given portion of a flow diagram and break it into more detailed component parts, just as one can take a thermostat and show how its various parts interact to change the furnace setting. Modeling a system in greater and greater detail as one learns more about its dynamics is equivalent to refining old hypotheses and constructing new ones to cover new data as empirical research progresses. And as with theories, there is no natural point at which to draw the line. One decides not to complicate the flow chart further when it shows what is required, just as one usually refines a theory only to the point necessary to answer one's questions about a system or subject.

The above description is unrealistically simple, and we do not discuss the mathematics involved, but see Cooke (1979) and Renfrew and Cooke (1979). In general, considerable analytical power is gained by transforming a flow diagram into a matrix of relationships or a series of equations. That is, flow diagrams have high heuristic value, but with adequate knowledge of a system, one can replace a flow chart with analytically more useful mathematical formulations.

While most of the mathematical considerations of systems models are far beyond our present concerns, a few relevant points are taken up at the end of this chapter. However, several additional issues and concepts must be considered first.

One recent effort to use a systemic approach is that of Hill (1977), who raises some very important points with respect to the application of systemic thinking to archeological data. However, he draws some conclusions that are incommensurate with our understanding of the systemic approach. Hill says that an adequate systems explanation of a particular cultural change has three essential characteristics. First, the positive feedback cycles between variables that promote change in the system must be identified; second, the environmental or cultural stimuli that set up and initiate the positive feedback relationships must be recognized; and third, the stabilizing regulating mechanisms that emerge to constrain and integrate the changes that take place must be described. The investigator who carries out these three steps must examine a change from its initiation through the establishment of a new stable condition.

One can take issue with several aspects of Hill's strictures. First, it can be misleading to consider only selected feedback cycles of a system. There may always be positive feedback cycles that are overridden by negative cycles so that the system remains stable. Then a breakdown of these negative cycles could be what leads to the systemic change; hence, concentrating on the positive cycles might cause one to miss the most important aspect of a systemic change.

Second, as noted above, the initial perturbation of either an environmental or a cultural system may be slight or even undetectable. It is not necessary to locate and describe the particular stimuli to understand the nature of systemic change. This is, in fact, one of the strengths of a systems approach, particularly for archeology.

Hill also raises the question of whether change should be viewed as internal to the system or as the result of external forces. This may at first appear to depend on whether one views a cultural system as open or closed. However, if systemic change seems always to result from external causes, then it would appear to be difficult to use systems analysis to explain the changes, and in this case a systemic approach would not be as useful as we might wish.

However, Renfrew (1981) and Low (1981) show that most cultural systems change from internal causes and not solely because of the effects on them of external forces. Catastrophe theory provides a model of very abrupt change that can be internally system-related, and this is by no means the only such model possible. A systemic approach and systems modeling can be very useful in describing cultural change.

There could be, in theory, two kinds of systemic change. On the one hand, external or internal initial forces could cause the system itself to change in the sense that at least some components and relationships would be modified, added, or deleted. However, these forces could also cause a system state to alter abruptly or very significantly without causing any changes in system components or relationships. It is obviously of interest to determine which kind of change occurs. Renfrew (1981) argues that archeologists traditionally assume that major cultural changes are system changes when many may be merely state changes. He is certainly correct that cultural changes are of both types and that we must distinguish between the two.

In summary, the contribution of systems theory to archeological research is that it is a way to formulate testable models of (i.e., complex hypotheses about) human social and cultural behavior. A model makes explicit just what variables and significant hypotheses have been selected as relevant from an infinite number of possibilities and thus forces attention on what may be missing or irrelevant. The model itself then guides one's efforts toward productive research in a specific area. The key to effective formulation of systems models is ability and insight in constructing graphical representations of cultural systems. These are built up from logical deductions and from data already at hand; they are tested by calculating future behaviors of the systems, as modeled, and then by checking these predictions against the empirical situation. A model that explicitly shows the interconnections among the feedback loops and components of the system, on the one hand, and the relevant aspects of its environment, on the other, thus can be used to calculate the behavior of a system. The model is tested by comparing that expected behavior with the behavior represented in the archeological record. If the predictions appear to be largely accurate and cannot be falsified by the archeological evidence, then the researcher has some support for the claim that the hypothetical relationships postulated in the model pertained in the real past. There is here, as always in empirical science, a kind of circular procedure as one postulates hypotheses on the basis of data, and then both tests the hypotheses on the basis of those data and interprets those data on the basis of the hypotheses. No vicious circle is involved in this process, as shown by the fact that it advances understanding by progressively increasing the explanatory and predictive powers of scientific models and theories.

Thus, utilizing "systems theory," or a "systemic approach," as the phrases are used here, means constructing models and diagrammatic summaries of some portions of a society. These simplified flow charts or directed graphs define, express, and describe hypotheses about functions and relationships. These hypotheses, like any others, then serve as the bases for prediction about the nature of the archeological record pertaining to the societies in question. The testing of such hypotheses is essential for establishing and expanding knowledge of these prehistoric societies. As noted above, the hypotheses are checked by comparing them with the known archeological record.

One means of carrying out this procedure is to use *computer simulation* of portions of the cultural systems in question (Doran 1970; Hodder 1978; Sabloff 1981). We now consider simulation, and the circumstrances under which simulation is the most effective approach to an archeological problem.

Simulation

Simulation is a computer-based technique that has considerable potential utility for archeologists. In this section we enumerate a number of uses of simulation, assess the power of the technique, and evaluate some of the published examples of simulation in archeology.

Simulations are produced in a computer by programming it to carry out the relational operations represented by arrows in flow diagrams. A simulation is begun by assigning initial values for each of the components (for example, so many people, so much stored food, so many temples built, so many different settlements) at an initial time (t_0). The relationships affect the values of each component in specified ways to produce new sets of values for each succeeding time (t_1 to t_n). The simulation can be run for as long as desired, but the time is usually set in terms of years or generations, depending on what one wants to learn.

Two kinds of systemic models can be simulated. One kind has varying relationships among various components but all the relationships are definite, that is, they have no random aspects. The other kind of system model includes one or more relationships that have random or stochastic properties. For example, we can specify a relationship whereby the population increase per cycle is 2 percent more than it was at the end of the previous cycle. That is, the relationship between the old and new populations is completely determined. Or, we can model a system in which the population increase is 1 percent, 2 percent, or 3 percent, but which percentage actually pertains is random. That is, neither the state of the system nor the size of the population can be used to determine the population increase because a stochastic element has been introduced into the model.

A model in which all the relationships are completely determined and that has no stochastic elements exhibits a unique state at any one time. Hence by assigning some initial values to relationships in the model and letting the simulation proceed, we can obtain the state of the system for any subsequent time, and the state for each point is identical if we repeat the process. We use simulation to study such systems for two different reasons. First, although it may be theoretically possible to determine the state of the system mathematically at any point by treating each relationship as a simultaneous equation and solving the equation, this is often so complicated that it is easier to simulate the system. Second, and more importantly, we often study systems whose behaviors are properties of their initial values.

Systems Theory and Archaeology 87

For example, a system may be stable if the initial population is low but unstable if the initial population is high. Thus, we may want to look at the long-term operation of the system to determine the states that follow from different combinations of the initial values. In this case, it is usually best to write a very general computer program so that the initial values can be changed without having to rewrite the program. Then the model can be easily rerun under varied initial values. If there are four or five different components, we might want to change their values to make a hundred or more different runs of the model with different initial values. This is one of the great advantages of a simulation procedure: once the model is programmed, additional runs are easy to make. Cooke and Renfrew's simulation of the rise of civilization in the Aegean is a good example of a determined model that was run with a wide variety of initial component values (Cooke and Renfrew 1979).

The second broad category of simulation covers models that include random elements which are used to determine stochastic relationships. In this case there are no unique values for the successive states of a model; that is, even starting with the same initial values for the components, we will not necessarily obtain the same results for different runs. Examples are models in which population growth has random elements, or in which there are random droughts, or in which a leader's death is a random event. Or a model may include several random processes operating at the same time. What is of interest is not the results of any single run but the frequency and plausibility of the different results. For example, one might be interested in the percentage of time that the system is stable, or the percentage of time required for the population to double. In general, comparison of repeated runs provides knowledge of the statistical distribution of results at specific times.

Analyses can be compounded by varying the initial values of the system. To calculate stochastic results, one starts the model with initial values and runs it 100 times. Then the initial values are changed, and another 100 runs are made, and so on. For determination of stochastic results with varying initial values, the advantages of computer simulation are obviously very great. Examples of stochastic models are Thomas' Great Basin model (1972), the Wright–Zeder

(1977) trade model, Chadwick's (1978) Mycenaean settlement model, and O'Shea's (1978) Pawnee site development model.

Determined models are simple cases of the stochastic situation. Thus, for purposes of illustration, we assume a stochastic situation in which several relationships are operating at the same time, some or all of them according to random factors. Because of these random processes, the range of possible outputs from such a system is wide. However, certain of these outputs are more likely than others. Successive runs of the simulation model are made to determine not only what outcomes are possible but also which are the most likely.

Suppose food output is directly related to population size and vice versa. Further, suppose that food output is affected by rainfall and the length of the growing season. Then, if we know the rainfall and the length of the growing season for a given year, we can determine the rate of food production and the effect on the population size. If we know the rainfall and the length of growing season for a long series of years, we can determine whether and how much the population will increase or decrease. Suppose, however, we know only the probability for drought or early frost in any particular year. In such a case, we cannot determine the exact long-range effects of these events on the population. But with a stochastic simulation model of the system we can determine the probable effects on the population under various initial conditions.

The system is modeled by using the rules governing the relationships with values of the known or assumed probabilities for the various events. For this example, we choose a number randomly to determine whether the first year has adequate rainfall or not. For example, if there is a 30 percent chance of drought each year, we could draw from numbers between 1 and 10, with the specification that numbers 1 through 3 represent drought years. Hence, if the random number drawn is 1, 2, or 3, we start by assuming a drought year; if the number is 4 through 10, we assume a nondrought year. We then draw from a set of ten numbers again to determine whether there was an early frost. (If the chances are 50 percent, we could just flip a fair coin.) From these results we determine what the output was for the year and what the effects were on the population. This simulation experiment is repeated for as many years as one wishes to consider, say, 100 years. One thus determines the hypothetical net effects of drought and length of growing season on this population for the entire 100-year sequence.

However, other random drawings of numbers could produce entirely different sets of results. So the entire process must be repeated over and over. Suppose one made 100 runs, each simulating 100 years. The results might show, for example, that the population starves only two years out of 100, or that the population never loses a crop. Or one might find that the most common outcome of such a series of events (say, 90 percent of the time) is that the population starves within forty years. One can also change some or all of the initial assumptions of the model (that is, the probabilities of drought or early frost) and repeat the entire analysis.

The value of simulation modeling increases with the complexity of the situations studied. Fortunately, very complicated systems can be modeled on computers. Then hundreds of repeated simulations involving many different probabilities and representing hundreds of years can be run, all for very little cost.

Some Archeological Examples

For purposes of discussion, we divide recent simulation studies into three categories: (1) tests of relatively simple mathematical relationships (usually expressed as algebraic equations), such as those describing patterns of exchange or the effects of alternate sampling methods; (2) tests of complex hypothetical explanations, such as those derived to account for settlement or demographic patterns; (3) tests of hypothetical behavioral processes specified either as complex sets of decisions or as behavior of the system as a whole.

Examples of simulations of simple mathematical relationships are the most numerous and are very similar to some investigations previously simply called quantitative analysis. One series of these comprises attempts to determine the most effective field strategies to use in attaining various objectives. For example, Stephen Plog simulates a variety of different sampling designs for a regional survey to discover which unit size, sampling proportion, and type of procedure produces the closest approximation to a given population of archeological sites (Plog 1976; see also Plog, Plog, and Wait 1978). Ammerman, Gifford, and Voorrips (1978) simulate a variety of different excavation programs for investigating a recently abandoned hunting and gathering encampment to determine which procedures to use and how much of the site must be uncovered to accomplish accurate description of the material.

Other archeologists have used relatively simple simulations to examine particular past exchange systems and to test specific models of the operation of these systems. These studies began as nonsimulation models. In particular, Colin Renfrew (1972) describes the distribution of Anatolian obsidian at neolithic sites throughout the Near East. He finds that, once the sites are beyond a crucial zone surrounding the obsidian sources, the amount of obsidian present diminishes directly as the distance from the sources increases. Hence, he postulates a "down-the-line" mechanism for obsidian distribution during the Near Eastern neolithic. Ammerman, Matessi, and Cavelli-Sforza (1978) refine this particular solution and present a fall-off curve to describe the distribution of obsidian in the Near East and in neolithic southern Italy.

To construct and explain the fall-off curve for the frequency of obsidian at each village successively farther from a source area, archeologists assume that each village retains some obsidian—a portion of which ultimately becomes part of the archeological deposit—and passes some on to the next village. This leads to two types of simulation studies. One type is illustrated by Wright and Zeder (1977), who explore some of the economic consequences of a simple down-the-line exchange model; they point out (as Sahlins [1972] proposes) that such systems are more complex than initially appears to be the case. The other type is represented by Hodder and Orton (1976), who assume trade goods like obsidian to be spread by a diverse series of mechanisms; they use a random-walk technique to simulate the movements of these goods. They find that different movement models may produce the same ultimate distributions, such as those including barriers to trade versus those without trade barriers. Their model also allows them to distinguish between goods that move many steps (probably luxury items; see also Elliot, Ellman, and Hodder [1978]) and those (presumably utilitarian) that move only a few steps.

Complex processes—such as those involved in population growth or population spread—often involve the simultaneous operation of a series of relationships including both environmental and social variables. Archaeologists investigate these situations by looking at only one segment of the system, or by holding constant a series of variables. For example, Ammerman and Cavelli-Sforza (1973, 1979) posit that the spread of village farming economy from the Near East was caused, at least in part, by actual population movements involving people who were practicing this technology. They compare the archeological information for the earliest appearance of farming villages in different European areas with predictions derived from a "wave of advance" model based on certain assumptions about demographic growth and the spread of individual settlements.

Other such simulation analyses involve both population and site location, for example, that of Chadwick (1978).

It must be stressed that these kinds of simulations—of great archeological importance—do not especially derive from systems theory or especially represent a systemic approach. They are simply ways of solving problems by programming computers with recursive relations in a process generally known as simulation modeling.

While there is no sharp dividing line, we separate less complex simulations like those described above from simulations that represent systemically all or some significant part of a cultural system (type 3 of the series listed at the beginning of this section). These do derive explicitly from a systemic approach. While there are a considerable number of published analytic simulations, there are only a few overtly systemic simulations, and we discuss most of them below.

Systemic simulation analyses are often focused on site location and resource production and/or exchange, often expressed as sets of decisions made by individuals or groups of individuals. The best-known example is that conducted by David Thomas (1972, 1973), who compares the prehistoric with the ethnohistoric subsistence behavior of the hunting and gathering Shoshonean bands in the Great Basin. To test Julian Steward's construction (based on ethnohistorical research, Steward 1938) of the seasonal rounds of Great Basin groups, Thomas devises a flow chart of alternate subsistence-settlement location decisions made during each season of a yearly round. The simulation model closely approximates Steward's description of procurement systems for piñon nuts, Indian rice grass, and antelope employed by the Shoshone at the time of contact. By means of this model Thomas projects data on population, site types, and site locations for a thousand-year period. He then compares the simulated result with the actual archeological information collected during a series of surveys in the region and finds a fairly close fit between predictions derived from the model, on the one hand, and archeological reality, on the other. Two other, less well-known models of similar complexity are worth considering in more detail.

THE AEGEAN MODEL

Renfrew (1972) proposes that the rise of civilization in the Aegean can be conceptualized usefully as a case of a system experiencing rapid change because of the operation of a series of positive feedback relationships among several key components. He and Cooke simulate this postulated system to study the takeoff process (Cooke and Renfrew 1979). Their effort is an excellent example because it illustrates most of the limitations archeologists face in the simulation and modeling of systems. This is not to suggest that they do not do a good job; quite to the contrary, they are very methodical and very thorough in their simulations, and they fully realize the limitations of the results they obtain.

They begin by defining six subsystems: subsistence, metallurgical, craft technology, social, symbolic, and trade. Cooke and Renfrew then characterize the relationships between the subsystems, as shown in table 2.1.

In order to simulate the system, they develop a matrix defined as follows: "Wherever no interaction is indicated we place a 0. Wherever a favoring mechanism appears, we place +1. Wherever an inhibiting mechanism appears we place a -1." This results in the matrix shown in figure 2.6.

We now come to the crux of the problem of characterizing and simulating archeological systems. How are the quantitative values given to each of these relationships to be determined? What is meant by an increase in the metallurgical subsystem and in the symbolic

Table 2.1.
Matrix of Interactions between the Subsystems of the Culture System (with Population)

	|	|	|	x	|	|	|
y	Subsistence	Metallurgy	Craft Technology	Social Systems	Projective and Symbolic Systems	Trade and Communication	Population
Subsistence	—	B_1	B_5	B_2, B_3, B_4	B_7	B_6	B_8
Metallurgy		—	C_1	C_2, C_3, C_4		C_5	
Craft technology	D_1	D_4	—	D_2	D_5	D_6	D_3
Social systems	E_1	E_2, E_3, E_4	E_2, E_3	—	E_5		E_6
Projective and symbolic systems			F_1, F_5	F_2, F_3	—	F_4	F_6
Trade and communication	G_1	G_2, G_3	G_4, G_5	G_6	G_7	—	
Population	A_1		A_4	A_2, A_5	A_3		—

SOURCE: After Renfrew (1972:488).
NOTE: Growth in subsystem y favored by growth in subsystem x through the mechanism indicated in the matrix. (Compare list in Renfrew 1972:489–494).

one? Cooke and Renfrew define the metallurgical subsystem as the "per capita" number of metal artifacts produced within the territory of the society. But does jewelry count equally with swords, or swords equally with axes or saws? However this problem is resolved, clearly we do not know what the actual number of artifacts is for any year, let alone for each year. What Cooke and Renfrew do is assume that a percentage increase in one subsystem results in exactly the same percentage increase in each subsystem it affects. This is the essential meaning of matrix A. Cooke and Renfrew fully realize how great a

$$A = \begin{pmatrix} 0 & 1 & 1 & 1 & 1 & 1 & 1 \\ 0 & 0 & 1 & 1 & 0 & 1 & 0 \\ 1 & 1 & 0 & 1 & 1 & 1 & 1 \\ 1 & 1 & 1 & 0 & 1 & 0 & 1 \\ 0 & 0 & 1 & 1 & 0 & 1 & 1 \\ 1 & 1 & 1 & 1 & 1 & 0 & 0 \\ 1 & 0 & 1 & 1 & 1 & 0 & 0 \end{pmatrix}$$

Figure 2.6

SOURCE: Cooke and Renfrew (1979:332)

simplification (if not actual inaccuracy) this procedure represents. The question is whether they can still learn something true of the system despite this simplification. In fact, they modify the matrix by appealing to knowledge of the archeological record, economics, common sense, and what verges on wild guessing to improve their modeling of the subsystem relationships. For example, they argue that an increase in the subsistence resources of craft specialists would have a relatively much greater impact on the metallurgical subsystem than on population growth. A series of reevaluations of this sort changes the relationship matrix to that shown in figure 2.7.

$$B = \begin{pmatrix} 0 & .5 & .5 & 1.0 & .25 & .75 & .75 \\ 0 & 0 & .75 & 2.0 & 0 & 1.0 & 0 \\ .5 & .75 & 0 & .5 & .5 & .25 & .25 \\ .25 & .75 & .5 & 0 & .1 & 0 & .5 \\ 0 & 0 & .25 & .75 & 0 & .25 & .5 \\ .25 & 1.0 & .75 & .35 & .1 & 0 & 0 \\ .75 & 0 & .1 & .85 & .1 & 0 & 0 \end{pmatrix}$$

Figure 2.7

SOURCE: Cooke and Renfrew (1979:335)

This, of course, is still a very simplified (even if generally correct) model of the actual system. But before running a simulation they must solve yet another problem. What values should be assigned to the system components at the beginning? How should the relation of population to metallurgical production be defined at the outset? Fortunately, this important problem—although it cannot be solved directly—can be met in an indirect manner. Cooke and Renfrew simply run the simulation many times, changing the initial values each time. This, of course, does not show which set of values is correct. However, what is shown in this case is that, regardless of the initial values, the system behaves essentially the same way. Hence, Cooke and Renfrew need not worry about choice of initial values.

The reader may have observed that all the components in this model have positive relationships; there are no negative loops. Thus, it is not surprising that Cooke and Renfrew find that the values in the system keep increasing. And even when they add a negative subcomponent—piracy—the system continues to grow regardless of the

Systems Theory and Archaeology

input values used. The authors conclude that the behavior of their model is not the behavior expected for such a cultural system and that the model is, in some way, deficient.

This example is thus a test that leads to the disconfirmation of a model. Renfrew might now modify his model of Aegean civilization, perhaps by adding more subsystems, especially negative ones. In hindsight, the absence of negative components from the original interpretation perhaps should lead one to expect that the simulation would be inadequate in mimicking real world behavior. Alternatively, perhaps adequate subsystems were chosen but the relationships between them were inaccurately modeled. Why should population growth and subsistence output increase directly with one another? Our general understanding of these processes suggests that, as population grows, it is increasingly difficult to increase per capita output. The problem of describing these relationships realistically is clearly recognized by the authors. Often there are not enough data to define such complex relationships. In any event, the Aegean study is an important deterministic simulation effort. The problems archeologists face are clearly evident, as are the efforts required and the results obtained.

THE MAYAN COLLAPSE

A second example of system simulation is that of the Classic Mayan collapse. Hosler, Sabloff, and Runge (1977) model a part of the Mayan system in great detail, making considerable effort to determine the nature of the component relationships as accurately as possible.

The simulation is based on a verbal description of the Mayan collapse produced by Willey and Shimkin (1973). The collapse is presented as the result of a combination of internal and external pressures. A major internal pressure was competition among elite leadership groups resulting in increased amounts of prestigious building activities (monument construction). The efforts invested in such constructions differed according to the population size. When the population was small, only a small amount of monument construction was undertaken; as the population grew, there was increased emphasis on building activities. When the population was very large, everyone worked on monument building to the detriment of agriculture, and this led to increased malnutrition and disease. The elite were incapable of managing the situation. They reacted by putting still more emphasis on monument building, thus intensifying the deviation-amplifying cycle and causing the destruction of the entire system. Destabilization was intensified by the breakdown of external trade, which was important to the maintenance of the Mayan elite.

Hosler, Sabloff, and Runge construct a simulation model of this system to determine whether it would indeed collapse and, if so, when. Care is taken to incorporate a large number of relationships (e.g., crop production per person per year) in the detailed model.

The final flow chart is given in figure 2.8. Perhaps the most important discovery the authors make is that many of the relationships are not linear; that is, the *proportions* among the elements in some of the relationships do not remain fixed as the *values* of the elements change. Hence, they include nonlinear relationships in which the proportions among the elements change as the values of the elements change. For example, they argue that as the population increases there is a fall-off in per capita food production and also that the advantage gained by the elite from the building of additional monuments is not strictly linear. But the most important relationship is that, as food production declines, the hardships suffered by the commoners threaten the elite. The elite attempt to remedy this situation by building more monuments, taking still more people out of food production, and thus causing still more hardship.

The authors conduct two simulations. In the first, they assume that there is a long delay before the elite try to repair the instabilities caused by the population's inability to keep up with the demand for more monuments. This leads to a systemic collapse. In the second simulation, they shorten the correction time by the elite, and in this case the system may begin to decay but does recover.

Their procedure in carrying out this simulation raises several problems. In order to develop their model, not only do they have to distinguish linear from nonlinear relationships, but also they must assign values in nonlinear relationships to such things as the birth rate (given as 4.1 percent) and the average life of a commoner (given

Systems Theory and Archaeology

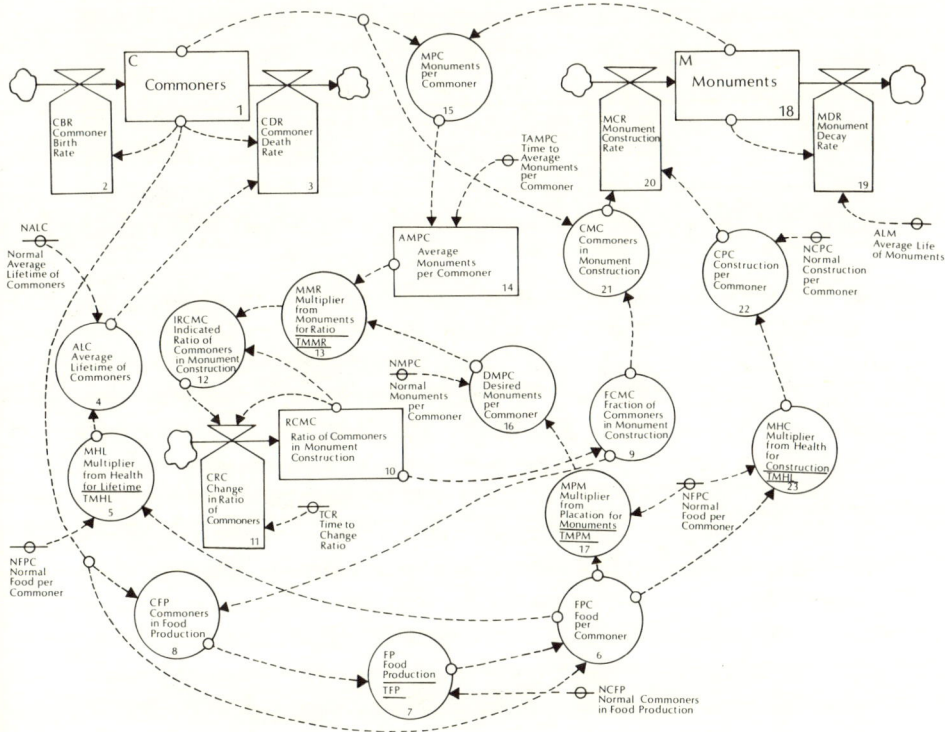

Figure 2.8. Flow Chart
SOURCE: Hosler, Sabloff, and Runge (1977:575)

as twenty-five years). How much would the results have been changed had they used plausible alternatives for these values, such as 4.5 percent and thirty years, respectively? The point is that, when a very detailed model is being constructed, one must *estimate* many parameter values. Rarely is there sufficient information to justify much confidence in any choice of a particular parameter value. Thus, one must determine the effects of running the simulation using plausible alternative values of the parameters. If the results turn out to be the same for a range of parameter values, this supports the conclusion that the model adequately reflects the real world. This would also solve the problem of what initial values to assign. The Mayan model is much more complicated than the Aegean model, so there are more values to be estimated and the entire problem is more complex.

A second problem inherent in this type of simulation stems from the fact that only part of a system is simulated. For example, the effects of potential warfare are not included, nor is the possibility of increasing agricultural potential via the building of ridged fields or other means of intensified agriculture. The problem is that one or more very important feedback loops that would have changed the results of the simulation drastically might be left out when only part of a system is modeled.

A final question about this simulation is whether the feedback loop of decreased food production leading to increased monument construction leading to still further decreases in food production is realistic. There may have been alternative strategies. The Mayan elite could have continued to build monuments at an even faster rate without an increase in workers by decreasing monument quality or size. Or, they could have developed public works such as ridged fields or causeways that would enhance food production. The elite-monument-commoner model of Hosler, Sabloff, and Runge is not the only one that could be constructed for the Mayan area, nor are the relationships they simulate the only ones that might lead to systemic collapse. Their model does show that some elite-monument-commoner relationships might lead to systemic collapse. But one might choose to propose other models that result in collapse before devising empirical tests of this one.

In a sense, the Aegean and Mayan models are complementary. The entire Aegean system (very broadly defined) is modeled on the basis of quite simple relationships between generalized elements. However, these parameters are varied under successive simulation runs. On the other hand, only a portion of the Mayan system is simulated, but with much greater specification of the relationships among elements than in the Aegean example. In each case there are serious questions as to whether these models are accurate reflections of the actual systems.

One is tempted to suggest that the solution is to construct a simulation as complete as the Aegean one but with as much detail and careful depiction of relationships as in the Mayan model, and then run it repeatedly with different parameter values. This would be a staggering undertaking because the model would be huge and would require a great deal of computer time to run. It would also require the estimation of many parameter values, thus increasing the potential for estimation errors and the need for enormous numbers of simulation runs. Simulations of cultural systems are difficult because of their complexity and our limited knowledge of the relationships among the elements and of the parameter values. There are no easy solutions to these difficulties.

Conclusions

This brief introduction to simulation and discussion of a few examples provides the background for making several important points. One obvious concern is the question of how useful this technique actually is. The method is limited by our ability to produce accurate or realistic models. The first obvious problem is that, if we fail to recognize and account for even one major feedback loop, the model may be so far from reality that the exercise is futile. This problem is obvious but is not always solved satisfactorily. For example, the Mayan Collapse model is admittedly a simulation of only part of the system. Had the entire system been modeled, would its collapse have been shown to be as likely? Or again, the Aegean model lacks any negative feedback loops until a "piracy" loop is introduced; are there other important components not being modeled?

Another problem is the difficulty of defining relationships among the component parts accurately. Many models show merely whether or not the relationships among the elements are positive or negative or neutral. Others contain complex linear relationships, as does the second Aegean model, in which, for example, when population doubles, metallurgical output increases by a fixed lesser amount. Cooke and Renfrew point out that in reality many relationships would not be linear but would be nonlinear, with proportions changing as the values of the elements change. For example, subsistence output may at first grow rapidly with increased population, but as the population gets larger, subsistence output is likely to fall off, so that the relationship between population increase and subsistence increase is nonlinear. The Mayan Collapse model also includes complex nonlinear relationships of this kind. No problems arise from including complicated relationships in a simulation (although they do make programming more difficult). Rather, the difficulty is that often we have no good empirical or theoretical basis for deciding how the relationships should be characterized.

There may not yet be enough archeological data to support construction of simulations of complex systems that approximate reality closely enough to warrant constructing and running them. This does not mean that the kinds of simple simulations discussed above (having to do with distributions of trade goods, for example) are not useful; clearly they are. But those who produce simulations of complex systems like the Aegean and Mayan ones have yet to produce a resounding demonstration of their utility.

Even in simple simulations with simplified relationships between components, one needs to select a set of initial values. How does one know what values are realistic? And what if for some sets of values a system is stable and for others it collapses? This would show that a system is capable of collapse in the specified situations. But one might argue that the initial conditions under which the system collapsed are unrealistic. The value of any interpretation obviously depends on specifying initial conditions accurately.

Simulation is thus a difficult but useful technique. In theory it is possible to draw some conclusions about a system even if certain aspects of the relationships cannot be specified. However, application and interpretation of computer simulations are only as good as the data and archeological expertise that go into their construction.

Simulation is quite useful for testing models or interconnected sets of propositions that are proposed as simplified representations of all or part of a system. Such models are composed of series of assumptions, hypotheses, and perhaps even laws. That is, relationships among some components are assumed, others are hypotheses to be tested, and others are well-confirmed laws. Inferences are drawn from the hypotheses according to the assumptions and the laws. The model is then tested by checking the actual archeological data. If the actual data (not output from the simulation) are different from the simulation results, then the set of hypotheses is disconfirmed. Then either new hypotheses are proposed whose inferences are supported by the data, or the model itself is modified or rejected. In practice this process of testing can be very complicated. Even if the model produces a result confirmed by archeological data, this does not prove that the model is correct. Confidence in the model comes only after much back and forth testing and confirmation of hypotheses that provide understanding of the data.

Simulations containing stochastic relations are difficult to test. The tests require many runs of the simulation at different parameter values and an enormous amount of empirical data. For example, if we want to know what proportions of populations actually survive under various conditions, we must consider many different groups. This requires testing simulations of output generated by using various values and comparing the results with data from as many known historical situations as possible. For example, to test the predictive capability of a simulation model for prehistoric Southwestern pueblos during the Great Drought (late thirteenth century A.D.), the output should be compared with the known histories of several pueblos from that time period. Comparison with only one such pueblo is not likely to be very enlightening.

A very serious problem with systemic simulations is that, although almost all of a system may be correctly modeled, one mistake may cause the results to be unrealistic. Does one then reject the model? When something goes wrong it is often very difficult to determine which relationship or hypothesis or value is wrong, or whether several are, or whether the whole simulation is misconceived. This is, of course, a problem with testing any set of multiple hypotheses and is not unique to simulations. This point seems to have been missed by Bell (1981), who argues that the power of the scientific method is that it provides a method for refuting inadequate hypotheses and then goes on to argue that the power of simulations is that they provide a method for refuting inadequate models. Our point is that simulation itself is a technique of general scientific method. Further, these techniques are not methods of refuting hypotheses and systems (which technically is no more possible than proving them to be absolutely certain); rather, simulation is one way to test hypotheses and models in the process of trying to confirm or disconfirm them.

But when is a model confirmed or disconfirmed? We know that, practically speaking, we can never model something as complex as a cultural system with complete accuracy. Also, the empirical data with which a model is tested represent only a sample of reality. Thus, no model's output ever fits the actual world perfectly. We must both choose the data and decide when simulation results are adequate. Of course, this depends in part on our interests and even on arbitrary choices, but the subjective element is controlled by the clear and full presentation of both the model and the hypotheses and by the corrective interplay between the model and the data. The model suggests tests that require the collection of data, which, in turn, suggest modifications of the model, and so on. This explicitly scientific, general covering law procedure is neither subjective nor arbitrary. It leads to the fit between laws and theories on the abstract side and the real world on the concrete side; it is this fit that is the ground and content of our knowledge of the actual world and of our ability to understand, explain, and predict.

The Systemic Approach Versus General Systems Theory

So far we have described some advantages, uses, and problems of a systemic approach to cultural systems. Systemic flow diagrams and graphs very usefully enhance most archeological analyses. And simulation techniques permit the construction of quite complicated models, including stochastic models. These simulations simply work out, step by step, the relationships built into them. They greatly increase our ability to test a large variety and quantity of hypotheses, models, and theories. Simulation, as we show above, is one systemic technique encompassed by the general covering law approach.

One goal of General Systems Theory is to devise propositions about systems in general that can then be used to understand particular systems, regardless of their specific components. While there are a variety of such theorems or propositions, at present only two, stability analysis and catastrophe theory, appear to be useful for archeology.

Stability analysis does not cover the full workings of a system or its particular output or state but determines only whether or not a system will remain stable over some or all ranges of its input values. Stability analysis permits the determination of whether some systems are stable or not, without requiring full details of the relationships among their elements. In many cases, stability analysis makes it possible to determine whether or not a system is stable, even if we know only which relationships are linear or nonlinear and which are positive or negative. For example, a system with all negative feedback systems will not increase or collapse. The question is how much can be predicted about a system on the basis of so little information. Cooke (1979) indicates that the answer is "disappointingly little." There seem to be few systems with both positive and negative interactions whose stability can be predicted from knowledge only of the directions—amplifying or dampening—of the interactions.

Bell (1981) disagrees with this conclusion and suggests that knowledge of the direction of feedback loops rather than of their magnitude is of major importance. Unfortunately, he provides no evidence or theory to support this statement, and since it is easy to think of examples where the magnitude of a feedback loop is critical to the long-term output of a system, one cannot accept this conclusion as having broad applicability. All is not lost, however, because archeologists can provide much more detail about many systemic relationships than merely whether they are positive or negative. Also, if some systems having nonlinear relationships between components can be approximated by linear relationships, then we might be able to make numerous predictions about the actual systems. Techniques will be improved when more archeologists work with mathematicians cognizant of the limitations of archeological data, as Renfrew does.

Another General Systems Theory technique relevant to archeology is catastrophe theory. A few papers in Renfrew and Cooke (1979) (namely, Renfrew and Poston 1979; Renfrew 1979) include considerable discussion of the background and potential utility of catastrophe theory and also provide pertinent bibliographies. In brief, catastrophe theorists argue that some systems can undergo marked, abrupt alteration resulting from very small changes in some component values, without collapsing. Renfrew uses an example of a very dispersed settlement pattern that almost instantaneously (at least from an archeological perspective) changes to a highly nucleated pattern. One can imagine explanations for such cases. For example, there may be significant advantages to nucleation, but only if enough people do it. Therefore, there is no gradual nucleation, but once aggregation gets underway, nearly everyone joins in. Renfrew develops this hypothesis in terms of a catastrophe theory model. He also argues that many of the classical collapses—such as the Aegean and Mayan examples considered earlier in this chapter—are perhaps best explained in catastrophe theory terms. He argues that these were probably systems in states such that sudden jumps could and did occur within them. He suggests further that all such sudden changes need not be "downhill," but that the emergence of stable, complex organizations may in some cases be the result of "reverse catastrophes."

There is a large body of mathematical theory behind catastrophe theory, but it appears that we face the same problems using it that we do with most of the rest of systems theory (see also Wenke 1981:107–111). We are at present not able to characterize archeological systems with sufficient precision to enable use of extant mathematical theory. Nevertheless, we can utilize catastrophe theory heuristically as we do much of the rest of systems theory: it provides concepts, terminology, and ways of thinking about cultural systems that are heuristically valuable but that do not necessitate use of the formal theory itself. In this sense, catastrophe theory can be conceived of as simply one kind of systemic approach.

In general, use of these and other approaches to systems analysis are predicated on the assumption that all systems have general features that transcend their particular characteristics. The general methods and general principles of systems theory are useful for understanding particular archeological systems. There is, however, as yet little use for formalized General Systems Theory in archeology. That is, although some methods such as stability analysis are useful, there do not seem to be many formal laws or algorithms about systems in general that can be applied to systemic archeological data. This does not mean that one should not make an effort to use what is available from a General Systems point of view, but the results of such use are likely to be quite modest until we are able to produce archeological systems models much more detailed than any now available.

Systems Explanations and Functionalist Explanations

In a recent paper, Merrilee Salmon (1978) suggests that systems theory has such a strong appeal for anthropologists and archeologists because it provides a scientific-sounding way of talking about and presenting *functional explanations*. Whatever the motivation of advocates, we agree—as indicated in the first section of this chapter—that what was called functionalism in the 1930s and 1940s and what was called systems theory in the 1960s and 1970s are certainly very closely related.

The functionalism of Malinowski and Radcliffe-Brown is an analytical approach whereby one explains traits or complexes by delineating the roles they play (their functions) within the particular culture. For example, one of Radcliffe-Brown's most influential papers is about joking relationships and patterns of avoidance among certain kinds of kin in various societies. He explains both these widespread customs as means of facilitating crucial relationships—like those between in-laws—that must be maintained yet that contain built-in elements of conflict (Radcliffe-Brown 1940). In other words, the presence of joking and avoidance relationships in many societies is explained by the function these relationships play in mitigating potentially severe tensions by providing ready-made or prescribed behavior patterns for the people in such structurally necessary yet tension-filled positions. Thus, such customs are means by which possible severe perturbations threatening the steady-state or dynamic equilibrium of a society are damped and controlled. The society is, therefore, seen as a kind of self-regulating system.

Systems theory, as archeologists understand it, has strong components of cybernetics, "computerese," and quantitative techniques, but it is only a slightly metamorphosed form of functionalism. That is, we agree with Hempel (1959), who identifies functional analysis with the description of self-regulating systems in his analysis of functionalism, although he does not explicitly refer to systems theory.

Hence, we conclude our discussion of systems theory with brief reference to Hempel's discussion of "The Logic of Functional Analysis" (1959; see also Hempel's discussion of discrete state systems, 1965:403–405; Brown's discussion of function statements and self-persisting systems, 1963: ch. 9; and Rudner's analysis of functionalism, 1966: ch. 5). Hempel points out,

> The kind of phenomenon that a functional analysis is invoked to explain is typically some recurrent activity or some behavior pattern in an individual or a group, such as a physiological mechanism, a neurotic trait, a culture pattern, or a social institution. And the principal objective of the analysis is to exhibit the contribution which the behavior pattern makes to the preservation or the development of the individual or the group in which it occurs. Thus, functional analysis seeks to understand a behavior pattern or a sociocultural institution by determining the role it plays in keeping the given system in proper working order or maintaining it as a going concern. (Hempel 1965:304–305)

Hempel notes that the aim of functional analysis is usually to explain the phenomenon studied: What role does it play in maintaining the institution or society into which it is integrated? In investigating the explanatory import of functional analysis, Hempel finds that functional analyses result in conclusions of the type, "The trait, X, is present because it satisfies an important need, Y," and that these conclusions are arguments involving a basic logical fallacy.

To understand Hempel's reasoning, consider a particular custom like the joking relationship referred to above, or, for another example, the Irish wake. A functional explanation might lead to the conclusion that the conviviality of the traditional Irish wake serves to reaffirm the solidarity of the affected human group subsequent to a major potential or actual disruption: the permanent loss of one of its members. *However*, even if it is agreed that the Irish wake functions primarily as a social intensification rite, this does not explain its specific form or the many characteristics that distinguish it from postmortem rites of social intensification elsewhere in Euroamerican culture. In other words, trait X does not function uniquely to satisfy the important need Y; X_1 or X_2 or X_3, or even A or B, might also satisfy need Y. The original functional explanation says nothing about why X is present rather than one of the other possibilities, so it is not an explanation of X.

Hempel concludes that functional analysis provides no deductive argument for the presence of a particular item. After further discussion, he also concludes that functional analysis does not provide *inductively* adequate grounds for expecting X rather than X' or some other variant, nor does it enable prediction of the presence or absence of particular items. However, he says,

> If a precise hypothesis of self-regulation for systems of a specified kind is set forth, then it becomes possible to explain, and to predict categorically, the satisfaction of certain functional requirements simply on the basis of information concerning antecedent needs; and the hypothesis can then be objectively tested by an empirical check of its predictions. (Hempel 1965:317)

Thus, if we agree that by "system" we mean not merely a set of objects and the relationships among them but also that this grouping of objects and relationships operates in a self-regulatory fashion, then systemic explanations are, at least potentially, on firmer Hempelian ground than functional explanations in which no reference is made to, or that do not demonstrate, the presence of self-regulatory mechanisms.

Hempel goes on to stress that a proposed hypothesis of self-regulation must be empirically testable. He finds such definiteness lacking in the functionalist literature.

The rest of Hempel's paper is devoted to a discussion of two other shortcomings frequent in functionalist accounts: inadequate specification of scope (failure to describe clearly the kind of system to which the hypothesis of self-regulation refers, or failure to indicate the range of situations within which the systems are claimed to develop traits that will satisfy their functional requirements); and nonempirical use of key terms such as *need* and *adaptation* (that is, use of these words so vaguely or generally that their empirical referents—if any—are unknown and cannot be defined).

Thus, traditional functional analyses are very marginal endeavors when viewed from Hempelian perspective:

> A class of phenomena has been scientifically understood to the extent that they can be fitted into a testable, and adequately confirmed, theory or a system of laws; and the merits of functional analysis will eventually have to be judged by its ability to lead to that kind of understanding. (Hempel 1965:329)

However, Hempel is not entirely negative. He concludes his paper as follows:

> The functionalist mode of approach has proved illuminating, suggestive, and fruitful in many contexts. If the advantages it has to offer are to be reaped in full, it seems desirable and indeed necessary to pursue the investigation of specific functional relationships to the point where they can be expressed in terms of reasonably precise and objectively testable hypotheses. At least initially, these hypotheses will likely be of quite limited scope. But this would simply parallel the present situation in biology, where the kinds of self-regulation, and the uniformities they exhibit, vary from species to species. Eventually, such "empirical generalizations" of limited scope might provide a basis for a more general theory of self-regulating systems. To what extent these objectives can be reached cannot be decided in *a priori* fashion by logical analysis or philosophical reflection: the answer has to be found by intensive and rigorous scientific research. (Hempel 1965:330)

Merrilee Salmon and Wesley Salmon (1979) take an initially more optimistic view of functional analysis than Hempel does. They believe that functional explanations can be accommodated more adequately by the S-R model of explanation (see chapter 1 here) than by any of Hempel's models (D-N, D-S, I-S) because S-R explanations are not arguments. They say,

> One is under no mandate to construct a deductively valid or inductively correct inference from the statement that oxygen is transported from the lungs to other parts of the body to the conclusion that hemoglobin is present in the blood. Even if no such argument can be given, the transport of oxygen is relevant to the presence of hemoglobin (as one of the various substances which can perform that function) and this relevance may constitute the basis for an adequate S-R explanation. (Salmon and Salmon 1979)

Systems Theory and Archaeology

109

The Salmons claim that the S-R model is more useful to archeologists and other social scientists than the Hempelian models because the S-R model does not include the requirement—as the Hempelian models do—that sufficient conditions must be provided for the occurrence of an event; hence, the stringency of Hempel's insistence on the definition of hypotheses of self-regulation is relaxed. For these reasons, anthropologists and other social scientists especially concerned with functional analyses might wish to give close attention to the S-R conception of explanation as well as to Hempel's models. However, no matter which CL model of explanation is under consideration—D-N, D-S, I-S, S-R—if explanations are to be adequate, then the other two faults Hempel finds to be common in the older functionalist literature—lack of specification of scope and nonempirical use of key terms—must be corrected.

In sum, we believe that M. Salmon concludes correctly that much of systems theory is made-over functionalism and therefore contains the intuitive appeal and also the theoretical pitfalls of functionalism. Hence, we suggest that advocates of systems theory in archeology read Hempel's discussion of functionalism carefully as well as the other references listed above, and then examine the S-R model (Salmon 1967; 1971a, b, c; 1973). It is important to be well aware of the weaknesses as well as of the strengths of these approaches.

But although we may all agree that some early applications of the functionalist approach are of limited utility, this does not mean that there is no value in delineating the primary components of cultural subsystems, graphing their possible interactions, and simulating their behavior. On the contrary, these activities will at least help us understand the *consequences* of the functioning of these systems.

Both functionalism in the traditional sense and systems theory (i.e., the systemic approach) suffer from the limitation that they do not describe or explain the origins of the components of systems. For example, we learn nothing from Renfrew's Aegean model about the origins of metallurgy or why piracy developed. However, a systemic approach can lead to predictive, testable results if—as Hempel indicates—we are clear about terminology, about the scope of the postulated system, and about the empirical referents of descriptions of the system's behavior. We believe that, when these qualifications are taken into account, systems modeling can be a fruitful means of generating and defining hypotheses about past situations that can be tested by use of archeological data to increase our knowledge about past societies in particular, and about human sociocultural behavior in general.

Conclusion

We believe that the most important use of the systemic approach is heuristic. Thinking about cultures as systems, looking for feedback loops, and using catastrophe theory to understand how systems can change states abruptly and thoroughly are systemic ways of improving interpretations of the archeological record. Even if archeologists cannot yet use any of of the mathematical concepts of General Systems Theory or construct complete simulations, systems theory is useful in archeology. Moreover, although mathematical modeling of cultural systems is fraught with difficulties, attempts to do it should not be abandoned. Continued effort may well convert what are now only potentially successful simulations into procedures that yield useful hypotheses about how cultural systems work.

Archeologists who use and advocate a systemic approach to the archeological record should be aware of the theoretical issues briefly discussed in the preceding section. The major points are as follows:

First, systemic explanations are not logically distinct from CL explanations, and systemic approaches are specifications of the generalized CL approach.

Second, systems approaches are functionalist approaches.

Third, functionalist approaches are intuitively appealing to social scientists and have a long history within social science, but—as represented in the literature—have low explanatory value (Hempel 1959; Rudner 1966:107–109). The Salmons (Salmon and Salmon 1979; Salmon 1978) suggest that the statistical-relevance (S-R) model of scientific explanation (briefly discussed in chapter 1 of this book) differs from Hempel's D-N, D-S, and I-S models in ways that make the S-R model better able to accommodate functional explanations than do the Hempelian constructions.

Systems Theory and Archaeology

However, we again stress the heuristic value of a functionalist orientation (see also Rudner 1966:110–111). As practicing scientists, archeologists are free to use systems models and techniques or any other methods as long as they are explicit about what they are doing and why, and as long as the models and techniques are useful.

Practically speaking, the value of systems analysis to archeologists is limited by the completeness and accuracy with which we can model archeological systems. Difficulties in quantifying relationships (or transforming them in other ways) are present in archeology apart from the problems encountered in systems analysis. However, the fact that we must look at numerous relationships at the same time when employing a systemic approach and that we must be able to specify all these relationships accentuate the difficulties. These limitations are especially acute in computerized simulations but are not restricted to them. One of the best ways to combat these problems is to undertake extremely intensive, long-term projects in particular areas so that enough information can be collected to model entire systems. Systems theory will find a place in archeology to the extent that it is productive of understanding.

CHAPTER THREE
Ecology and Archeology

We discuss the ecological approach in archeology as a special topic for several reasons. Just as some have equated new archeology with systems theory, so also others have equated it with ecological archeology. In fact, ecological archeology incorporates both systems and ecological methods. We examine the ecological view separately to show how it is related to the other facets of archeology.

From an ecological perspective, one views culture within its biophysical environment and emphasizes the systemic nature of people's relations to their surroundings. The effect of this approach, like that of systems theory, is to shift major research efforts away from an emphasis on entities and toward a concern with relations. An artifact is no longer studied solely as an object in itself but also as a mediator between human beings and their surroundings. The various cultural subsystems—economic, political, religious—are seen in relation to one another and to the biophysical environment. This is a practical approach for archeologists in that it involves recovery of several independent categories of data, all of which are reasonably easy to infer from the archeological record. Consequently, an ecological approach yields many testable hypotheses concerning prehistoric cultural systems. Another important consideration is that the ecological approach can provide archeologists with substantial amounts of data independent of traditional categories. These ecological data are in turn useful in testing hypotheses that are central to the understanding of cultural processes.

Use of the terms *ecological data* or *environmental data* can lead to arguments over just what is meant by data of these types and to the formulation of elaborate, rigid definitions. In the past, similar attempts to define artifacts or their features precisely were often inconclusive. It seems obvious that use of such words as *artifact* or *feature* should and will vary depending on the problems at hand. Good definitions thus depend on careful attention to data collections and analyses (see chapters 4 and 5).

The same is true for the terms *ecological* or *environmental*. For the purposes of general discussion, rigid definitions of the environment are not very useful. What is needed for application to particular problems are working definitions. Thus, use of these terms implies a general concern with people–land relationships as opposed to person-to-person or community-to-community relationships. Our interest is in the total ecological system of which human beings are a part, in data relating to the means by which people extract and utilize energy, and in what traditionally has been studied as the integration of human beings with nature (Watson and Watson 1969).

Such definitions are vague and open to modification and precision. Systems theorists might argue that cultural systems are so interconnected that any part of them could be called ecological. Nevertheless there does seem to be a body of data and procedures that can be considered to be specifically ecological, although they are not inherently different from other data and are utilized in the same logical framework as are all other data relevant to archeological problems.

One of the general points of this chapter, then, is that an ecological approach does not lead to analyses basically different from the others we describe in this book. The ecological approach is useful because hypotheses concerned with the relation of a society to the natural environment are often far from obvious, yet are highly productive and testable. Ecological hypotheses are not intrinsically better than other hypotheses, but they certainly are extraordinarily useful in providing understanding of the past.

The ecological approach is important also because it is pervasive. Societies are easily affected by changes in their ecological relations. That is, although we might hypothesize that a particular society is not markedly affected by ecological or environmental factors, the alternative hypothesis is that this is always such a strong possibility that it must be tested. Thus even to test nonecological hypotheses one needs to collect and consider ecological data.

Hence, our view about the old (and not so old) ideas concerning environmental determinism is that they are worth considering if they can be framed as testable hypotheses, and if they can, then they should be tested. That is, it is one of the ultimate goals of anthropology to determine just how much cultural behavior is dependently related to environmental factors. One cannot merely assume that culture is or is not environmentally determined. Many archeologists believe as we do that much cultural behavior is in fact dependently related to environmental factors and that ecological hypotheses automatically have considerable plausibility. But only empirical tests can show whether or not environmental factors are determinative of cultural factors. As remarked, ecological hypotheses are eminently suitable for testing. Yet those who collect ecological data or discover dependent relations between environment and culture are not necessarily environmental determinists. Culture can be significantly independent of environment even when there are many dependent relations between the two.

The Development of the Ecological View

Emphasis on ecology and environmental variables and interest in paleo-environments and food sources go back almost as far as archeology itself. However, there has been large-scale systematic application of the ecological approach in studies of prehistory only since the end of World War II. The most influential publication in the postwar period exemplifying this approach is Grahame Clark's 1952 book, *Prehistoric Europe: The Economic Basis*. For 1950s archeologists this volume was a shining and substantive example of the productivity of analysis based on questions about subsistence and paleo-environment. Clark himself followed that book with another tour de force of paleo-environmental research—Star Carr (Clark 1954)—and firmly established a strong school of ecologically oriented prehistory at Cambridge University.

Elsewhere in the Old World, archeological research with an ecological emphasis was being carried out under the direction of R. J. Braidwood. He conceived of his Iraq-Jarmo project not as a simple site excavation but as an explicit attempt to solve the ecological problem of how plant and animal domestication originated in western Asia (Braidwood et al. 1960; Braidwood et al. 1983). Geologists, botanists, zoologists, and ceramic technologists were employed to study and analyze various subsystems within the general ecological framework. Remains of early forms of domesticated plants and animals were discovered at the prehistoric village of Jarmo in northern Iraq, and paleo-environmental research was initiated to provide data for use both in developing and in testing hypotheses about early domestication.

This interdisciplinary approach produced a large amount of natural historical data and stimulated great interest in environmental problems and approaches. Braidwood thus played a major role in establishing interdisciplinary expeditions as the norm for modern archeological research. The main fieldwork objectives of such a project are to collect data concerning the physical geography, the prehistoric flora and fauna, the climate, and the distribution of archeological sites. A recent example of interdisciplinary archeological work in the Near East with a strong paleo-environmental/ecological orientation is the research directed by Frank Hole in southwestern Iran (Hole and Flannery 1967; Hole, Flannery, and Neely 1969; Hole 1977, 1978, 1979).

In the New World, one of the most influential of the pioneer archeologists, Alfred V. Kidder, argued persuasively in favor of interdisciplinary fieldwork as early as the mid-1930s (Kidder 1937). But it was not until much later that interdisciplinary fieldwork was systematically carried out, one of the earliest such projects being the Glen Canyon research begun in the 1950s under the direction of Jesse Jennings (1966).

Richard S. MacNeish has undertaken interdisciplinary investigations of the problem of early plant domestication in the New World. During several seasons of work in the Tehuacan Valley of Mexico, MacNeish's team found evidence of a progressively developing series of early cultigens including maize. Using environmental data from a number of excavated sites, he and his collaborators describe a nine-millennia-long cultural-historical sequence of adaptations and settlement for the valley (MacNeish 1964, 1967).

Ecology and Archeology   117

These interdisciplinary expeditions laid the groundwork for the current ecological approach to archeological interpretation by demonstrating the productive results of close cooperation—in the field as well as in the laboratory—of archeologists with natural scientists and the value of environmental data for understanding the prehistoric record.

At the same time, Lewis Binford, in his highly influential theoretical papers of the 1960s (see especially Binford 1964), persuasively recommended the fielding of ecologically oriented archeological investigations. By the end of that decade Americanist archeology was almost entirely dominated by the ecological approach. Further examples of recent research in this tradition are the long-term projects directed by Stuart Struever in the Illinois River Valley (1968a and b, 1978), Kent Flannery in Oaxaca (Flannery, ed. 1976, and several publications by project personnel in the University of Michigan Museum of Anthropology Memoirs series, 1973 to the present). In the Old World, some classical archeologists have also adopted an ecological approach (Jacobsen 1973, 1981; McDonald and Rapp 1972).

The emphasis of many interdisciplinary studies is on selected kinds of botanical, zoological, and geological evidence only. However, the original rather narrow focus of interdisciplinary endeavor in archeology has now broadened greatly to include, for example, specialists in soils and microstratigraphy, in trace element analyses of many different kinds on a wide variety of materials to demonstrate source areas and trade routes, and in fairly esoteric niches within zoology (such as an aspect of malacology devoted to the study of tiny snails, some species of which are sensitive climatic indicators) and botany (such as the study of fossil pollen to learn about ancient vegetation and climate, or the examination of phytoliths—microscopic opalized fragments of plant cells sometimes present where pollen is not preserved—that may enable identification of vegetation contemporaneous with the prehistoric occupation of a site).

The theoretical point we would like to stress here is that, although a large variety and amount of environmental-ecological information is now potentially obtainable, this does not mean that every archeologist must somehow seek to gather all this information at every site investigated. It *does* mean that archeologists must—more than ever—keep clearly in mind what sorts of data are relevant to the problems being investigated at any site or series of sites so that the research can be designed appropriately and efficiently. It is not possible for the archeologists in an interdisciplinary project to concern themselves exclusively with artifacts, as the term was once used (stone, bone, basketry, wood, pottery tools or utensils, and architectual remains). The range of data relevant to ecologically oriented archeological research is immense, and hence the challenge of designing that research effectively—usually within fairly stringent budget limitations—is highly demanding. In this chapter we treat the concept of ecology as it relates to archeology and to explanation in archeology, the relationship of an ecological approach to a systems approach, and the contemporary practice of ecological archeology with special attention to problems and difficulties.

The vast increase in potential data recovery techniques (many, but not all in the environmental-ecological realm) requires that archeologists choose carefully those that will produce the most useful data for the problem under investigation.

However, the usefulness of these techniques is highly dependent on the research designs employed by archeologists. Almost all these techniques require that an interpretive framework be built into the overall research program. Furthermore, one must operate under the assumption that all data categories—artifactual and ecofactual—can lead to hypotheses from which testable implications can be inferred. Thus, archeological reality requires us to decide how to use all the potentially available data and at the same time to be realistic about what can be expected and analyzed usefully. This is usually impossible to do a priori, and thus one's collection strategies and even research designs must evolve to some degree as fieldwork and analysis proceed.

Ecology and the Ecological View of Culture

As noted above, the ecological view of culture is widely believed to be one of the most productive of understanding in archeology and anthropology. Ecology is defined as the science of the interrelations between living organisms and their environment, or as the study of the structure and function of nature (Odum 1953:3; 1963:3). Human beings are a part of this natural system; the study of our relations with other organisms and our physical environment has come to be known as human ecology (Bates 1953).

The interaction of most organisms with their environment is closely determined by their biological needs and genetic composition. However, human beings have developed culture in a large variety of forms to act as a mediator between them and their environment. Leslie White expresses this functional view when he defines culture as man's extrasomatic means of adaptation (1959:8). Some archeologists also adopt this view and consider cultural ecology to be the study of the culturally dependent relationships between human groups and their physical environment. June Helm describes this ecological view as stressing "the adaptive and exploitative relations, through the agency of technology, of the human group to its habitat, and the demographic and sociocultural consequences of those relations" (1962:630).

There are two main ways of relating cultural behavior to environmental situations: "either showing that items of cultural behavior function as part of systems that also include environmental phenomena or else showing that the environmental phenomena are responsible in some manner for the origin or development of the cultural behavior under investigation" (Vayda 1969:xi). Historically, archeologists have been especially interested in the possibilities of explaining the development of new economic adaptations in cultural historical sequences by reference to environmental relationships and changes.

As Marston Bates points out, it is probably more useful to "regard ecology as a pervasive point of view rather than as a special subject matter" (1953:701). To utilize this perspective one views culture in its environment and emphasizes the systemic nature of people's relations to that environment. The effect this has on archeology, as we said about systems theory, is to shift major research efforts away from an emphasis on entities and toward a concern with relations. An artifact is no longer seen solely as an object in itself but as a mediator between human beings and their environment. Various cultural subsystems—economic, political, religious—are viewed in relation to one another and to the biophysical environment.

The ecological approach to interpreting relations between human beings and their environment can lead to the specific view of environmental or geographic determinism. That the environment is in some sense determinative of culture and sets the boundaries of human existence is patently obvious (Cannon 1939), but equally obviously, there is a wide variety of possible lifeways within the range of temperature, air pressure, and so on that humans can survive. Likewise, there is a wide variety of cultures, each of which is consistent with any given environment. Earlier proponents of environmental determinism such as Ellsworth Huntington (1907, 1915, 1945) sometimes state their views in the form of laws, asserting that in an environmental situation of a given type a given culture develops. This rigid formulation with its lack of allowance for the complex nature of environments and the interaction of cultures with them is disconfirmed by the facts of anthropology and archeology. In the broad sense that humans and culture are limited by environmental factors, the thesis is obviously true, but it is not usually productive of detailed hypotheses.

A variation of environmental determinism is that of "possibilism." The environment sets limits that provide opportunities for culture but does not directly determine cultural details. Inherent in this view is the idea that culture and environment are two relatively independent spheres, so that culture can—within very broad limits—develop independently. Such a framework does not provide environmentally deterministic explanations of cultural proliferations, although environmental factors do set absolute limits on culture. Within the limits, any possible development can occur, and it is apparent, for example, that mountain peoples are prevented by the environment from developing a tradition of surf-riding, while oceanic people are encouraged (though not necessarily coerced) by their environment to make seafood a dietary staple. Because of the wide variety of cultural possibilities within even such rigid limits as those imposed, for instance, by polar or desert environments, possibilism is accepted as true but as too general to provide many hypotheses and explanations concerning the detail of cultural development.

The ecological approach, then, stresses the interpenetration and interdependence of culture and environment. The complexity of environmental situations and the detail and diversity of human adaptations to them are emphasized, together with the dynamic aspect of subsistence and other adaptive systems. The ecological approach has made viable and scientifically productive the old insight that the environment influences human behavior.

The approach of Julian Steward (1955) has strongly influenced ecologically oriented anthropological work. Steward studies cultures by examining their adaptations to their environments. He generates a taxonomic scheme comprising various levels of sociocultural complexity that incorporate the observed variability in subsistence techniques and social organization of numerous societies. Steward emphasizes the importance of the "culture core," by which he means recurrent constellations of similarly functioning basic features that are found around the world in a wide variety of cultures with comparable ecologies and similar social organization. By means of the culture core concept and of empirical generalizations about cultural-historical data, he seeks cross-cultural regularities in behavior patterns and in long-term developmental sequences for human societies. Steward is one of the earliest proponents of cultural ecology. For other expressions of this viewpoint, see Bennett (1976), Butzer (1982), Durham (1976), Helm (1962), and Watson and Watson (1969). Hardesty (1980) and Jochim (1979) provide recent summaries of the variety of ecological approaches used in archeology.

The ecological approach has given rise to other ideas about how anthropological research should be viewed. Edmond Leach was one of the first to question the traditional single community–single society approach of ethnological fieldworkers (1954). Ethnologists or archeologists investigating only an individual settlement cannot attain a complete picture of the processes characterizing the entire culture. To do this one must study the total system of interacting communities and their environmental milieus. Leach asserts that the individual communities as the primary units of study should be subordinated to study of the cultures of which they are a part.

Leach's recommendations have been followed by those archeologists who emphasize the regional approach to archeological survey and site excavation (for example, Binford 1964; Roper 1979; Struever 1968a and b). Binford says, "The methodology most appropriate for the task of isolating and studying processes of cultural change and evolution is one which is regional in scope" (Binford 1964:425).

With the acceptance of a regional approach and concern for relations with the environment, archeologists have also adopted a number of useful concepts from the biological sciences. Some archeologists follow Fredrik Barth's lead in utilizing the notion of the "ecological niche" of a community.

> Thus the "environment" of any one ethnic group is not only defined by natural conditions, but also by the presence and activities of the other ethnic groups on which it depends. Each group exploits only a section of the total environment, and leaves large parts of it open for other groups to exploit. . . . The present paper attempts to apply a more specific ecological approach to a case study of distribution by utilizing some of the concepts of animal ecology, particularly the concept of a *niche*—the place of a group in the total environment, its relations to resources and competitors (Barth 1956:1079).

This concept is a highly productive way of viewing related cultural systems and their environments. The biophysical environment is conceived of as one grand system, with cultures participating in different aspects of it and relating to one another and to their surroundings in a variety of ways.

Ecological niches must not be confused with either environmental zones or the simple geographic location of settlements. Environmental zones delimit regions occupied by related suites of plants and animals and are characterized by particular topographies, climates, and soils.

The ecological niche a culture occupies is not a portion of a geographic region but is a position within a complex of relationships. The possible ecological niches of a given environmental zone are theoretically limited only by the total resource base but in actuality are further limited by the range of those resources cultures have the technology to utilize, and even further by their choices of which to utilize. Thus, niches are occupied by cultures selectively according to their procurement systems and their other relations with plants, animals, and human neighbors. Accordingly, two cultures can exist side by side in the same environmental zone or habitat and occupy quite different ecological niches. Good examples of this are sedentary farmers and semisedentary pastoralists whose herds feed on the stubble in farmers' fields and on uncultivated tracts of land in the vicinity (Barth 1961).

Emphasis on ecological relationships between cultures and their biophysical environments, between subcultures within a larger cultural system, and between different cultures occupying the same geographical regions has led archeologists to undertake settlement pattern analyses (Willey 1953, 1956; Chang 1967; Binford 1964; Vita-Finzi and Higgs 1970); estimates of past population densities (Schacht 1981); and studies of trade networks (Adams 1974; Caldwell and Hall 1964; Earle and Ericson 1977; Sabloff and Lamberg-Karlovsky 1975; Renfrew 1969; Winters 1968; Wright 1969; Rathje 1975; Kohl 1981). One recent result of the pursuit of these subjects by archeologists is an interest in detailed, often quantified, models developed in other fields, especially in geography (locational analysis, including central place theory; see Fox and Smith 1982; Haggett 1965; King 1969; Johnson 1977; Crumley 1979; Smith 1982a, b, 1976), and economics (Runnels 1981) but also in engineering and sociology (information theory: Johnson 1978, Wobst 1977).

Now that we have provided some background information on ecology and archeology, we take up some important theoretical questions about the relationships between the ecological approach and the systems approach and the role played by ecology in archeological explanations.

The Ecological Approach in Archeology: Theory

Much of what has already been said about systems theory is applicable to the ecological approach. There are various advantages to looking at the systemic interactions of cultural systems, such as the relationships of the various parts of a cultural system to the environment. If one is using a systems approach, then ecological data are on a par with other data about the system, and the need to understand the feedbacks that exist between behavior and environment is obvious. Whether one is doing a systems analysis or not, the effects of the environment on cultural behavior must be taken into consideration.

Interest in ecological data extends beyond those who are actually doing systems analysis. This interest has a history almost as long as that of archeology. This is in part because ecological data are a priori easier to interpret than are many other kinds of archeological data, and it has long been recognized that there is a close relationship between the environment and cultural behavior. Numerous hypotheses about culture–environment relationships have already been tested and confirmed. Recent interest in ecological data has come about in part because of an increased interest in the functioning of entire cultures. A list of animal species for a site is often easier to interpret than a list of projectile point shapes. We may have more success interpreting what changes and variation in animal bone data mean than what differences in projectile point data represent because there is a much better developed body of information and theory about biological systems than about cultural systems.

Ecological analyses focused on reciprocal relationships between human societies and their biophysical and social environments exemplify a particular kind of systems approach. The systems being investigated are cultural systems and subsystems on one hand and biological (floral, faunal) and physical (topographic, climatic) systems and subsystems on the other. Because ecological analysis and explanation are a special class of systems analysis and explanation, an ecological explanation is a kind of functional explanation and hence is characterized by all the intuitive appeal and theoretical difficulties of functional explanations (see chapter 2).

A classic example of the application of the ecological approach is archeological research on the beginnings of food production in the Near East. We have already referred to Braidwood's Iraq-Jarmo project in the context of ecologically oriented, interdisciplinary fieldwork. In a theoretical paper, Binford (1968b) also offers an ecologically based, systems-oriented explanation of the origins of food production:

Aboriginal human groups in the Near East probably settled first in those areas where palatable and relatively accessible wild foods were most abundant. Indeed, Braidwood's investigations indicate that the

Ecology and Archeology

earliest agricultural and pastoral communities are in just such areas. Binford suggests, however, that the *antecedents* to these established food-producing communities—the incipient plant and animal cultivators—probably did not live in the heart of the optimum zone but rather on the *edges* or *margins* of that zone. Binford's answer to the question of why this should be so involves a chain of reasoning that comprises an ecologically based hypothetical explanation for the origins of food production in the Near East. The original human population in the optimum zone would grow to the limits of the natural resource base (plants, animals, and desirable occupation sites). Local hunting-gathering communities would then be forced to alter their behavior in some way to relieve the pressure on their resource base. A variety of procedures is possible (all are known ethnographically to have been used in various times and places). These include migration, infanticide, senilicide, and abortion. Perhaps only one or two or perhaps all were used, but in any case the simplest and most efficient is migration to the nearest unclaimed terrain. Within a few human generations this policy would result in colonialization of nonoptimal or marginal territory outside the heartland where traditional foods were most abundant. In coping with this less desirable environment, the marginal groups would eventually find it necessary to manipulate and modify that environment in nontraditional ways to make it yield at least some of the traditional plant and animal products in sufficient quantity. This would ultimately result in domestication of a number of plant and animal species. Once established, the food-producing techniques would be spread by various means beyond the marginal zone (and back into the original optimal zone) by example and further migration.

Basic to this hypothetical explanatory construct are a number of ecological-environmental-demographic assumptions: (1) That the natural foods in the aboriginal optimum zone were so abundant that there was no necessity to encourage their growth and reproduction there. Jack Harlan's experimental reaping of modern wild stands of a primitive wheat species gives limited but strong support to this assumption (Harlan 1967). (2) That successful human populations with relatively simple technologies (such as prehistoric hunter-gatherers) will inevitably increase to the limits of the carrying capacity of their environments. (3) That human societies are highly conservative in their economic behavior and will alter their subsistence pursuits only under stress; even then the alteration will be as minimal as possible.

Any or all of these premises can be challenged on factual grounds, as can various other portions of the hypothetical formulation developed from them. However, our points here are that Binford's postulated explanation for the origins of food production in the Near East is an initially plausible construct; but, to be on strong theoretical ground, archeologists interested in using the construct must show to their own satisfaction and that of their colleagues that human populations like that postulated as inhabiting the Near East circa 10,000 B.C. do indeed behave in the self-regulating way outlined by Binford. Then it would have to be shown that the presently available archeological evidence from the appropriate portions of the Near East does not disconfirm the hypothetical construct. The construct would also have to be tested by checking predictions made on its basis about new and independent archeological evidence from previously uninvestigated parts of the Near East. If new data fit the hypothesis, then it is so far confirmed.

We use this and other examples to illustrate the reasoning involved. Whether or not the model is correct is another matter. Readers of literature on archeological theory should not confuse these two matters. For example, Carter Ranch (Longacre 1968, 1970) has been repeatedly used as a takeoff point both for polemical discussions and as an example of archeological reasoning. Whether Longacre does or does not show that Carter Ranch is matrilocal is seldom relevant to these discussions. Most writers who consider the Carter Ranch study to be a useful example agree that he did not. Similarly, we use Binford's model to illustrate an ecological hypothesis, not to argue for or against its substance. In fact, despite Harlan's study, there is little reason to believe in general that the plant and animal species that were eventually domesticated provided the bulk of the diet in the optimum zones, and there may actually have been considerable motivation to manipulate these species to increase their contribution to the diet of human groups within those zones. Further, with present dating techniques it would be difficult to determine whether or not domestication originated in marginal areas prior to its occurrence in

Ecology and Archeology   127

optimal ones. Nevertheless, the model is provocative and is testable in principle.

One more example illustrates the range of ecologically based explanations used by contemporary archeologists. It provides a transition from theoretical concerns to the meshing of theory and practice.

In a volume edited by Wood and McMillan (1976), Bruce McMillan discusses the interrelationships of climate and human adaptation at Rodgers Shelter in western Missouri (McMillan 1976). Using vegetation patterns inferred from U.S. Federal Land Survey records of the 1840s, but also with some support from the sedimentology of the shelter deposits (Ahler 1976) and from the faunal remains there (Parmalee, McMillan, and King 1976), McMillan postulates that there was a shift from forest-edge environment to a grassland or prairie vegetation cover during the earlier period of occupation at Rodgers Shelter (about 8000 B.P. to 6300 B.P.), and then a second shift back to a forest-edge biotype after 3000 B.P. (McMillan 1976:227–228). Faunal analyses reveal an emphasis on deer during the earliest period of occupation (Dalton) and the next to latest (Late Archaic), but during the intervening Middle Archaic "a reduced emphasis on deer hunting and the increase of diversity of species taken, especially small game" (McMillan 1976:230). The explanation offered for the shift from deer to small mammals and back to deer is the change in environment from more wooded to more open and then back to woodland again.

> We believe the "less efficient system" (that is, increasing the diversity of species hunted and emphasizing small game) was a necessary stress response—set in motion by a deteriorating effective environment. . . . The Late Archaic adaptation reflects a return to environmental conditions supporting deer herds and, concomitantly, to a procurement system designed to exploit these animals. (McMillan 1976:230)

Although there is some circularity in the explanation (faunal evidence is one of the bases from which environmental change is inferred, and faunal fluctuations are then explained by reference to the environmental change), the proposition is carefully worked out, plausible, and intuitively satisfying. It is a good example of an ecologically based hypothetical explanation that would be generally regarded as satisfactory by McMillan's colleagues (one of us used a similar construction for a different archeological situation; Watson 1974a:235–238). On the other hand, it is not an explanation of why people stayed at Rodgers Shelter rather than, say, moving far enough to stay in the arboreal zone. One might say that they stay because there is still a food supply, even if a different one from before. But this suffers from the weakness Hempel finds characteristic of all functional explanations in that it provides a plausible reason why *something like* X is present but it does not specify why X happened rather than X_1 or X_2 or X_3. Why, for example, did the people not move east far enough to stay in a wooded region? It is always necessary to pose hypotheses about why people adapt one functionally satisfactory solution rather than another.

In the case of Rodgers Shelter, one might hypothesize that the people stay there because it is such a good shelter. This, added to the hypothesis that, although the deer went away there remained adequate small game for food, is still a functional explanation, but it is strengthened by the conjunction of the two reasons.

But is even the primary ecological explanation well confirmed? Explanations for the faunal remains other than shifts in climate and back-and-forth migration of the arboreal zone are possible. For example, perhaps the climate supported a mixed open and forest zone. Perhaps the people at Rodgers Shelter simply preferred deer for a while for some reason, and then small game a while for some other reason. If this were the case, then the faunal data would not support the hypothesis of climate change and arboreal zone migration. Can any research programs be devised to test the two alternative hypotheses for explaining change in the faunal remains, one postulating climate change and the other postulating cultural change? Yes. Pollen analytic and flotation techniques, for example, can be applied to sediments in and near the shelter to determine the vegetation sequence during the entire time of occupation. A general point here is that single hypotheses, no matter how well confirmed, are not so strong as they would be if their confirmation involved at the same time disconfirmation of plausible alternative hypotheses. The preferred procedure is therefore known as the method of multiple working hypotheses (Chamberlin 1890).

Practical limitations on archeological field and laboratory work often place severe restraints on comprehensiveness and thoroughness. Hence, again and again archeological reports provide abbreviated, truncated, or otherwise incomplete interpretations and explanations. Some of these abbreviated explanations—such as McMillan's—are as solid and sound as the state of archeological knowledge permits. However, those archeologists who are unaware of the weaknesses inherent in functional explanations are more likely to produce inadequate or just plain bad interpretations than those who are aware of these limitations. One should systematically consider all feasible functional alternatives and then try to construct hypotheses explaining why the one adopted was chosen. Because such hypotheses are numerous and frequently difficult to test by field or laboratory work, they are often tested only by working out plausible lines of argument. In any case, the evidence and reasoning supporting even tentative conclusions should be clearly reported.

Hence, we come again to the conclusion we have reached from a variety of directions before and will reach several times again: Archeologists should begin with clearly stated problems and then formulate testable hypothetical solutions. The degree of confirmation of conclusions should then be exhibited by describing fully the field and laboratory data and the reasoning used to support these conclusions. This is what we mean by an explicitly scientific archeological method.

Inherent Dangers of the Ecological Approach

A fundamental point is that archeologists must state and test their hypotheses and assumptions explicitly. While it is obvious that social organization is closely tied to environmental factors, our basic assumptions about the relationships between culture and behavior must be tested. As already noted, we must be able to reject hypotheses as well as confirm them. *Assuming* without testing that a close relationship exists between environmental factors and human behavior may conceal disconfirming data. It may seem to be highly plausible that changes in projectile point shape relate to changes in fauna being hunted, but eventually someone must examine alternative explanations for these shifts in point form, such as changes in craft specialization or in social organization.

The general question of just how large-scale cultural changes—such as major alterations in population distribution or the initial domestication of plants and animals—are related to changes in the environment poses some of the most basic and important problems in archeology. Setting up the problems and constructing sets of alternatively possible hypothetical solutions is often difficult. Fortunately, however, the collection of environmental data to test these hypotheses is usually straightforward. It is far easier to demonstrate that there was a drought in the Southwest than that there was a migration, but this does not mean that a particular migration might not have been much more important than a particular drought. Although environmental data are usually important and are relatively straightforward to obtain, there is no a priori reason to assume that they are categorically more significant than nonenvironmental information. Both cultural and environmental data taken together are necessary to test hypothetical explanations.

What one must keep in mind is that, from an archeological viewpoint, the collection of ecological data is not an end in itself. Collecting some pollen samples, doing some flotation (see below), and saving all the animal bone does not automatically result in scientific archeology. Environmental data must be collected for the purpose of solving archeological problems. They are extraneous unless they are used in constructing and testing hypotheses and theories. Archeologists using the ecological approach must be careful not to fall into the trap of merely producing environmental data per se.

The Ecological Approach in Archeology: Practice

The primary focus of 1960s and 1970s ecological archeology is on subsistence and paleo-environment, but recently—as already noted—ecological archeology has broadened to include systematic investigation of other loosely related topics such as trade and settlement patterns. (Under the broad heading of settlement pattern analysis we include locational analysis, paleodemography, and site catchment

Ecology and Archeology 131

analysis). We do not discuss trade or settlement pattern studies here (see the references listed above) but do make some general points about the use of ecological and environmental data before taking up the subject of how these data are obtained.

The justification for concern with empirical information about subsistence and paleo-environment is that one must know how a prehistoric society made its living if one is to achieve understanding of that society. One cannot learn about the subsistence patterns of a prehistoric society unless one also knows about the environment within which the society functioned. Further, in any kind of diachronic (through time) analysis of primitive (that is, nonindustrialized, nonurbanized, small, relatively homogeneous) societies, one must take into account the possibility that changes in the environment affected the development of technology and other aspects of those societies. (Such societies may sometimes have affected their environments significantly, but this is more difficult to detect archeologically than the reverse, although it has sometimes been the object of serious study: Inversen 1956; Martin and Wright 1967; Minnis 1978). Hence, the preoccupation of ecologically oriented archeologists with questions of diet, food procurement, and the environmental settings of prehistoric cultures is understandable. Long gone in Americanist archeology are the days when ethnobotanist Hugh Cutler had to go from backdirt pile to backdirt pile in Arizona and New Mexico to retrieve important botanical remains shoveled out by archeologists in quest of architecture and artifacts, as the latter were then defined. Floral and faunal remains ("ecofacts") are now collected routinely with a wide variety of techniques such as fine screening, water screening, water separation and flotation, and collection of soil samples for pollen, phytoliths, and/or microgastropod extraction in the laboratory. However, there are a number of important practical problems that nearly all ecologically oriented archeologists face, and we give some attention to these because how (or whether) these problems are solved by fieldworkers directly affects archeological interpretation and is relevant to the issue at the core of our concern in this book: archeological theory and its implementation in the field and in the laboratory.

We discuss briefly three topics that should be of serious concern to nearly every archeologist carrying out a research project within an ecological framework: (1) funding; (2) locating and coordinating personnel; and (3) practical concerns in sampling and retrieval procedures for ecofactual data.

Funding

Ecological archeology is very expensive. It is now apparent that the 1960s was the heyday of large, relatively generously funded, academically based interdisciplinary projects, and that that heyday is over. Nearly all of the money for the projects listed as examples earlier in this chapter came from the U.S. government, the bulk of it from the National Science Foundation. This form of financial backing is now much reduced and will remain so for the foreseeable future. Consequently, precisely because the majority of practicing archeologists in the United States are convinced of the theoretical and practical value of ecologically oriented, interdisciplinary work—although it is far more expensive in every way than the old-style approach in which each archeologist was a jack-of-all-trades and did his or her own surveying, photography, or whatever else was thought necessary—such academically based interdisciplinary work is becoming harder and harder to maintain. There is greater and greater competition for less and less money from the government funding agencies that receive the bulk of the research proposals from archeologists: the National Science Foundation and the National Endowment for the Humanities.

Since 1974 when the Archeological Conservation Act was passed, two kinds of solutions to funding problems have emerged: (1) research supported by grants and by the work of volunteers; and (2) contract or conservation archeology.

The first solution consists more or less of free-lance research based on U.S. or state government grants (nearly always smaller than those of the 1960s) combined with a high proportion of volunteer labor and other support, as well as private funding (for example, outright donations obtained by soliciting private individuals or corporations, or money obtained from students or interested laypersons enrolled in a field school at one's site). A few notable examples of successful, large-scale use of this tactic are Stuart Struever's research organization in Kampsville, Illinois (1978); Cynthia Irwin-Williams's center in the Four Corners area of the Southwest (Irwin-Williams et al. 1975); and Steven LeBlanc's Mimbres Project (LeBlanc 1983). A smaller-scale example of the same tactic is the Shellmound Archeological Project/Cave Research Foundation Archeological Project in Kentucky and Tennessee (Watson ed. 1974; Marquardt and Watson 1979, 1983; Watson 1977, 1978).

The second solution, contract or conservation archeology, is a highly important phenomenon that now dominates archeological fieldwork in the United States. Because we are here addressing matters of actual archeological practice as well as archeological theory, we take up such pragmatic topics as the ramifications of the Archeological Conservation Act and related U.S. government legislation. Those unfamiliar with the recent history of antiquities legislation in the United States should consult Fowler (1982); Lipe (1977); King, Hickman, and Berg (1977); Schiffer and House (1975); Schiffer and Gumerman (1977); and Wildesen (1982), as well as McGimsey (1972). Very briefly, the Archeological Conservation Act authorizes up to 1 percent of the federal funds budgeted for construction projects that disturb the landscape to be spent for location and documentation by appropriate experts (including archeologists) of cultural historical materials in the path of that construction. Related legislation requires that archeological surveys be carried out in conjunction with the other environmental impact studies necessitated before such construction projects can even be begun.

The terminology often used to distinguish archeological research stemming from the antiquities legislation from that funded by other means is "conservation" or "public" or "contract" archeology or occasionally "salvage" archeology versus "academic" or "ivory tower" archeology.

The immediate result of the antiquities legislation was to open up a large source of federal funds for archeological work that could be tapped by archeologists with research competence in regions where federally subsidized construction (for dams, interstate highways, etc.) was planned. We do not discuss here all the effects this legislation has had and is having on the archeological community in the United States (see chapter 6), but we note in the context of funding for ecological archeology that by the end of the 1970s well over 90 percent of all archeological work done in the United States was partially or wholly subsidized from this source and that many archeologists doing contract work do some form of interdisciplinary contract work.

In any case, if federally funded construction is slated for some portion of one's geographical or topical research area, one can potentially obtain rather generous sums to carry out archeological research there, but usually with a number of important strings attached. These constraints include delineation of the research area by the agency rather than by the archeologist, hard-and-fast deadlines for completion of fieldwork and laboratory work, and written reports on that work.

The point we wish to make with respect to the current funding situation in the United States is that archeological research strategy is more heavily influenced by available funds now than ten or fifteen years ago when the ecological approach was first burgeoning. In both contract and academic archeology, however, successful proposals are those that are clearly written descriptions of well-conceived research designs aimed at well-defined, significant problems. Hence, at the crucial, practical level of funding as well as at the level of archeological knowledge accumulation, the suggestions made throughout this book about adherence to explicitly scientific methodology are relevant. Well-organized and clearly written proposals are more likely to be funded than are badly organized, poorly written ones.

Locating and Coordinating Personnel

This is a ubiquitous and critical problem, but we do not discuss it at length here because others have already done so (Brown and Struever 1973; Butzer 1975, 1978, 1980; Schoenwetter 1981; Struever 1968a, 1971; Taylor 1957; Wiseman 1980). Also it has been and still is almost entirely a logistical matter that must be resolved via the personal networks of individual investigators. We do stress, however, that the nature and number of staff personnel sought by an archeologist wishing to carry out an interdisciplinary project are directly dependent on the exact problem or problems being investigated and on the kind of work planned to solve those problems. Once again, the questions to be studied and the data necessary to answer these questions must be as clearly conceived as possible before the work begins. It may be that a particular problem would necessitate the closest cooperation between, and joint directorship of the project by, an archeologist and a botanist, or an archeologist and a geologist, or two or three botanists and two or three archeologists, or some other combination. It is also quite likely that different phases of the work will necessitate different combinations of expertise in the directorial staff. In any case, it is of course essential that some one person—in the context of the present discussion, this person would be an archeologist—or a very few people, be responsible for the long-term conceptualization and carrying out of the work.

We have only one more observation to make about personnel here, and that is to reinforce the cautionary statements of such experienced collaborators as Karl Butzer (1975). Although large-scale, interdisciplinary research in archeology has been going on for almost twenty years, the number of projects that have produced results commensurate with their cost in time, effort, and money is distressingly small. The main reason for the failures, the near-failures, and the heavily qualified successes is lack of coordination or poor coordination among the experts involved. Some of the coordination problems derive from personality clashes or from lack of communication on the part of individual scholars. These sorts of difficulties will always be present to some degree and must be overcome as they occur.

The most destructive difficulties, however, arise from unclarity about who is in charge of the overall project, who is to do what, and just how each segment of the work fits into the total research strategy to move the investigation toward solutions to the questions being investigated. In the present context, the archeologist is in charge and defines the overall research plan for the purpose of solving archeological problems. It may be a very difficult matter to figure out how to avoid hard feelings when the necessity arises—as it often does—of reminding enthusiastic cooperating scientists from other fields that the archeological project comes first and that they are not in the field to pursue their work for its own sake. Sometimes one cannot subordinate cooperating scientists from other fields. In some cases one must join them in cooperative expeditions during which their basic research—for example, in paleoclimatology or paleobotany—provides data useful for archeologists but is not specifically collected to solve archeological problems. However cooperation may be established, it is always necessary.

Major communication problems are inherent in interdisciplinary work and must be continually guarded against by those directing such work. Techniques used by various archeologists to ameliorate these problems include regular face-to-face group meetings (called specially, or held on the occasion of national and regional professional meetings), frequent letters and phone calls, and newsletters. We cannot stress too strongly the importance of a clear, mutual understanding of the role to be played by each group member and of continual dialogue among the cooperating experts with one another and with the project directors.

Practical Concerns in Sampling and Retrieval Procedures for Ecofactual Data

As with the questions of funding and personnel, this topic is vital to ecologically oriented archeological research. Detailed consideration of it would be out of place in this book, but good detailed publications are readily available (see the references in this chapter and in chapter 4).

We must stress once more, however, that which sampling and recovery techniques are used for ecofactual materials depends very heavily on the overall research design. Flotation of archeological deposits to recover charred botanial remains is a good example. Should one save all dug deposit for flotation? Or float 50 percent of it? Or 25 percent? Or should one float only the contents of the pits and hearths? What flotation system should be used: the Apple Creek immersion technique, the garbage can or oil drum technique, or some motorized technique using a water pump and a variety of plumbing equipment? (See P. Watson 1976; Dye and Moore 1978; Minnis and LeBlanc 1976; Wagner 1982). Should the dirt be weighed before floating, or measured volumetrically, or both? Should the heavy fraction be treated chemically to help sort dense botanical remains like hickory nutshell from the even heavier microremains (small bones and bone fragments, chert bits, pebbles, etc.)? Should the light fractions be packaged in newspaper or cloth? The possible questions are endless for all ecofactual realms of investigation (pollen, macro- and microfauna, sediments, and depositional analyses, etc.). The way out of this potential methodological chaos is the same one we stress throughout this book: investigators must know exactly what questions they are asking so that they can determine the kinds of data needed to answer those questions and, in turn, the procedures needed to obtain these data. Although practical details may be multitudinous and often troublesome, these logistical problems can be solved successfully once the theoretical framework that defines them is clearly understood.

One more point should be made about recovery techniques. Because archeologists and their interdisciplinary collaborators are still in the early stages of working out refinements—and, in some cases, even the essentials—of retrieval procedures for ecofactual data, it is especially important to include in archeological reports fairly detailed accounts of the actual sampling systems and recovery techniques used. These descriptions are necessary to ensure public access to techniques and methods as well as to results, so that the results can be evaluated and so that investigators working on similar problems can benefit from the experiences of their colleagues. Knowledge can accumulate in no other way.

Nature of the Data

Having discussed some theoretical aspects of paleo-ecological research, we now describe, in a pragmatic or operational vein, various pertinent classes of data to show their roles in that research. As noted above, archeological data are not limited to artifacts in the traditional meaning of that word but include anything introduced into an archeological site by human activities. In fact, even this definition is too narrow because we need to include all "natural" materials that can provide evidence about the environment in which human beings operate. The varied and ingenious means developed for extracting information about the environment is one of the brightest spots in archeology, and there is a rather large literature on the recovery of paleo-environmental data. Our concern is not with these methods per se but rather with the means of using them to test hypotheses, so we consider them from that perspective.

Some techniques such as pollen analysis or faunal analysis are familiar to all archeologists but nevertheless present many problems in interpretation. For example, pollen records are difficult to work with because they are always influenced by at least three factors: (1) the composition of the undisturbed prehistoric biotic community; (2) the composition of the biotic community resulting from human activities of all kinds; and (3) the differential use of plants (including pollen itself) by human inhabitants of the settlement that later becomes an archeological site.

Thus in order to use pollen for information about any one of these three facets we must be able to control for the other two, a very formidable task. If we find a high proportion of weed pollen in a sample, does this mean that weeds were increasing because of farming activities, or because patches of disturbed soil were common at and near the site itself; or were the weeds themselves (for example, sunflower, chenopodium, knotweed) being cultivated? Is the abundance of weed pollen a result of overall environmental changes; or were certain weeds used ceremonially, or as kindling or bedding or building materials in the particular location from which the pollen sample came? While some of these possibilities can usually be eliminated by taking multiple samples and by comparative checks against other types of pollen, it should be clear that the final interpretation is inherently rather difficult.

Faunal analysis also presents considerable problems. For example, do the rodent bones present on a site represent game, or contemporary or postoccupation residence by a population of free-living rodents? Or does a *lack* of rodent bone represent little or no hunting of these animals, or poor preservation of their small and fragile bones, or only inadequate recovery techniques? One way to reduce these problems is to collect environmental data in several different categories. For example, flotation and analysis of paleofecal material as well as pollen analysis can be used to determine ancient floral communities. Flotation is especially useful in that all sizes of seeds are automatically recovered, eliminating the enormous bias present in collecting only those macroplant remains that the collector happens to see. There are a number of sites in the Southwest where only fragments of corn and a few beans were recovered by trowel-using excavators; but from similar sites where flotation was used great quantities and varieties of botanical material were recovered.

Many kinds of rather esoteric biological data are now sought and examined by archeologists for a variety of purposes (for example, to determine seasonality; Monks 1981). Such data categories may include submicroscopic gastropod shells and the rings on fish scales or in thin sections of marine bivalve shells, for example, but there are still other important data categories that are often neglected, such as human skeletal material, pollen cores from off-site locations, and firewood analysis. Skeletal material is a particularly good example because it can provide data that are very sensitive indicators of the manner in which a human population is affected by its social and physical environment (Buikstra 1976; Huss-Ashmore, Goodman, and Armelegos 1982; Tainter 1978).

The use of pollen cores from wet areas not directly associated with sites raises an interesting point. In investigating past environments, archeologists are often overly attracted to the sites themselves as sources of information, but there are distinct advantages in collecting data from areas away from prehistoric human activities. Stratigraphic tests should be made at places apart from sites, and evidence such as pollen should be collected from them. This is rarely done by archeologists, although palynologists routinely collect numerous samples of the modern pollen rain to compare with the ancient pollen they are collecting from bogs or lakes. The excavation of uninhabited caves or rockshelters as controls for interpreting the deposits in inhabited shelters is another technique that is rarely used (see, however, Thomas 1974; also Nance 1980). In fact, there is so much potential information about the environments of prehistoric sites (and about their formation processes) in the geology of their regional settings that a field of study called *geoarcheology* has developed to take a position beside archeozoology and archeobotany (Gladfelter 1981, Rapp and Gifford 1982; see also Wood and Johnson 1978; Butzer 1980 presents a thoughtful critique of this new subdiscipline).

Modern Environmental Data

Data about modern environmental conditions are of great importance for archeologists trying to understand ancient ones. Such data fall into two classes: observations on present ecosystems and how they work; and generalizations about yields, hunting and farming strategies, energy requirements, and so on drawn from ethnographic information and from experimentation. The pitfalls and limitations of relying on these modern data to help interpret the past are numerous, but information on recent ecological processes is essential to archeologists. We need to be familiar with modern ecological parameters that are plausible analogs for the aboriginal circumstances under investigation, but we also need to be cautious in using these analogs. On the basis of modern data we can estimate prehistoric corn yields or the labor required to build a certain type of canal, but if the estimates are for corn different from modern varieties or for tools that differ significantly from those used in the past, then they may be seriously misleading.

Some generalizations (for example, the caloric values of different foods) are quite reliable, others (the yields of different crops) are much less reliable. In general, however, archeologists fail to utilize these kinds of data to their fullest for two reasons. First of all, archeologists have simply not fully exploited the large bodies of data that do exist (Thomas's study discussed in chapter 2 is an exception). Harlan's experimental wheat reaping in southeastern Turkey (Harlan 1967) has been recounted so many times partly because the results came as such a surprise to so many archeologists.

Secondly, few archeologists are themselves farmers or hunters, hence, few have any intuitive understanding of these subsistence

Ecology and Archeology 141

purusits. A case in point is the requirements of irrigation, which go far beyond the construction of a few barrages and ditches. Questions of adaptability of plants to irrigation, needs for soil drainage, and effects of water on soil compaction and salinity must be understood before the cost-effectiveness of a particular irrigation pattern can be estimated. Under certain circumstances, the adverse effects of some of these factors can significantly increase the labor requirements for irrigation over dry farming, and this must be understood in order to explain why irrigation was practiced at some times and places and not at others.

The need for modern data is undeniable, but they require careful documentation. Both the sources of estimates and delineation of probable errors are very important, as are the short-term and long-term ranges of variation characterizing them. Thus, statements about crop yields or about annual rainfall must be accompanied by estimates of how these values deviate from the norm over many years.

Uses of Ecological Data

We have mentioned several possible sources of environmental information; we now discuss how this information can be used. In a sense this topic is not deserving of a special heading because environmental data should be used as are any other kind: to aid in the creation of theories and in the formulation and testing of hypotheses potentially explanatory of the archeological record and of the human past.

Our primary need is for data relevant to particular research goals, and there is no a priori reason why pollen samples or flotation samples must be comprehensively collected from every site. Some classes of data such as faunal remains are useful for many purposes and should be collected from any site. But the use of very fine-mesh screens to collect all rodent bones from all excavated deposits requires special justification. The principal purpose of recovering and analyzing rodent bones is to enable inferences about paleoclimate, and they may be critical for interpreting Pleistocene cave sites but less crucial for a site like Teotihuacan. Thus the decision as to whether or not to recover and analyze rodent bones depends on the site and the problem.

Practical Considerations

Environmental data must almost always be quantified to be useful. It is of interest to know whether or not various species of plants or animals are present or absent, but only if we know the quantitative relations of specimens examined can we say that a particular plant or animal was wild or domesticated. Changes in species composition can be used to infer past environments and adaptations. Complete replacement is unusual, so presence of a now-extinct species at a site is interesting information regardless of its frequency. But to determine the total exploitive strategy of the human group under consideration, we must know the relations of all the animals present. To understand the Paleo-Indians we need to understand what animals they collected and in what proportions they collected them, not just that they killed some big game. Thus, nonquantified and noninterpreted species lists are rarely of much use.

However, environmental data that are appropriately collected possess great potential for testing a wide variety of hypotheses and hence for helping to solve many problems. Questions of seasonality, changes in diet, changes in climate, and changes in the environment induced by humans are some of the most obvious. Different classes of environmental data can provide independent means for testing the same hypothesis. A hypothesis about seasonality, for example, can be tested by considering animal and botanical remains independently, such as the presence or absence of certain kinds of immature animals, or of one type of pollen spectrum, or of varying suites of plant remains, or of floral and faunal constituents of human paleofecal material.

Each of these data categories is independent of the others, and while some may be lacking or may give equivocal results, together they may provide a full picture of the past environment. Thus, quantified environmental data of various related sorts are of great use to archeologists. However, there is such abundance and variety of collectable environmental data that an archeologist must always have clear research goals asnd specific hypotheses to guide the collection of ecological information.

Because of the vagaries of the archeological record, data must usually be collected from numerous related sites to obtain a full paleoenvironmental picture of a past culture. But suppose one is restricted to a single site; should large amounts of ecological data be collected from it?

The practical answer to this question is that we must begin somewhere; simple accumulation of data is justifiable in some cases. As noted in the following chapter, just what and how much environmental data one should collect for descriptive purposes alone are extremely difficult problems. But a case can be made for obtaining abundant quantified data of the kinds that have generally been found to be useful in other areas. At least one should attempt to determine quantities and varieties of plants and animals. This initial step can help future workers decide what problems can be solved for a site or region.

This is an example of the operational inseparability of induction and deduction. Before substantive problems relating to the paleoenvironment can be solved, we must collect a substantial amount of environmental data. Fortunately, a considerable amount of information is already available for several areas such as the Near East, Western Europe, and the U.S. Southwest. Not only is there a large quantity of high quality data, but also there are regional syntheses that make possible specialized problem-oriented research and data collection.

Ecological Data as Artifacts

Environmental data are seldom evenly distributed over a particular site. This makes their interpretation difficult and significantly affects the manner in which such data should be collected. This differential distribution of data is usually at least partially a reflection of human behavior and provides important information about that behavior. Thus, analyses of the differential distribution of ecological or biological data are important.

Environmental data can be treated just like any other class of artifacts. Note that one of the implications from Hill's model (Hill 1968) is about the distribution of pollen between classes of rooms, and another concerns differences in the distribution of corrugated pottery. Environmental or biological data are useful for testing hypotheses about both the environment and people's relationship to it. These data yield both environmental and cultural information, and the effects of variability both in the environment and in human behavior must be considered. Hill's data on pollen provide information not only about room function (storeroom versus living room) but also species lists detailing what was being put into these storerooms.

It is thus apparent that knowledge of intrasite variability is necessary to interpret data in an ecological framework. Intrasite variability shows the range of cultural adaptation. Storage methods, divisions of labor, and regional economic specializations vary. Environmental data can also be used to delineate social groups within or between sites. Miksicek (1975) suggests that different groups in prehistoric Southwestern pueblos use slightly different strains of corn and beans; thus, the distribution of these strains in the archeobotanical remains should reflect the locations of these groups.

It is possible, of course, that differences in the frequency of occurrence or composition of ecological variables on a site merely represent different rates of deposition or intensity of human activity. As always, one must be alert to recognize and allow for the effects of extraneous variables on depositional patterns.

Modern Ecological Data in Model Building

Modern ecological data are collected to provide a basis for interpreting prehistoric data. For example, only by understanding modern pollen rain can we infer the meaning of past pollen spectra. Here we are using a body of established biological theory (although the degree to which many of these theories and relationships are well confirmed varies) to explain a particular data set.

Modern data can also be used as a basis for formulating hypotheses about possible strategies of past behavior. From a hypothesized model of possible strategies we can infer just what patterns and kinds of remains we should expect to find or what kinds of data we need to collect to test them.

The geographic boundaries of ecological models can be chosen on various grounds. A model can be bounded, for example, by the catchment area of the site. This is an area (of a size that previous archeological and ethnographic information indicates is usually exploited) utilized for specific activities such as hunting, farming, or shellfish collecting. Then, given the catchment area for exploitation of a particular resource at a particular site or series of sites, one can define possible strategies. If more than one strategy is possible—and this is usually the case—models are constructed for each strategy. From these models one can derive implications for testing to compare the various models. For example, if collecting one resource conflicts with collecting another because they can be obtained only at one time of the year, then the presence of one and the absence of the other in the archeological record shows which model best fits actual past behavior. In practice, of course, the results of most tests of various models are not this conclusive.

The most important use of modern ecological data associated with archeological sites is to combine them with previously established biological principles to construct models from which interrelated hypotheses can be inferred and tested. With modern ecological data, one can even compute rewards and costs of different strategies. This, of course, requires some kind of systemic analysis. Usually cost accounting is done for only a portion of an entire system. Models can show how one strategy is theoretically superior to the others and then one can check to see whether or not it was utilized. One can also determine whether or not a strategy was even viable, that is, whether or not a subsistence procurement system, as we envision it, will provide the necessary calories for the group over the long run. If the optimum strategy was, in fact, not utilized, or a model we have shown to result in starvation actually fits the archeological data, then either our basic assumptions are incorrect or we have ignored some important part of the system. Or, perhaps, people were not operating in a way we take to be rational. In any case, the model must be modified or rejected.

As is true of systems analysis in general, a quantified model can lead to important conclusions prior to its testing against the data. Such a model can often show that, unless additional variables are included, the results will be unrealistic. Of course, past people may have behaved in ways that we consider to be unrealistic, but in general we can make fieldwork more efficient if we reject models with highly implausible results. Or we may realize that unless we include additional information about the environment the model will not be useful for determining an optimum or even a possible strategy. For example, if we have no idea of the variability of a system from year to year, then we have no idea about the need for storage or alternative strategies during years of stress, yet many ecological models require an understanding of the role of these two practices in the system as a whole.

In fact, in practice we usually employ a combination of various procedures. We use both modern and prehistoric data in constructing models, which we test against both prehistoric data and logical conclusions drawn from the models.

For example, we may use modern site catchment data together with prehistoric pollen and flotation evidence as well as animal bone and artifact distributions to construct a model of a subsistence strategy. Modern data may show that certain amounts of land per person are required for farm production. This may lead to estimates of maximum population for the catchment area that can be checked archeologically against population estimates for the site. If the projected population of the site seems large compared to the computed productivity, we might construct a model of "marginality." This model might indicate that the population was too large for the carrying capacity and hence was operating with some difficulty. There would be evidence for different strategies and different kinds of plant and animal remains, different population structures, and so on, if this were not the case. Modern data about nonfarming strategies utilized in the site catchment area today might suggest modifications of the model. Having made appropriate changes in the model, we would again turn to the archeological record to test it. Several models might be constructed and compared as we go back and forth many times among modern data, archeological data, and hypotheses about the interrelationships of environment and culture.

Special Considerations About Ecological Data

Before making some additional generalizations about ecological data and their relation to archeology, we need to consider some special aspects of the nature of such data.

Synchronous Versus Diachronous Use of Ecological Data

How does one use ecological data to determine quantitative aspects of past subsistence economies? It is often difficult to translate recovered data into quantitative statements about past systems. For example, how does one determine what quantities of original animals and plants are represented by the remains of animal bone, flotation material, and plant and animal fragments from dry caves? How many deer does one deer bone represent? How much corn does one charred corn cob represent? Except under the most favorable conditions (shellmiddens possibly being one of them for certain kinds of data), these questions are almost impossible to answer with much accuracy. Of course, the data are still worthwhile, but one must be cautious about the inferences drawn from them.

It is far easier to use such data to detect proportional changes over time than to determine actual quantities for any given time (an approach considered in more detail in chapter 4). Many generalizations about the rates of preservation, loss, and so on are required to relate the numbers of bones or charred seeds or dried cactus fruits to the numbers of animals or plants originally collected. Thus, it is difficult to be assured about estimates, for example, of the ratio between animal and plant resources or between domestic and wild species for a given time period, but it is not so difficult to determine whether or not there were changes in the ratios over time.

Sometimes, however, determination of the proportions or relative composition of diet at a given time can be made relatively readily. Also, the proportional use of species of approximately the same size or preservability can often be readily inferred, for example, the proportion of reindeer to horse in a paleolithic site, or the proportion of fish to mussels in a shellmidden. In each case, however, one would have to show or assume that rates of deposition are the same for each species. Were the sites seasonal and hence the remains not representative of the total annual diet? Were the butchering practices the same for horse and reindeer, or were more reindeer bones brought to the site than horse bones? Were the fish cleaned on the shellmound, or were the scales and most of the bones deposited elsewhere? If we can answer these kinds of questions satisfactorily, then we may reasonably infer the caloric ratios of the pairs of resources in question.

The above comments are not to suggest that the problem of estimating actual quantities of various components of a subsistence base is unsolvable. It does seem true, nevertheless, that hypotheses about changes in subsistence strategies over time are more readily testable than hypotheses about the detailed composition of the subsistence base for any given time.

Ease of Collection Versus Cost of Analysis

One of the main difficulties in excavating a site from a limited problem base is, as noted above, that in doing so material is destroyed that is necessary to solve many other problems not under consideration. Because it is impossible to save or record everything, samples should be taken of as many varieties of the data categories represented at the site as possible. This is usually easier to do for environmental data such as pollen, plant remains, animal bones, shells, paleofeces, and so on than for artifactual or architectural material such as that from kivas, temples, and burials.

There are many excellent sampling techniques that in fact lead to

Ecology and Archeology

more rational use of archeological resources than attempts to collect or record all data fully. A well-sampled site can obviously be described more fully than one in which one aspect is covered exhaustively to the neglect of many others. But one problem with extensive sampling of environmental data is that it is often difficult and expensive to analyze all the samples. No archeologist can analyze and interpret all categories of material himself or herself. For example, comprehensive comparative collections of plant and animal remains are required, as is expertise in many specialized fields. Identification of Old World sheep versus goat or bison versus cow is far from easy. Distinguishing among the various kinds of birds and between domestic and wild turkey is very difficult. Identification of rodent remains requires expertise and excellent comparative collections. Such needs make interdisciplinary cooperation imperative.

So although it may not take excessive amounts of time and money to collect sufficient samples of subsistence data, the time and costs of analyzing these data may be great. Often there are either insufficient funds or insufficient personnel available to work on the ecological data. This practical consideration is becoming a major stumbling block to ecologically oriented research, and serious efforts are needed to overcome it. Again, fielding a cooperative interdisciplinary project is one of the best ways to proceed.

Special Considerations About Different Classes of Data

There are specific problems in working with each type of ecological data. For example, there are classic arguments over how to count economic versus noneconomic pollen and whether to make minimal counts of individual animals or total counts of bones. While some of these differences are important in themselves, some of the controversies reflect lack of problem-oriented research. What data should be collected depends in large part on the problems one sets out to solve. (The requirement of minimal sampling of all major types of data is based on the assumption that the general problem being addressed in all archeological work is to reach comprehensive understanding of the site or material.)

For example, neither the minimum number of individuals represented nor the total count of bone is categorically a "superior analytic variable." The methods of determining each differ, as do the problems the acquired data can be used to solve. Further, the significance of samples from a refuse midden obviously differs from that of samples from kill sites. Sampling methods and materials sampled thus differ according to type of site as well as according to the problems in mind.

While it is clear that a given archeologist cannot possibly be expert enough to analyze all classes of environmental data, he or she cannot leave the final interpretation of the results solely in the hands of the specialists who examine them. To use these results intelligently, an archeologist must understand the assumptions, powers, and limitations of the analytic methods. For example, one need not know how to run radiocarbon determinations oneself, but one must know how to collect samples correctly, and one must know the limitations and reliabilities of various techniques on different materials (see Browman 1981, for example).

Another use of ecological data is in locating activity areas within sites. The activities carried out at a site are often related to seasons or subsistence strategy. In particular, it is important to discover nonobvious activities. While we might infer from artifacts such as projectile points and animal bones that a site was a hunting camp, the further discovery of tools for processing vegetable material at the same site could make us alter our interpretation of the group's overall subsistence pattern.

On the other hand, if one already knows that a group farms cereals and grinds grain, the mere discovery of grinding equipment in particular rooms, or that some rooms were storerooms, does not add to our knowledge about the group's domestic economy, although the numbers and volumes of storage areas may. But room data can provide information about the composition of social groups. The spatial locations and temporal shifts of such "obvious" activity areas can be used to determine whether there was craft specialization, whether strategies shifted over time, whether more or less storage was related to environmental or social changes, and so on. Thus, the mere demonstration that certain activities were performed is important information about some sites, while for other sites this is not enough, but knowledge of the spatial or temporal distributions of these activities is of considerable importance.

Environmental data are essential for studying the interaction of subsistence strategies and social systems. Obviously, as mentioned above, there is no logical distinction between "ecological" or "subsistence" analysis and "systems" analysis. Just as understanding of site dynamics helps one interpret environmental or ecological data, so subsistence data are used to test hypotheses about processes and such specifics as estimates of family size. Distinguishing floor deposits from refuse deposits helps to decipher the environmental situation, and distinguishing roasting pits from storage pits by use of ecological data helps to define the social structure of a group.

We have again reached the conclusion that ecological data are part and parcel of archeological data in general and that "ecological" analyses are integral with "social organizational" analyses. Environmental and cultural factors are so interrelated that the analyses of their remains cannot be separated without falsifying the results.

Some Generalizations About Human Ecological Relationships

Several conclusions can be drawn about the nature of human ecological adaptations. These are conclusions in the form of hypotheses or statements describing possible empirical regularities that bear testing.

One suggestion is that people often adapt by exploiting multiple ecosystems. That is, they do not concentrate on just one zone but use a variety of techniques to exploit several zones seasonally or at the same time through division of labor. To the extent that this generalization is true, we must design both our surveys and our excavations with it in mind. For example, we should expect that the settlement systems of any one cultural system (note that a settlement system is not the same as a settlement pattern) will include seasonal or other shifts in exploitive strategies and the presence of important—although superficially minor—strategies that can be easily overlooked. For example, ancient farmers usually depend more upon wild resources than one might assume. One must look for data to test the general assumptions as well as to test the specific hypotheses inferred from them.

Rational Behavior

There is strong evidence that people behave rationally in a real economic sense, although there are, of course, numerous examples where human beings ignore "economic" considerations to satisfy other goals, such as a desire for prestige. In the long run, however, human beings do not seem to depart very far from relatively efficient strategies. The main criterion for rational behavior seems to be acting to minimize short-term loss. Thus, it is still rational behavior if long-term potential is sacrificed to maximize short-term yields. Models representing efficient loss-minimizing behavior are thus useful in archeological interpretation.

Testing models of rational behavior is itself, of course, a matter for empirical research. Statements about human rationality are themselves hypotheses and *not* statements of fact. Clearly, how people make decisions about maximizing or minimizing risk relates both to the environmental systems being exploited and to the social organization of the exploiting groups.

Level of Sophistication

It is absolutely essential to remember that most of us have a tendency to think that prehistoric people were much less sophisticated and intelligent than they really were. We must assume (again as a hypothesis) that they were as intelligent as we are and that they were capable of highly sophisticated responses to circumstances given their stage of cultural development. That Upper Paleolithic people herded reindeer or had seaworthy boats are quite plausible hypotheses. Further, we must assume that prehistoric people exploited resources in ingenious ways we do not use or know of at present. Hawaiian fish farms, Peruvian sunken gardens, Mayan ridged fields, and Aztec floating gardens involve techniques that are anything but obvious to most archeologists. While we must and do use ethnographic analogy to model many exploitive strategies, we must also try to imagine other possibilities. For example, areas that are seasonally utilized historically may have been occupied on a yearly basis prehistorically (Odner 1972). There are other areas where staple crops can be grown that are quite different from those presently relied upon (manioc versus corn in Venezuela, for instance). It can be shown that, although corn is being utilized today, manioc provided an effective crop in the past, and thus it is wrong to assume that local subsistence strategies necessitated exclusive reliance on either one (Zucchi 1973). Although modern analogies furnish vital information, they rarely provide directly the full range of models we need to consider.

The Subtlety of Subsistence Strategies

Another important consideration is that extractive processes are usually very subtle. That is, the actual decision making involved in selecting strategies often takes into account more factors than are easily discerned in the archeological record. Thus, our models of extractive processes may be inadequate.

As already noted, the dynamics of even relatively elementary irrigation systems are surprisingly complex. For example, considerable energy is required to break up fine-grained soils to allow the spread of irrigation water. Irrigation increases the transport of salts to the surface, where they are deposited with significant effects on overall fertility, and on the balance of species raised. For example, it is thought barley became the favorite small grain in Bronze Age southern Mesopotamia at least partly because it is more salt-tolerant than wheat. Just where, when, and for how long it is rational to irrigate is far more difficult to determine than one might suspect.

We conclude that one of the major requirements of any ecologically oriented (and perhaps of any) archeological research project is detailed understanding of the natural environment and how it varies spatially and temporally. This is necessary to one's understanding of just what strategies could and should be employed and of how each possible strategy might work. That is, one needs to know what the costs, rewards, and risks are and how a strategy would affect and be affected by other aspects of the environmental and cultural system as a whole.

Environmental Change as Prime Mover

In the previous discussion we have paid little attention to overall changes in the environment over time, but much of the power of archeological analysis is in diachronic comparisons. To the extent that diachronic changes in culture are being investigated, we obviously need to understand changes in the environment through time.

In any study of cultural change we must investigate the possibility that it is related to environmental change. It is seldom adequate to explain cultural change simply by correlating it with climatic or other environmental change. For example, even if it is true for a certain region that villages became less numerous but their sizes increased as a long drought continued, this generalization does not illuminate the detail of the processes involved. However, knowledge that this relationship existed does set the problem of understanding the processes of establishing the new settlement pattern. The point is that ecological (or systemic) analysis begins with the discovery of covariation between environmental and cultural phenomena. We then seek detailed understanding of the possible causal relationships between culture and environment. We believe that cultural systems are always intimately and complexly related to the overall ecology and that even slight changes in the environment (which may be natural or may be caused by human activities) can have enormous effects on the cultural systems integrated with it. Thus, although we agree that not all changes in cultural systems are directly tied to environmental changes, we believe that most environmental changes are reflected in the workings of cultural systems. Archeological remains record these environmental effects, and knowledge of past environmental changes is of help in interpreting archeological remains. The study of the past by means of archeology is the study of interrelations between culture and environment.

CHAPTER FOUR

The Archeological Record and the Designing of Archeological Research

So far we have considered, for the most part, rather broad issues concerning the logic of science and archeology as a science. In this chapter we turn to some very specific topics to indicate what is entailed methodologically if archeologists assume the theoretical position discussed in the preceding chapters. The question of analytical techniques is very important because epistemological sophistication is of little use if one does not have adequate means for testing hypotheses or acquiring the information necessary to build useful models. In fact, one can make the argument that epistemological sensitivity among archeologists has already outstripped general methodological ability. Present efforts should be concentrated on improving techniques before further refining archeological theory (for the present state of the art, see the excellent survey by Salmon 1982).

In this section on archeological research design we suggest some answers to the questions, What techniques are available to archeologists? and What are the implications, assumptions, and uses of the techniques now employed? We make no claim to cover these subjects exhaustively, and our omission of various techniques in no way implies that we consider them insignificant. We concentrate on those topics we have found to produce the most questions and misunderstandings and relate them as clearly as possible to our preceding arguments. We first consider the archeological record.

Nature of the Archeological Record

The traditional approach to the archeological record usually stresses the limits of the information available to archeologists because of lack of preservation. "What we have at our disposal, as prehistorians, is the accidentally surviving durable remnants of material culture, which we interpret as best we may, and inevitably the peculiar quality of this evidence dictates the sort of information we can obtain from it" (Piggott 1965:5).

Today, there is greater emphasis on the positive potential for eliciting systematic order from the archeological record. Archeological remains are always patterned to a greater or lesser degree, and these patterns are related to prehistoric activities and events in ways the archeologist can ascertain. Thus, we can obtain from the archeological record information on many aspects of past cultural systems:

> It has often been suggested that we cannot dig up a social system or ideology. Granted we cannot excavate a kinship terminology or a philosophy, but we can and do excavate the material items which functioned together with these more behavioral elements within the appropriate cultural subsystems. The formal structure of artifact assemblages together with the between element contextual relationships should and do present a systemic and understandable picture of the total extinct cultural system. (Binford 1962:218–219)

Binford is far from being the first or the most extreme in holding this view. In *The Ninth Bridgewater Treatise,* Babbage argues that every human action is permanently recorded in the air and water and rocks of the earth:

> No motion impressed by natural causes, or by human agency, is ever obliterated. . . .
> The solid substance of the globe itself, whether we regard the minutest movement of the soft clay which receives its impression from the foot of animals, or the concussion arising from the fall of mountains rent by earthquakes, equally communicates and retains, through all its countless atoms, their apportioned shares of the motions so impressed.
> Whilst the atmosphere we breathe is the everliving witness of the sentiments we have uttered, the waters, and the more solid materials of the globe, bear equally enduring testimony of the acts we have committed. (Babbage 1838:114, 115)

The Record and Designing Research

For archeologists, the materials in the ground and their spatial distributions theoretically represent all the behavioral patterns of the ancient culture. Practically speaking, however, there are limitations in the nature and amount of data for various times and places; for example, there may not be enough data to permit independent tests of certain hypotheses that therefore must remain unconfirmed.

The problem of negative evidence also frequently arises. That evidence of an element or complex is not directly observable does not mean that it did not exist in the living culture whose remains we are examining, nor does it mean that we cannot infer its presence some other way. If, in the course of investigation of some particular problem, negative evidence becomes pertinent to the testing of a hypothesis, one's first approach should be to try to find an independent test based on positive evidence. For example, it has often been noted that bone tools are abundant and varied in the Upper Paleolithic industries of Europe, whereas in the preceding Mousterian bone tools are virtually absent. Traditionally, it is claimed that there is a major break between these two manifestations. If it could be established that the absence of bone in Mousterian industries is a real lack and not just the result of differential preservation, then this would help confirm the major break hypothesis. On the other hand, if it could be established that bone is absent because of differential preservation, then the hypothesis would be disconfirmed.

Or one could choose not to use the bone data (or lack of it) directly in testing a hypothesis because of the inconclusiveness of negative evidence. Instead, one might seek some means of inferring information about bone that is reflected in other preserved items, for example, in distinctive wear on stone tools used to work bone.

In general, archeologists should take the optimistic position that the archeological record does somehow contain information pertinent to almost all archeological problems and that it is the investigator's task to devise means to extract it.

> The practical limitations on our knowledge of the past are not inherent in the nature of the archeological record; the limitations lie in our methodological naivete, in our lack of development of principles determining the relevance of archeological remains to propositions regarding processes and events of the past. (Binford 1968a:23)

To formulate hypotheses, to test implications concerning such intangibles as the prehistoric social organization, and to articulate these with the actual debris recovered from the ground—even in the absence of major postaboriginal disturbance—requires great care and ingenuity. But there *are always* relations between the debris and the actions of ancient peoples and the events and social structures that characterize particular ancient societies. It is up to us to work out ways to define them.

Having said this, we can also recognize that sometimes we simply do not have enough data to test certain hypotheses. Some information may be lost before the site is ever investigated because of such phenomena as slope wash, weathering of exposed items, and disturbance by animals and humans. More and more attention is currently being paid to the processes that transform the debris of functioning societies into the material remains that confront archeologists years or millennia later (Schiffer 1972, 1976; see also Gifford 1978, Lyman 1982, and Wood and Johnson 1978). The relations between the present remains and the original objects (and even between the absence of remains and the original objects) and the relations between the original objects and social structure are there. Archeologists must find methods of discovering and interpreting these relations. In general—except in cases of extensive postoccupational disturbance—the difficulties of interpretation do not derive from inadequate material but from inadequate interpretive techniques or from archeologists' inability to apply them.

One approach is simply to intensify the application of standard techniques. First, one can increase the number of samples analyzed. For example, if chronological relationships are unclear, many overlapping radiocarbon determinations will produce tighter time sequences. One can also apply more, and more sophisticated, analytic techniques. For example, seemingly confused data on artifact or site distribution may in fact contain patterns that can be discovered by use of factor analysis or some similar statistical technique.

Another approach is to find multiple ways to extract the same information. While each technique alone may produce too little information from which to draw firm conclusions, combinations of several techniques may produce enough. For example, flotation and pollen analysis used together can give information that neither technique alone could satisfactorily produce.

Yet another technique is to formulate questions in such a way that they can be answered with data from the archeological record. These data may be ill-suited for answering questions formulated in one way but may be rich in information for answering alternative formulations of the same questions. For example, the archeological record is notoriously recalcitrant in yielding data on amounts. It is exceedingly difficult to determine absolute population size, length of occupation, or amount of meat consumed with any useful accuracy in any great number of cases. However, if the questions are modified to ask about rates—how much the population increased or decreased, whether occupations increased in duration, or whether the proportions of various products in the diet shifted—then answers are much easier to obtain. Uncertain assumptions that must be made with regard to the determination of the actual *amounts* are not necessary when *rates* are considered. Thus, if the main problem can be solved by determining rates rather than amounts, a shift of question is justified.

For example, consider the great number of assumptions necessary to estimate the amount of meat consumed by a human group that hunts deer and rabbits. Are deer and rabbit bones preserved? Did all the bones of animals killed and eaten actually reach the site under investigation? If not, is the selection process patterned so that accurate estimates can be made of the numbers of individual animals consumed? Are the available modern figures on pounds or kilograms of meat per animal reliable? If so, do they apply to a prehistoric society whose food processing techniques are poorly known but were surely different from those of modern hunters? Failure to answer these and similar questions accurately may make any estimates grossly erroneous.

However, if the original question is rephrased to ask whether deer becomes more common at the expense of rabbit over time, then we need make assumptions only of constancy (for example, that butchering techniques and bone destruction are roughly constant over the times involved). That is, one may choose to answer a less detailed question with a much higher level of confidence than is possible if one tries to answer a more detailed one. The variety of data available usually makes it possible to answer some version of most questions archeologists ask, if they are sufficiently ingenious.

In fact, today we have a paradoxical situation. There is much recent archeological concern about the inadequate extraction of information from the record, and new or improved field recovery techniques are called for. New techniques are welcome, but the retrieval of adequate information in many cases can be achieved by employing *more* analytic techniques more thoroughly. Most archeological reports contain far fewer analyses than could usefully have been applied to the materials in hand. This is particularly true for many contract archeological reports, where description, rather than analysis, is often the end product.

The point, again, is that the archeological record is not usually insufficient per se but must be approached with appropriate questions, methods, techniques, and resources. This raises the problem of just what archeological data should be collected.

Relevant Data

Relevant archeological data consist of anything observable that pertains to the solving of a particular problem. In order to determine what data to collect, archeologists must formulate hypotheses and infer implications from them to test. Relevant data are then those data necessary to check the implications and may include anything observable at the archeological site as well as information obtained elsewhere. At the site, relevant data may include architecture and artifacts, the condition of artifacts, and ecofactual remains such as pollen, splinters of animal bone from ancient garbage dumps, bits of carbonized plant parts, impressions of plant remains in mud walls and floors, the chemical constituents of various strata at a site, and so on. The spatial distributions and associations of objects in the site may be especially relevant. There are also whole realms of archeologically relevant data, completely outside the boundaries of any archeological site, embodied in ethnographic situations all over the world (Kleindienst and Watson 1956; Donnan and Clewlow 1974; Binford

1978b; Gould, 1978, 1980; Kramer 1979; Watson 1979a; Yellen 1977). Other relevant data can be obtained from controlled experiments that may be quite detached from actual archeological sites (Coles 1979; Hester and Heizer 1973; Ingersoll, Yellen, and Macdonald 1977; Tringham et al. 1974). Finally, information on the flora and fauna, land forms and available raw materials, soil conditions, and other environmental factors not immediately at the site can be extremely relevant.

However, whether inside the archeological site or outside it, only data considered to be relevant will ordinarily be collected. One seldom collects what one is not looking for. For example, before the development of the radiocarbon dating technique in the late 1940s, little or no attention was paid to bits of charcoal in archeological excavations. After 1948, however, charcoal was eagerly sought and carefully collected for submission to radiocarbon laboratories. And before the tiny stone tools called microliths were known to exist in open sites in southwestern Asia, thousands of them were shoveled out of excavations without being noticed. After attention was called to them, excavators found them in quantities. More recent examples also exist. Flotation techniques for recovery of many classes of small artifacts have come into widespread use only in the last fifteen years. This technique permits recovery of large numbers of specimens where previously few were thought to be present. Even more recently phytoliths, inorganic residues distinctive of different species of plants, have been found in archeological and geological deposits (Pearsall 1982; Rovner 1983) and extend our abilities to recover evidence of long-vanished vegetation.

The question of what data to collect must be answered for each excavation and site survey. One cannot possibly record all artifactual and nonartifactual information or even be sure that every "artifact" is properly perceived as such. One must decide which categories of data to collect and which sampling strategies are appropriate to the problem at hand. Some archeologists may still insist that one should just dig and record standard data, then let the facts speak for themselves. But this is to allow unexamined tradition to set the problems, and "standard" data are often inadequate for answering even the traditional problems.

Because it is literally impossible to record everything, one must formulate problems carefully and design one's research to solve those problems. Only certain categories of data will then be collected. But other data will be destroyed in the digging. One's responsibility to the profession as a whole requires that some time and money be committed to collecting and recording samples of those data categories not directly pertinent to the problems being considered.

Of course the extremes of both positions—recording all data and recording only relevant data—are impossible to achieve. Because it is impossible for an investigator to determine beforehand exactly how much and what kind of data are relevant, he or she always tries to record more than appears necessary to answer the original questions. It is also true that, by use of some ingenuity and sophistication, one can wring quantities of information from relatively minor data items. For example, a single fish scale may be sufficient to reveal the season when the fish was caught and the ecological essentials of the stream or other body of water from which it came. And always there is the critical issue of archeological ethics alluded to above: How much data must one collect that is not called for in one's own research plan but is obviously useful to the work of other archeologists? This problem must be resolved by every archeologist in a way that does not jeopardize his or her own fieldwork and that does not result in irrecoverable loss of information from the archeological record.

The basic method advocated here is very simple in outline: First, the archeological investigator should decide exactly what questions are being asked and, next, what kinds of information are needed to answer those questions. The questions must be specific. To express interest in broad, general topics such as "urbanization" is not sufficient; these interests or topics should be approached through specific hypotheses. Third, the investigator must devise ways to get the information from the ground. Information, again, can be anything observable that helps answer the research questions and may be quite remote from the traditional categories of "material culture." At Star Carr, for example, a large percentage of the analysis was devoted to ecofactual material such as cast-off antlers used to determine the season the site was occupied (J.G.D. Clark 1954).

The Record and Designing Research

As discussed in the Research Design section below and in chapter 5, the idea that one needs a particular question or hypothesis to guide one's research is one of the most difficult concepts for archeologists to accept and one of the most misunderstood. As cannot be stated too strongly, one can and is likely to change one's questions repeatedly as one digs or surveys. One may ask very particular questions such as, "Is this level the floor of a storeroom?" which in turn necessitate recovery of particular classes of data in particular ways. If one discovers that artifacts have been displaced by water, this may require a change of recovery techniques and give rise to new questions. From the practical point of view, what is crucial is that the research questions serve as specific guides for recovery procedures.

An Expanded Concept of Data

An expanded concept of archeological data is necessary to include those not originating at the sites themselves. As already noted, ethnographic data and data from replicative or imitative experiments can be used.

Archeological data from a site consist of observable artifactual items (bone and stone tools, pottery, and so on), architecture and ecofactual remains (animal bones, carbonized botanical remains or impressions of plant parts, soil chemistry, pollen, and so on), and other observable attributes of artifacts (wear patterns, charring, and so on), and the spatial relationships of all these. The basic spatial relationships are orientation and position of artifactual and ecofactual materials with relation to architecture, depositional matrix, cardinal directions, and other features.

This network of interrelationships makes up the structure of the site; in particular, spatial relationships are crucial in delineating depositional history. It is important not merely to record the stratigraphic levels of a site but also to *excavate* the site with respect to these levels. The basic assumption is that the vertical and horizontal distribution of all material making up an archeological site is as important as the material itself because—in the absence of postdepositional disturbance—that distribution reflects patterned human cultural activity just as much as do artifactual forms, style, and manufacturing techniques.

Descriptions of spatial relationships make it possible to delimit *activity areas* by plotting precise proveniences of tool types and other artifacts with respect to ground matrix, architectural features, and one another. For examples of activity clusters and activity areas see Hill (1966), Hole, Flannery, and Neely (1969: fig. 10), de Lumley (1969), J. D. Clark (1969: pl. 14), South (1977: ch. 3).

Descriptions of activity-specific tool kits lead to questions about social organization and social stratification. The classic example is Deetz's description of differential distribution of items made and used by men as opposed to those made by women among the Chumash Indians:

> Baskets and milling equipment among the southern California Chumash of the early nineteenth century, and perhaps even earlier, are quite uniform over the entire area known to have been occupied by these people. Such uniformity contrasts sharply with the diversity seen in such artifacts as arrowheads, which differ considerably from site to site. The pattern is one of widespread rules for female manufactures, and isolated sets of somewhat different rules for male manufactures. . . . This can only mean that women were "widespread" and men "isolated." (Deetz 1967: 94–95)

Deetz infers this artifact distribution results from the Chumash customs of patrilocal residence and local exogamy. The men, and hence their skills and manufactures, stay in the villages where they were born, whereas the women (and their skills and manufactures) move to the villages of their husbands. As a result, items made and used by men have a discrete distribution and each village is characterized by its own style of projectile points, while items made and used by women are widely distributed.

Thus, from the distribution of tool types and clusters identified as female and male specific, Deetz arrives at conclusions concerning the social organization of the human group that left the remains. Hill (1968:133) and Longacre (1968:97–98) also identify male- and female-associated items and use them in their analyses. These are good examples of inferring social organization from artifact distribution, but

The Record and Designing Research 165

the lack of artifact distributions should not deter attempts to delineate social organization by other means.

The nature and distribution of grave goods have long been studied by archeologists. For example, in his examination of social evolution in ancient Sumer, Adams utilizes as an important line of evidence the differential quantities of luxury goods found in excavated graves.

> In the late Ubaid period significant differentiation in grave wealth was almost entirely absent. . . . [But by Early Dynastic times] the impression of differentiation [given by architectural remains] is confirmed and amplified by a study of tomb furniture. One of the clearest indices to wealth is the presence of copper, as well as more precious metals. . . . The previously unparalleled concentrations of metal that appear in a few graves . . . must indicate a correspondingly increased range of differentiation in wealth. And while copper becomes *le métal d'échange par excellence* by the Early Dynastic III period . . . on the whole it remained of so high a value that ordinary craftsmen and even minor bureaucrats were limited to at most a few implements of this material for which they were at pains to keep an accounting. . . . In other words, copper implements and vessels (to say nothing of gold or silver) qualitatively increase the implication of wealth for the burial assemblages in which they occur, as opposed to those in which they are lacking. (Adams 1966:95, 98–99)

Adams then examines known graves of the Early Dynastic period at several sites and finds that, "In sum, insofar as grave goods reflect the general distribution of wealth, there is evidence for the decisive increase in social differentiation in the cities during the course of the Early Dynastic period" (Adams 1966:100).

At Grasshopper Pueblo in Arizona, the differential distribution of grave goods is low so does not provide much evidence for social stratification (G. Clark 1969; Longacre 1975). However, by using dental traits from Puebloan skeletons Birkby infers that burial distributions within some pueblos reflect a matrilocal residence pattern (Birkby 1973).

Remains of activity areas are distributed in sites both horizontally and vertically. Various members of a single culture may perform different activities in different parts of the same site at about the same time. The resulting horizontal distribution of cultural debris and features might indicate or delineate butchering, cooking, sleeping, and toolmaking activity areas, which the archeologist would probably interpret correctly as different activities of the same people. However, it is quite possible that in some sites (rockshelters, for example, or riverbank shellmounds) debris from various activities may accumulate vertically and that diachronic inferences may be mistakenly drawn from them. For example, members of the same culture may return to the same place several times over a period of a few months or a few years and undertake varying activities there (sleeping and cooking one time, butchering another, toolmaking on a third occasion, butchering and cooking on a fourth, and so on). The result is a vertical distribution of cultural debris that actually reflects only changes in activities of a single culture over a short period of time, but that might be interpreted as successive replacements of one culture by others over a much longer period of time. Rockshelters provide the most obvious (yet not always recognized) potential situations of this type. As a cave or shelter is filled with deposit, available space is reduced. Thus certain types of activity may be eliminated with no real change in the actual total range of group activities.

Mistakenly interpreting vertical ordering of activity clusters or areas as a diachronic sequence of cultural replacement is especially likely in studies based on seriation because the basic assumption of seriational studies is that sharp changes in artifact types and frequencies indicate cultural breaks or transitions. For further details about the possible complexities in the distribution of activity areas, see Yellen (1977) and Gifford (1978, 1981).

In this section so far we have made the following points:

1. For problem-oriented archeologists, data are any observable items or attributes that help to solve the problem.

2. Because the main data that will be recorded and/or collected are those considered to be relevant to the problem, one should proceed by explicitly defining the problem to be solved or question to be answered, explicitly defining the data needed to solve the problem, and explicitly defining the techniques necessary to collect those data.

3. Because a problem often requires collection of only a limited set of data categories, archeologists must sample and record data from the other main categories that are destroyed by digging.

The importance of contextual relationships of artifacts and architecture is strongly emphasized by Walter W. Taylor (1948) in his discussion of the conjunctive approach, which is, as indicated by the examples in this chapter (Deetz, Adams, Longacre, Clark), indispensable to contemporary problem-oriented archeology. Hence, fundamental field recording is the area of greatest continuity between past and present developments in archeology. Walter W. Taylor's conjunctive approach and Sir Mortimer Wheeler's discussions of the importance of natural stratigraphic relationships set standards for all archeologists everywhere.

New techniques and equipment (resistivity devices and magnetometers, flotation and water separation, the multitude of dating techniques, computers) have been developed, but basic field techniques have remained the same. What has changed are the problems. This was pointed out many years ago by Struever, who said, "If a major purpose of archeology is to elucidate cultural process by *explaining* prehistoric episodes of change or stability, then the strategy of archeology must shift to long-term programs of fieldwork and analysis" (Struever 1968a:133).

He discusses in detail his own research program in the lower Illinois Valley to illustrate his basic point that the traditional organization of archeological research is not adequate for solving what are considered to be the most important research problems today, nor can it incorporate adequately the new techniques available to solve them. We touch on this difficulty here in chapter 4 and discuss it further in chapter 6.

Research Design

The general plan of a project is usually called the research design. A research design contains definitions of problems, of the major strategies (methods) devised to solve them, and of the survey or excavation, sampling, recording, and analytical procedures. A research design defines the work to be done by placing it within a theoretical framework and by describing how it will be carried out.

Because resources are always limited (including those of the archeological record itself), we suggest that their use be organized according to the following strictures: (1) The diversity and accuracy of the data should be sufficient for answering the research question. Technically this means the data should be adequate to confirm or disconfirm the various hypotheses. (2) The accuracy of each data set should be relatively homogeneous. A data chain is no stronger than the weakest link, so, optimally, all parts should be of equal reliability. (3) Bias in the data must be kept to acceptable levels. (4) One must be able to estimate both the accuracy and the bias of the data.

When and how does one prepare a research design? A tentative plan is prepared before beginning work. The hypotheses being tested (which are drawn from the research questions the archeologist is trying to answer) as well as the entire scheme for testing the hypotheses (together these make up the research design) are always subject to revision. As the work progresses and data accumulate, the research design will almost certainly be altered, perhaps drastically. As stressed in chapter 1 of this book, it is essential that one formulate hypotheses to guide one's research, but readiness to modify the hypotheses as the work progresses is also essential. Similarly, an explicit research design is necessary at every stage of the work, but the investigator must be willing to modify the design at any time in the light of the data being accumulated.

It is particularly important to differentiate between the questions being asked and the research design itself. Archeology like other sciences abounds with interesting and important hypotheses. The heart of science is to figure out how to test them. A research design is a scheme for carrying out the tests.

Extreme care in formulating research designs is particularly important in contract archeology. This is because of the constraints that result from being restricted to limited sites or portions of sites, to surveying only particular areas, and to being required to prepare strict budgets for analysis of materials you *may* recover, with little margin for work on what you actually *do* recover if it differs greatly from what you expected.

Data Collection

An archeologist must determine both the quantity of data necessary and how "good" they need to be. There are three criteria for judging "goodness" of data: the levels of *random error,* of *regular error* or *bias,* and of *gross error* present in them. We consider these matters only briefly here, but an excellent detailed discussion of this aspect of research design is provided by Daniels (1972; see also Blalock 1972). Random error means the effects of accidents and variation in the original production and dispersal of the artifacts and other remains, as well as the effects of mistakes made during collection and analysis of data. Random alteration of the data by such agents is referred to in scientific jargon as "noise." For archeological data, noise is a combination of cultural, depositional, and analytic factors.

The conviction that data containing noise, whatever the cause, are not valuable or that noisy data are necessarily inaccurate is mistaken. All data include some noise; the noise can be accommodated by considering the quantity of data collected and the kind of information being extracted from them. Even extremely noisy data can yield quite precise information as long as the noise is random and sample sizes are large enough. For example, the fact that each individual painted line on a given piece of pottery varies in width (cultural noise) does not prevent one from obtaining useful data by taking a single measurement of the width of each line. Even if individual potters make lines that vary more than a millimeter in width at different points on a line, and potters in one village make lines only half a millimeter smaller on the average than those in another village, one can still distinguish pottery from the two villages if sufficiently large samples are measured. It is certainly the case that noise may make analysis difficult, but it can be controlled for if we are aware of it and if we do not unnecessarily add to it during analysis.

Regular error, or bias, in data is much more insidious than random error. Even very slight regular error can have significant consequences. Natural sorting procedures on the site may move large artifacts differently from small ones. When surveying, one may collect light-colored sherds more readily than dark ones. One pottery-design recorder may measure the narrowest part of a line and another may measure the widest part. If their measurements are combined, the results will be either weak or imprecise. Both bias in the data caused by natural and cultural forces and bias that arises in the analytical process must be controlled by proper research design.

The basic control technique is to randomize the workers' relationship to the data. For analytical procedures, this can be done relatively simply by randomizing which data are examined by which worker; that is, worker effects are not eliminated but are turned into random error. During excavation, however, procedures of this sort are less practical. In particular, moving people frequently from one excavation unit to another is counterproductive to the understanding of the archeological situation in each unit and, often, to the general esprit de corps of the dig crew as well. A more feasible alternative is to use standardized recording forms. Of course, careful training and supervision of field and laboratory workers is necessary in any case. However, no training can be expected to eliminate behavioral biases that are not perceived.

Gross errors are big mistakes of all kinds that occasionally occur. These include mislabeling bags, omitting labels, misplacing decimals, and so on. Such errors can be minimized by double labeling, rechecking, and using standardized procedures.

A successful research design must provide controls for these kinds of error in a variety of ways. We should strive to reduce bias wherever possible, but efforts to reduce random error must be carefully tempered. Data are no better than the worst error they incorporate, hence reduction of some random error to low values while leaving other random error high may not improve accuracy sufficiently to be worth the effort. For data that are especially subject to analytic error, repeated readings by different personnel greatly increase accuracy. However, for data that are intrinsically noisy because of depositional factors, repeated measurements may be a waste of effort.

Stratified refuse deposited by many randomizing processes is a case in point. If one requires a representative collection of artifactual materials from such a context, then very careful excavation to find and remove all artifacts at the cost of working slowly may, in fact, result in greater error than would result from rapid excavation with more missed artifacts. If one loses a few percent of the artifacts randomly but doubles the sample size in the process, accuracy may actually be increased. Thus, if labor input is equal, the automatic use of one-eighth-inch screen, with the tremendous increase in time required, may actually be more inaccurate than using a one-fourth-inch screen. In practice, however, other constraints usually enter into one's considerations. If rodent bones are important for the faunal analysis, then use of a one-eighth-inch screen may be necessary even though a one-fourth-inch screen is adequate for collecting the pottery sherds.

An estimate of error is needed to enable assessment of the overall accuracy of the results. At the very least, one must take into account random or regular sampling errors. It is usually possible to estimate, on a probabilistic basis, how representative a collection is of the total universe being investigated. In considering overall error, we should also make an estimate of *experimental error.* Experimental error is a measure of the difference between what archeological material is actually there and what is eventually recorded. Sherds lost during excavation, sites missed during survey, and artifacts misclassified in the laboratory are all forms of experimental error that can be either random or regular.

Usually the most practical way to estimate these errors is to recollect and reanalyze wherever possible. For example, resurveying particular quadrants to find what was missed the first time will give a good idea of the accuracy of initial survey data. Similarly, artifact samples can be reanalyzed. Such repeats should be done both by the individuals who performed the original analysis and by others so that one can estimate the consistency among workers. In some cases, simple but effective checks of accuracy can be devised. For example, archeobotanist Gail Wagner tests the recovery of various flotation setups at Midwestern sites by adding carefully calibrated doses of one hundred poppy seeds each to certain flotation samples (Wagner 1982). The number of these small but unmistakable seeds that show up (or not) in the floated plant remains dramatically reveals the rate of success or failure of the particular flotation rig and its operators.

At excavations, some checks of recovery can be made by such techniques as rescreening backdirt. Of course, the cost in time, energy, and labor for all these efforts to estimate error is sometimes high, so they are rarely implemented to any great degree. The lack of concern many archeologists have about estimating error is probably due in part to the general lack of interest in problems of quantification that was once widespread and still exists here and there. Indeed, if one knows the general magnitude of error, then there is no need to determine it exactly. For example, the sorting of flint from obsidian is usually exceedingly accurate and one's error in doing so need not be estimated. However, the correctness of conclusions is dependent upon the accuracy of error estimates, whether they are explicitly computed or not. One must try to estimate all errors and control all sources of error. Efforts to reduce sampling error drastically while ignoring experimental error, for example, are of little value.

One way archeologists and other scientists solve the problem of error is with overkill. By recording many more artifacts, or by digging greater percentages of a site than is necessary, one can elicit clear patterns despite poor knowledge about error rates. However, as both costs and concern about conserving the data base increase, ways to calculate error rates become increasingly important.

Multistage Designs

The particulars of research design formulation are beyond the scope of this chapter, but two fundamental generalizations about research designs must be included. If any lesson has been learned about how to do successful archeology, it is that a multistage technique is the most useful procedure (Redman 1973).

Multistage design calls for a series of procedural steps: hypothesis formulation, data collection, data analysis, hypothesis test, new hypothesis formulation. The same procedural steps pertain at a variety of research levels. Even site survey is most effective when one's sampling (including taking a 100 percent sample) is not done all at once but is done piecemeal with intervening analyses and redesigning of recording and collecting procedures. Similar stepwise procedures are best for excavation strategies. Most archeologists agree that there are great advantages to a regional approach, and thus site survey combined with excavation on more than one site is becoming much more common than in the past. It is far more productive to do some survey and some excavation followed by some analysis and

The Record and Designing Research 173

testing of hypotheses, and then to reconsider and perhaps to modify the research design, than it is to do all the survey, then all the excavation, then all the analyses, and finally all the testing of hypotheses. It is poor scientific method to follow a rigid sequence with no opportunities to evaluate and modify the research design.

Within each component of research—survey, excavation, analysis, testing of hypotheses—further multistage steps are appropriate. Making a very small survey sample, or even recording a few known sites, is an excellent way to test the usefulness of collecting and recording procedures. For excavation, even more recorded steps are advantageous. One can take initial samples from deposits of different ages, from structures, from use areas, and so on. Further excavations can be based in part on the results of these tests. Moreover, during each of these preliminary excavations the units themselves need not be dug in their entirety. Portions of each can be excavated, the material and stratigraphy evaluated, procedures adjusted, and excavation continued.

Such a stepwise procedure is useful in analysis, too. By starting with a small sample of artifacts, one can check schemes for evaluating or coding attributes to see whether they are adequate for the materials at hand. This can be done each time a new question is addressed by using the same artifact collection.

In long-term projects such a multistage procedure can reach quite large proportions. Five years of research by the Mimbres Foundation in southwestern New Mexico provides an example. Site survey was begun by recording previously known sites. Then for the next three seasons areas were repeatedly resampled by taking both random and grab samples (see chapter 5 for definitions of these sampling procedures). Each year new recording forms were devised to reflect changes in what variables were recorded and how they were recorded. Collection strategies were also revised repeatedly. Excavations were conducted at twenty-five different sites. Only a test trench or two were dug at some sites, but, at the other extreme, one site was excavated for five field seasons. Changes in where and how this site was excavated were repeatedly made based on previous seasons' work. Most sites were excavated for at least two seasons.

This procedure is in sharp contrast to excavation of a single site carried out according to a fixed plan in one continuous field season, as was common in the past and sometimes occurs today in contract archeology. It is in contract archeology that the greatest problems in implementing multistage research designs are likely to arise. All too frequently work is initiated with a single-pass survey, followed by intensive excavation and a rapid one-stage analysis of the artifacts. All the power of multistage designs is thus lost.

Multistage design is necessary even for areas with which one is already quite familiar. In such cases, one already has protocols of how and what to collect and how to select survey and excavation locales. But procedures do not remain constant just because recent work has been done in an area. First, as excavation proceeds, more is learned about the materials and the situation. On the basis of this new information, hypotheses are modified. As hypotheses are altered, data collection efforts and analytic approaches must also be changed. Second, we should not expect all sites in a region to yield similar classes of information. There is always the possibility that one will encounter a site with preservation characteristics or stratigraphic relationships different from those previously known. One must expect the unexpected or one will not detect it. Using a multistage research design is an effective means of allowing for the unanticipated.

In designing a research program, one must keep in mind the numerous factors that cause variability of the archeological record. The more obvious include site location, level and nature of technology, cultural preferences, and differential preservation. We must control for as many of these factors as possible to determine the effects of those remaining. For example, if two sites differ both in time period and locality, then differences in the archeological materials they contain may result from either cultural or environmental factors. If two sites are the same in either time period or locality, then we can control for the common factor and measure the effects of the other.

The development of such controls is extremely important to archeological research design. The general point is that controls must be planned. Otherwise interpretation will be inadequate if not actually wrong. As discussed below, analytic comparisons between sites, between parts of sites, between artifacts, between features, and so on are highly productive of understanding. Independent methods of making these comparisons are thus very useful.

In designing research, then, we must give special attention to what comparisons we intend to make and to how comparisons of different types of material may be integrated. For example, two sites in different locales may be in geological situations similar enough so that differences in lithics can be compared without one's having to consider the compounding effects of differences in availability of lithic raw materials. However, the sites may be in different vegetative zones, so that differences in recovered plant remains are not so easily interpreted. Any or all of such considerations may be important in deciding which sites to excavate.

In summary, research design formulation is the most important practical step in archeological research. We must describe problems and methods for tests, controls, comparisons, analyses, and interpretations. Multistage designs have many advantages and should be implemented at all levels of research.

To recapitulate the main points made in the preceding discussion: Archeological data include random and/or regular errors due to idiosyncratic cultural behavior in the past and to the vagaries of deposition and preservation. Sampling errors are controlled by using estimates of the accuracy with which the samples represent the sampled universe. Making estimates of this kind of error is a major function of statistics. To control for "transformational error" (introduced randomly or regularly by the natural and cultural processes that change the debris from human activities into archeological remains), we must obtain information on refuse disposal patterns, taphonomic, weathering, and many other relevant processes (Schiffer 1972; Stanislawski 1969b; Gifford 1978, 1981; Lyon 1970; Kent 1981; Evans and Limbrey 1974; Jewell and Dimbleby 1966). Experimental and recording errors are controlled with standardizing and checking techniques.

All overall research designs, like all hypotheses, should be constantly evaluated and modified as new information comes to light. In archeological investigation a multistage research design is the most productive overall approach, and multiple steps should be employed at every level. A research design must designate controls separating the effects of many simultaneous processes so that accurate interpretations can be made. This is why carefully controlled comparison is the basic analytic method in archeology.

Archeological Sampling

Once a problem is defined, the research design is focused on the kinds and quantities of data needed to solve the problem, and the question of sampling immediately arises. Archeologists sample continuously: even choosing a site to excavate is sampling the universe of excavatable sites. Moreover, sites are very rarely entirely excavated, hence what is excavated is a sample of a site. Sampling is a compromise; it is a way of getting an adequate representation of some universe of data without having to work through all the data in that universe. It is unnecessary to recover *all* the data of any one kind, even if this were possible. But it is important to make the sampling process, at whatever level, explicit, systematic, and efficient. Sampling is an integral part of research design.

Sampling is not just a device for choosing where to survey or what squares to excavate. Sampling is crucial also in the analysis of recovered artifacts. For example, if a unit containing two thousand sherds is to be compared for basic similarities and differences with one containing two hundred sherds, it is probably unnecessary to consider all two thousand sherds from the first unit; a sample of them will suffice for the comparison.

One of the most important conclusions drawn from proper sampling and analysis is about the traditional practice of excavating arbitrary levels of uniform thickness in sites where no natural strata can be distinguished. This practice is based on a false assumption; it mixes data from different proveniences, and thus leads to incorrect interpretations. There is almost never any reason to assume that depth of deposit is directly proportionate to time.

A better procedure is to excavate in equal samples, thus producing a series of levels, each of which yields roughly the same artifact and/or ecofact counts. This optimizes the comparisons between them. This procedure requires—prior to excavation—an adequate idea of the nature of the material to be recovered and of the analytic methods to be employed. Given this information one can define an arbitrary level by stipulating, not a given thickness of deposit, but a given count (or possibly a given weight) of artifacts and ecofacts for each level. Similar reasoning can be applied to surface surveys. For some purposes, surface collections are more useful if artifacts are collected from units whose dimensions are determined by the artifact density, so that each collection consists of approximately the same number of artifacts.

This discussion raises the question of how large a sample should be. Decisions about sample size are based on the nature of the problem to be solved and on the desired degree of confirmation of hypothetical solutions to it. There is no standard percentage figure that automatically yields a valid sample size. If a systematic surface collection is to be made of a sample of the five hundred grid squares on some particular site, then a 10 percent sample is probably statistically adequate. But if a universe consists not of five hundred grid squares on a site surface but of twenty rooms in a prehistoric pueblo, then a 10 percent sample is probably not adequate because a sample of two is an absolute number too small to support statistical inferences. It is also highly unlikely that there are only one or two different kinds of rooms in the whole pueblo; hence no two rooms could possibly be representative of the whole. However, this does not mean that a sample of two is worthless. If these two rooms were burned, or contain burials or storage pits, then one has at least answered the questions: Were some rooms of the pueblo burned? Did some have burials or storage pits? But if neither of the two rooms was burned or contained storage pits or burials, then our data are inadequate for determining the likelihood of burning, burials, or storage pits in the other rooms.

In general, the accuracy with which a sample represents a universe being sampled increases as the absolute sample size increases. But after a certain minimally adequate sample size is reached, a point of diminishing returns is also quickly reached, so that, for example, doubling the sample size does not double the reliability of the characterization. For more complete and detailed discussions of this and other questions about sampling, see Deming (1950), Haggett (1965), Mueller (1975), Ragir (1967), Redman (1974).

Sampling strategies are often influenced by cost factors. The larger the universe under consideration, the greater the advantages of sampling, whether the universe comprises an archeological region, an archeological site, or a body of artifacts. Sampling is basically a means of saving work, time, and money, and the designing of a sampling strategy must reflect this fact. The goal of any sample is to get as good a picture as possible of the universe in question for a given amount of energy input. It is always the case that, as knowledge about the data increases, one is in an increasingly better position to handle them more effectively. And as one's understanding of the universe under investigation changes, so should one's sampling procedures. Therefore, there is no right way to sample for any given problem because most problems change. Thus, as one proceeds with an investigation, one necessarily changes sampling strategies.

This is especially true when one is delineating the kind of sample to be taken. The better one understands the actual nature of the variation in the universe in question, the better one is able to measure it. This fact must be kept in mind in designing archeological sampling strategies. In sampling one need not and should not ignore what one already knows about the data. If a sampling procedure does not incorporate what is known, it is likely to be an incorrect approach. Also, one must consider whether or not sampling will increase one's knowledge enough to justify the cost. In particular, one should have a procedure for stopping the sampling of certain categories of data once they are adequate for providing the information sought. One does not do good archeology simply because one samples. However, it is unlikely that one is doing as good work as possible if sampling is not being carefully considered.

Besides savings in cost and improved interpretive ability, there is another extremely important reason for using effective sampling procedures: sampling saves portions of sites for future research. As techniques improve, the ability to extract more information from sites increases, thus it is very important to leave sites for future excavation and analysis. This is so basic and obvious that it is hard to believe any practicing archeologist would not subscribe to it. And in fact, nearly all archeologists do. But occasionally one encounters archeologists who believe that many "equivalent" sites exist and that one can safely extract all the extant information from a given site because of the presence of equivalent information at other sites. It is probably very seldom true that a particular site can be excavated in its entirety because comparable sites remain for future work. One may,

The Record and Designing Research

for example, excavate a site completely only to find that it was much more unusual than originally believed. Moreover, if we view sites as parts of systems, then there is much less basis for believing that large numbers of sites are "equivalent." Techniques for analyzing and interpreting the unique aspects of sites are bound to improve. In sum, we are morally and scientifically obligated to preserve large parts of most archeological sites for future work.

Quite apart from the need to conserve archeological resources in any particular case, there is also a pressing need to learn how to conserve sites. That is, because conservation is important in general, it behooves all researchers to help improve our techniques for conservation. We must learn to extract more information from what we excavate and to improve our ability to sample properly. Finally, we must work for legislation and public education to protect and preserve archeological sites.

Strategies of Sampling

One important requirement for any scientific sampling procedure is that it avoid bias. This can often be accomplished by using some form of probabilistic sampling design. Another technique is to use a large, nonprobabilistic sample, but it is difficult to be sure one has succeeded in doing so. Alternatively one may deliberately sample nonrandomly with respect to some variable, for example, nearness to water, then make analytic corrections for this later. The most basic probabilistic sampling design is to take a random sample of the universe being investigated, and many statisticians argue that for many problems this is superior to more complicated designs. For example, if the universe to be sampled is a series of projectile points of which the investigator measures only the perfect specimens to determine average dimensions, that sample may be badly skewed (biased). The perfect ones may comprise a nonrandom sample because their perfection is controlled by some additional factor (such as nature of the raw material) other than the attributes ostensibly being measured (length, width, and so on).

Spatial universes, for example, survey areas or site areas, require consideration not just of the attributes of a particular unit (the number of sites in a transect, the number of sherds in a surface collection) but also of the relationship of this unit to other units. For example, in a study of the relationship of surface to subsurface archeological material at two prehistoric sites in Turkey (Redman and Watson 1970), we found that the simple random sample of grid squares that we proposed to collect at our first site (Çayönü) was not satisfactory because it resulted in "blank spots" on the site where no sample squares happened to fall (figure 4.1). This random sample eliminated bias, but because our purpose was not merely to sample the total assemblage but also to trace the variation in distributional patterns across the site, we modified a random sample to fit our purposes. At the second site (Girikihaciyan) we used such a modified random sample, called a stratified unaligned systematic sample, which eliminates the disadvantage just noted for the random sample but retains its unbiased nature (figure 4.2).

Often one knows or suspects something about part of the universe under question. One has an idea that certain land forms were put to different uses, or that large sites are significantly different in function from smaller sites. In such common cases as these, one often needs to divide the overall universe into subuniverses, which statisticians call strata. One then defines strategies for sampling these subuniverses. Most questions about sampling here concern the def-

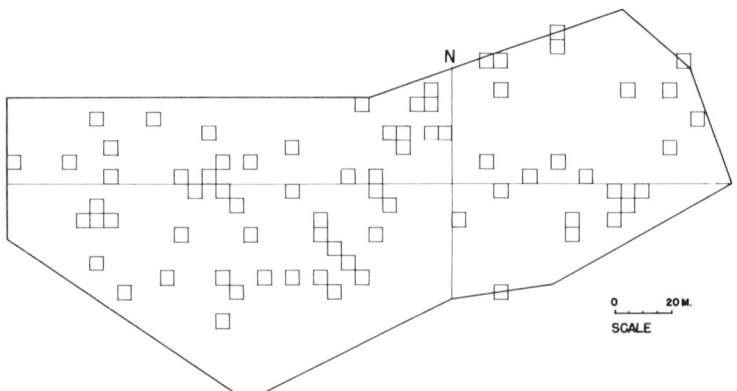

Figure 4.1. Outline Map of Archeological Site of Çayönü

The Record and Designing Research   181

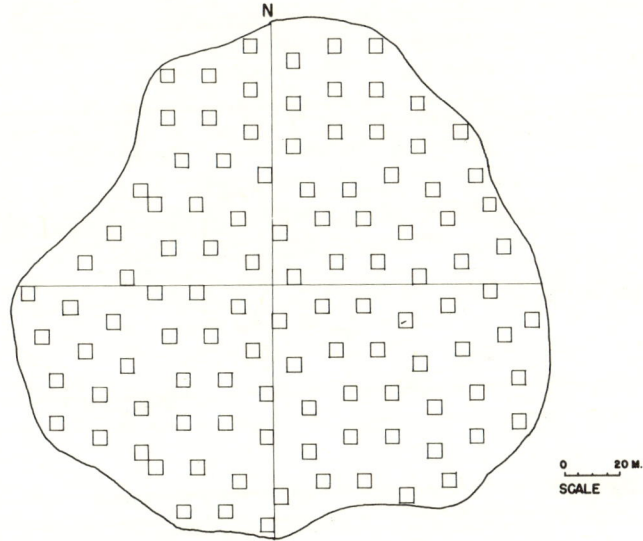

Figure 4.2. Outline Map of Archeological Site of Girikihaciyan

inition of the strata to be chosen for analysis and the intensity with which those chosen are to be measured. One has a continuum of choices in these matters. At one extreme, one can divide the universe into strata and take a small (e.g., one) sample from each stratum. At the other extreme, one chooses a few of these strata and takes many samples from each.

The surface collection from Girikihaciyan referred to above is an example of the first approach. Here 109 strata (blocks of nine grid squares each) were laid out, and one square from each stratum was chosen as the sample to be collected. An example of the alternative strategy would be to define each grid square at Teotihuacan as a stratum and then to choose one (or a few) of these blocks and take many different surface collections from buildings in the chosen square (or squares).

Each of these strategies has concrete advantages depending on variations in the universe under consideration. If each stratum defined is relatively homogeneous and there is much variability between strata, then sampling many strata with only a few samples per stratum is the best procedure.

For the surface survey of Girikihaciyan, we assumed that there was little variation in artifact counts over short distances (up to fifteen meters), therefore a few samples (in this case, only one) were believed adequate to represent each stratum. Such a sample is usually referred to as a stratified sample. In the case of a very large site, it may be that each block is relatively similar to every other block on the whole but that within each block there is a great deal of complexity. One sample from each block does not help much in understanding this complexity. However, if one block is surface-collected intensively (or, more realistically, excavated), then it may be possible to understand its organization and extrapolate to the other blocks. Such a sample is usually referred to as a cluster sample.

Several points should be made about these different strategies: First, a significant amount of information is required to implement them properly. The assumption that each block is essentially similar to every other can be accepted only if there are adequate data to support it. Second, surface collections are usually of the many-strata/few-samples-per-stratum type, and the usual traditional excavation strategy is to choose a "typical" site that is excavated intensively (thus traditional surface collection and excavation exemplify alternative methodological extremes). In the absence of explicit justification, there is no good reason why these traditional trends should continue to prevail, whereas there are often good reasons for employing sampling strategies different from these traditional ones. Third, the two methods outlined here are extremes, and, in many cases, compromise strategies employing both methods are to be preferred.

In making any decision about sampling design—as is true for determining sample size—pragmatic considerations are important. One must weigh the cost of obtaining a sample against the value of the data recovered. For example, if the portion of a site selected for excavation by a sampling procedure is covered by a tree or by large boulders, the time and money involved in sampling it may be prohibitive. Selecting another sample area by some nonbiased means is usually the best solution. The important point is that pragmatic considerations should not be the primary determinants of procedure and should not be allowed to bias the sample. Conversely, one should not completely ignore pragmatic considerations. One value of sampling is to save energy, and taking pragmatic considerations into account can often help save energy without increasing bias.

It follows from this discussion and from our discussion of multistage research design that it is usually worthwhile to sample the same (or parts of the same) universe more than once. We may choose an initial survey sample and then, on the basis of these results, define new strata, and then sample and survey again. Similarly, we may choose to excavate a small number of test trenches and, on the basis of these results, choose a new sample of areas to excavate. Thus, multistage research design and multiple sampling are closely intertwined. Our sampling goals, however, remain the same: to use available knowledge to devise the next sample design; to seek to conserve work resources; and to reduce bias with proper sampling.

The above points on sampling may be fairly obvious, but they are by no means universally accepted, let alone universally practiced. In fact, some archeologists have a certain tendency to be "against" sampling. The grounds for objections to the use of sampling procedures range from intuitive feelings that sampling is somehow inaccurate to sophisticated statements to the effect that 100 percent samples are necessary to solve certain kinds of problems. Some archeologists argue that we have not yet "learned how" to sample in archeology so should not do it until we learn.

Most of the arguments against archeological sampling are weak, but a few points about these criticisms are worth considering. The theory of sampling was worked out long ago, and the present level of sophistication is far higher than archeologists will need for a long time to come; current sampling methods are better than most analytic methods in archeology. While some minor questions about sampling have not been completely answered for archeology—such as how results differ between transect surveys and block surveys—most necessary aspects are well understood. For example, we may need to experiment somewhat with the shapes of survey blocks, but most of the differential effects are understood. When sampling blocks are long and narrow, or small, then they have a large amount of edge per unit area. That is a quarter-section square has 1 mile of edge, but an equivalent size transect 100 yards wide by 7,744 yards long has 8.9 miles of edge. If sites are counted that are only partially within the sample area, then the higher the edge-to-area ratio of a sampling block, the more sites will be found per sampling block surveyed (Plog 1976). Thus, if other things are equal (which they seldom are) and one's goal is merely to find sites (which is not always the case), then transects are perferable to squares. But transect site discovery strategies may not result in data that are representative of the frequency distribution of sites for a given area. For this, a square might be better. The point is that such effects should be taken into account when planning survey procedures.

It is not our intent to discuss all aspects of site survey sampling schemes, but it is worthwhile to note that most schemes are chosen as compromises between conflicting needs. Large sampling units are more efficient than small ones because the cost of getting to them and locating them is relatively lower; small units are more efficient because of edge effects; long, narrow units are more efficient because of edge effects; square units allow for more "nearest neighbor" types of analysis; and so on. Clearly, no general sample solution exists, nor is there a "right" way to sample any given terrain.

The theory of archeological sampling is well established, but we certainly are far from understanding the relative costs of various procedures. How much time do we waste trying to locate very small units? How useful is edge effect in practice? Because much of the site survey done today is under contract, there is a strong economic incentive to learn the answers to such questions. Close cost accounting of these operations potentially provides the means to get the answers. It would be of great help in designing surveys rationally if archeologists would include cost data in survey and site reports.

The relative advantages of cluster vs. stratified sampling are also well established, and no experimentation with different kinds of these sampling designs is necessary. Similarly, questions as to what sample sizes are adequate can be answered from an already existing body of statistical theory. We need no experimentation to learn what sample sizes are appropriate for archeology in particular.

The real problems with sampling are rarely considered. We often confront universes—areas or sites—that are so large and diverse that we cannot sample them adequately with the resources generally available. To accumulate enough sampling units we would have to make them so small that we would be unable to interpret their contexts. To understand some structures or fragments of architectural remains, we need to excavate a very high proportion (often 100 percent) of these features. This often requires use of so many work resources that the remainder of the site can be excavated only inadequately. Of course, this difficulty has nothing to do with sampling per se but instead is a problem of adjusting available work resources to the extent and detail of archeological problems.

To summarize, we emphasize aspects of sampling that must be considered in any research design: (1) All data collection is sampling at some level and must be recognized as such. (2) Sampling is a means of conserving resources, and the cost and value of data collection must always be kept in mind. Too small a sample gives poor or inadequate information; too large a sample wastes irreplaceable data and resources. Sampling strategies must not be so time consuming that they waste more effort than they save. (3) Different assumptions about the underlying universe lead to different kinds of sampling procedures. When information is sparse, a strong case can be made for simple random sampling. As one learns more, this information should be utilized appropriately to design more complex sampling procedures. (4) An important but not exclusive goal of sampling is to reduce bias.

CHAPTER FIVE
Archeological Analysis

Given the data, how should they be analyzed? This fundamental question—as repeatedly noted throughout this volume—must be asked before the data are collected because the analytical techniques determine what, how, and how much data should be obtained. Let us assume that one has formulated a research design and with hypotheses in mind has chosen digging and recording methods and techniques based on adequate sampling procedures. As excavation proceeds and as data accumulate and are analyzed, one may alter the original hypotheses to bring them into line with new information. When this happens, digging and recording will probably also be altered, as will the analytical techniques.

Most excavators follow the general outlines of this procedure, altering their excavation techniques as data accumulate, but sometimes there is a long lag between digging (data accumulation), analysis of data, and modification of methods of data accumulation. Ideally, a short feedback cycle should be maintained so that analysis keeps pace with fieldwork and the two constantly influence each other. New data are analyzed and the results are used immediately to assess the basic hypotheses and the implications for excavation that these entail. If either hypotheses or implications need to be altered in the light of recovered data, then digging and recording methods must also be altered.

In practice this is extremely difficult to do fully during a typical field season. The best balance of cycles is between short digging and long analytical seasons, that is, one should dig for a few weeks or months, analyze for the rest of the year, then repeat the process.

Contract archeological situations often do not allow for this optimal balance. Excavations are frequently compressed into one continuous session, a situation that may seriously impede archaeological analysis. However, for the purpose of considering analytic techniques, we assume that a body of data is already at hand.

Comparisons and Scales

Underlying all analysis is the basic procedure of making comparisons. A fundamental aspect of this procedure is that *two objects can never be meaningfully compared*. The similarities and differences of two objects can be listed, but formal comparison requires that they be measured with respect to a third object. There are two ways to proceed with a comparison: One can compare more than two objects and make statements such as, "A is more similar to B than it is to C."

Alternatively, one can compare (measure) A or B with a scale, so that the scale serves as a referent third object (or set of objects). A scale is essentially a standard record of a previously performed set of comparisons that is used to facilitate additional comparisons. There are three major kinds of scales, as explained below, and all three types serve this basic function. But because analytic methods differ according to the scales (means of measurement) used in recording the data to be analyzed, we must examine the different scales that are available. These are: interval, ordinal, and nominal. Scales are discussed in detail in Blalock (1972) and Kolstoe (1969). Ratio scales are included with interval scales because, for our purposes, the distinction between them is not important.

In a review of our book *Explanation in Archeology* (1971), Leaf (1973) states that ignoring of the distinctions between ratio and interval scales would "cause a mathematician to shrink in horror; . . . the distinction between interval and ratio scales is critically important because the mathematical manipulation of data measured in these two ways is quite different." This is not correct. Blalock states:

> In practically all instances known to the writer the distinction between interval and ratio scales is purely academic, however, as it is extremely difficult to find a legitimate interval scale which is not also a ratio scale.

. . . Thus in practically all instances where a unit is available it will be legitimate to use all the ordinary operations of arithmetic. (Blalock 1972:18)

The point is that one does not need to know very much mathematics to be a good archaeologist, and the mathematical knowledge one does need is not very difficult.

The interval scale is the most familiar. An interval scale is any type of measurement device with fixed and equal intervals. Rulers, thermometers, stopwatches, and so on are used to make measurements of fixed intervals. As an archaeological example, consider three projectile points with lengths of 8, 9, and 10 cm. Not only do we know the absolute lengths of the points with reference to a standard means of measurement, but also we know that the difference in length between the 8 cm. and 10 cm. points is twice that between the 8 cm. and the 9 cm. points. Interval scales can be used to obtain quantitative data of any degree of precision, and, in general, the most powerful statistics are those based on data collected with interval scales.

The second kind of scale is the ordinal, or rank, scale. With an ordinal scale, one can make only relative comparisons of items with one another. An example is Moh's Hardness Scale for minerals. For another illustration, suppose we decide to rank ten projectile points according to length and to assign them numbers 1 through 10, from longest to shortest. We know that a projectile point given a value of 7 is longer than one given a value of 8, but we do not know how much longer it is. There is no specified amount of difference between the units of the scale. The projectile points ranked 4 and 5 could differ by one centimeter while those ranked 9 and 10 could differ by 5 cm. It is obvious that the ordinal scale provides less data about the comparative lengths of the projectile points than does the interval scale. Statistical techniques that can be applied to ordinal scale data are different from those that can be used with interval scale data. In general, statistical methods for interval scale data are more thoroughly understood and have produced a more voluminous literature than have methods applicable to ordinal scale data. This implies that *whenever interval scale data are appropriate to the subject matter* (a very important qualification), they should be obtained. However, if interval scale data are inappropriate or unobtainable, interesting and valuable analyses can still be carried out.

The third scale is the nominal scale. Nominal scales merely order items in discrete categories without specifying anything about the differences between the categories. A nominal scale might have divisions based on shape, color, religion, or basis of descent reckoning. Any scale that measures the presence or absence of some attribute is a nominal scale. For example, we could divide the projectile points into two classes, "long" and "not long," by defining "long" as 10 cm. or more in length. Such an ordering would then be according to a nominal scale and would convey less detailed information about the point lengths than do the other two scales. Presence–absence or other dichotomous scales are simply particular kinds of nominal scales. A dichotomous nominal scale can be conceived of as a two-valued (presence–absence) interval scale, but the limited interval techniques that can be used offer no advantages over nominal techniques, so there is seldom any reason to make this move. In general, the statistical techniques that can be used with nominal scale data provide the least information of the three. Table 5.1 is a comparison of the three scales for the ten projectile points.

One objective of any general scientific method is to collect data appropriate for solving the problems set. Therefore, every effort should be made to collect data by means of scales appropriate for obtaining the information needed and adequate for the statistical techniques one wants to apply. Interval scales provide the greatest quantity of

Table 5.1.
Scales

	Interval Scale (cm)	*Ordinal Scale*	*Nominal Scale*
A	5	1	short
B	5.5	2	short
C	12	8	long
D	8	5	short
E	9	6	short
F	7	4	short
G	10	7	long
H	6	3	short
I	20	10	long
J	15	9	long

statistically meaningful information, but tabulating data by use of interval scales is usually more difficult and time-consuming than tabulation using ordinal or nominal scales. Hence, there is often a greater tendency to use ordinal or nominal scales than interval scales. For example, nominal scales are often used in describing pottery. However, much information is lost when nominal scales are used, and a question arising later in the analysis that could have been answered if an interval scale had been devised and used for recording the original data might remain unanswered forever. As always, cost considerations may be decisive. Recording on interval scales is usually more expensive of time and effort. Hence, the advantages of interval measurements must be weighed against their cost.

Because of differential preservation and the effects of postoccupational disturbances of many different kinds, information originally contained in artifacts and in their features and distributions may be hidden or even lost. Digging also destroys data, so it is crucial to obtain as much information as possible from archaeological data. Therefore, one should always use the most powerful scale possible in recording those data to recover as much as possible of the potential information. However, for both theoretical and practical reasons, not all the data can be recorded by means of interval scales, so much archaeological data will always be recorded by use of nominal or ordinal scales. Thus, archaeologists should be aware of existing techniques for analyzing nominal and ordinal data and, where possible, should develop new ones.

Archaeologists are often confronted with data measurable only with nominal scales. The distinction between bowls and jars, or between various types of stone raw materials are classic cases. One should be alert for different ways of viewing these materials. Vessel shape can be converted to volume that can be measured with an interval scale. Also, one can rank raw materials with an ordinal scale based on ease of chipping or the relative effort required to obtain them. In neither case is the new scale equivalent to the old nominal scale, but for some questions it may be far superior to it.

It is very difficult to analyze a single class of material, say, projectile points, whose different attributes have been recorded on different types of scales. In such cases one is usually forced to reduce interval data to nominal data in order to compare them, thus wasting the energy that went into recording with an interval scale in the first place. However, if several measurements are made on interval scales, then appropriate analyses can be done on these, and some of the resulting information can be transformed by use of ordinal or nominal scales so that it can be compared with other ordinal or nominal data. The point, as usual, is that one must plan the entire analysis before completing the first steps. The techniques that will eventually be employed must be defined before work begins because they determine which scales are to be used. The most efficient and optimal combination of scales and techniques can be achieved only when they are considered together.

Dimensions, Variables, Attributes, and Cases

A scale is used to measure a particular aspect of the data. Spaulding (1960) uses the term *dimension* to designate the aspect measured, but *variable* is the word more commonly used now. Physicists sometimes use *variable* to refer specifically to interval scale data. However, *variable* is used by statisticians and workers in other fields to indicate aspects measured with nominal and ordinal scales as well as with interval scales; we use the term with this wide scope.

Another common term is *attribute,* usually used to specify ordinal and nominal data. An attribute is a specific state of a particular variable. Thus, for pottery, we might have the variable (or dimension) "pottery color" and the attributes "red" or "white." Doran and Hodson (1975), however, use *attribute* synonymously with *variable* when discussing nominal or ordinal scales, and then use *attribute state* to connote the specific form, such as "red pottery."

While any of the various terms can be used as long as their definitions are clear, the simplest procedure is to use *variable* to mean the type of phenomenon being measured and *attribute* to mean a particular state.

A variable, then, is some formally defined aspect of the objects being studied. Every variable is measured in terms of a scale, and the mutually exclusive attributes of the variable are indicated by the units of the scale.

Quantitative attributes can be defined by reference to the equal units of an interval scale designed to measure them. Once this is done, the attribute is merely the value of the measurement. For example, variable: length in centimeters; attribute: 10.5 centimeters. For nominal and ordinal scales, mutually exclusive attributes must be defined for each variable so that only one attribute can pertain for each variable at a given time. For example, for any one specimen the variable "projectile point length" can include only one of the mutually exclusive attributes "short" and "long."

One can record the attributes of a projectile point by reference to the variables of length, width, thickness, weight, color, number of retouch scars, and so on. Attributes such as poor or good workmanship can be measured also if they are clearly defined with respect to the variable "workmanship." That is, empirical criteria for good and bad points must be defined so that the same judgment is reached by different workers using these criteria. If this is done, the attributes of workmanship are just as objective as those of length.

Each variable is a particular aspect of a *case*. A case can be an artifact, a portion of an artifact (each design motif could be a separate case), a site, a region, or a culture. A case can also be a collection. Thus, all the pottery from one level or room may be a case for certain analytic purposes. A case is occasionally called an entity, but case seems the preferable term. Data recording usually comprises measuring—by means of attributes—a number of variables (dimensions) for each member of a collection of cases.

Descriptive Analysis

In general, before proceeding to any actual analysis, one should examine the data collected from each case and variable to check for errors, to estimate the accuracy of the measurements, to describe the data succinctly, and to determine approximately how the cases are distributed, variable by variable.

One initially looks for extreme values or outliers ("ringers") in the data because they may be recording errors and should be checked; if they are not errors they are likely to be of special interest. Spot-checks of the original data tabulations should also be made to determine the accuracy of the procedures and measurements before detailed analysis begins.

The techniques of descriptive statistics can then be employed to represent the data clearly and concisely. Means, medians, modes, standard deviations, percents, histograms, and so on are all forms of data description. For purposes of comparison, a mean or a standard deviation alone is of little value. A researcher can draw a conclusion from a mean only by comparing it with previously collected means. Such statistical descriptions are essential to archeological analysis but do not themselves constitute either archeological interpretations or solutions to archeological problems.

The final step in the preliminary examination of data is to note exactly how the cases of each variable are distributed. If all or almost all the cases of a variable fall at the same point along a scale (a not uncommon situation with nominal scales), this variable may be of little or no analytical use, but variables whose cases have normal, bimodal, or other such distributions are likely to be useful analytically.

There are unlimited numbers of variables and attributes for almost any data set. Which ones should be chosen for study? Those that are clearly relevant to the questions being asked. However, two further considerations are necessary. Just because a variable has the potential of being relevant is no guarantee that it *is* relevant. We may hypothesize that there will be differences in pottery found in elite structures as compared with pottery found in nonelite structures and that vessel temper is a variable that will reflect such differences. However, it may turn out that all vessels have the same temper. On the other hand, vessel color may indicate the hypothesized difference. Thus, sometimes one must examine variables not originally thought to be relevant. Obviously, these new variables must occur in enough different attribute states to make them analytically useful. In sum, which variables and attributes we choose to study is primarily a function of our questions, but however we select these variables they must not be so homogeneous over the cases in question that they cannot be used analytically.

One purpose of a multistage analytic approach is to avoid recording thousands of attributes only to discover that their values do not differ sufficiently to warrant analysis. This difficulty can often be avoided by drawing and analyzing an initial sample.

One might select, say, a 5 percent sample of artifacts for initial attribute recording to determine whether the attributes selected are useful. We did something like this for ceramics from the site of Girikihaciyan in Turkey. We examined the attributes of pottery temper and discovered a very low occurrence of chaff temper in the sample. It was proportionally so rare that it was "clearly" analytically useless; hence, we dropped chaff temper as an attribute and recorded all the sherds without reference to chaff versus grit temper. Later that one small area of the site was found to have considerable percentages of chaff-tempered pottery, but because this area is small it contributed almost nothing to the initial 5 percent sample. In fact, this pottery represents a later occupation of the site and thus chaff temper is an important attribute. This example shows that rare attributes may be highly significant archaeologically and that simple random samples are not always ideal. One could argue that the initial 5 percent sample should have been stratified on the basis of which units were most likely to be dissimilar.

Thus we see again that the questions and the analyses are integrated, and that a multistage approach is best.

Variable Analysis and Case Analysis

Scientists in many fields are primarily concerned to discover and describe relationships among variables. Physicists, for example, are not interested in individual atoms; they study classes or groups of objects. Archaeologists also are interested in discovering and describing regular relationships among variables. In addition, archaeologists are concerned to describe individual cases. We are interested both in regularities and similarities and in the individual historical development of sites, architecture, and artifacts. While all scientists must work with both case and variable analysis, many archaeologists are more concerned with case analysis. And, of course, case analysis is at the foundation of behavioral interpretation. Case analyses support generalizations about social complexity, carrying capacity, and other abstract variables. Unfortunately, most methods of case analysis are less fully developed than are those for variable analysis.

We consider variable analysis and case analysis under separate headings below, but one cannot always carry out case and variable analysis separately. Obviously, which cases are found to be similar depends on the variables used to compare them. Also, obvious patterns in the cases influence the choice of variables measured. However, problems arising from such interactions are beyond the scope of the present work and do not usually result from the kinds of archaeological comparisons discussed here.

Up to this point, the word *variable* has been used in a rather nonspecific way. In practice, there are two different kinds of variables: those that are actually measured, and those that are transformations of these original, measured or scaled variables. For example, rates and percents, which are particularly useful in archeological analyses, are transformed variables, as is a ratio such as that between two attributes when the value of one is divided by that of the other. This ratio is an abstract variable that can be used for complex comparisons. One consideration in choosing variables to record is how they can be transformed into variables that are more useful analytically. In the remaining sections we use the word *variable* to mean both the original and the transformed variables.

Variable Analysis: Measuring Relationships Among Variables

A full discussion of this topic and those that follow is beyond the scope of this book. We intend here only to touch on those issues that are particularly pertinent to topics treated in the previous chapters or that frequently cause difficulty.

Variables are measured and compared for the purpose of discovering general relationships among cases. We test such hypothetical relationships as the following: "As population increases, volume of trade decreases." "As pueblo size increases, size of pueblo rooms decreases." "As the proportion of flint to obsidian increases, so does the proportion of time spent in farming."

Archeological Analysis

If we confirm one of these relationships, we explore it further. However, something like, "As kiva diameter increases, so does the circumference," is not an empirical discovery but is tautologically true. Measuring diameter and circumference are just two logically connected ways of measuring the size of a circular building. It is quite possible to measure the same aspect of a given set of data along several different dimensions. Therefore, some relationships represent necessary logical relations and not new empirical discoveries. They can be useful in analysis, however, and it might be easier, for example, to measure diameter than to measure circumference.

Analytic techniques as such do not indicate which relationships are significant in the sense of providing understanding. But there is a variety of formal comparisons that can provide precise or clear or graphic representations of relationships so that they can be understood and integrated. The results of these analyses can also suggest new hypothetical relationships to be checked. But always it is up to archeologists to *evaluate* the significance of the confirmed relationships. Analyses themselves are merely ways of arranging and making inferences from data.

With this caveat in mind, we can consider how to go about finding relationships among variables.

In general, efforts to find relationships among variables are divided into two classes: two-variable analyses concerned with the relationships between only two variables at one time; and multivariate analyses in which many variables are considered simultaneously. Application of multivariate analysis is an ultimate goal in archeology because most of the situations that concern us are complex enough to require the consideration of many variables at once. However, the fundamental principles involved are much the same regardless of the number of variables, and it is easier to describe some of these principles for the two-variable situation, hence we start with it. Some of the techniques of multivariate analysis are discussed briefly later in this chapter.

These analytical techniques are used to find out whether or not there are relationships among variables. If we find that some of the variables are related, we try to determine the strength and form of the relationships. These are quite different steps, however, and this fact must be kept in mind. If two interval variables are known to be related, a statistical test of correlation such as Pearson's r is commonly used to determine the strength of the relationship between them, and then we use other statistical tests to determine whether or not the observed relation has a high or low probability of occurring by chance (that is, is the relationship a temporary chance occurrence or abnormal conjunction, or is it a permanent or normal conjunction of variables?).

For ordinal data the procedure is the same except that a different coefficient (for example, Spearman's rank order coefficient) is used, and the probability statements are computed on the basis of different assumptions. For nominal data only the measures change. The chi-squared test is usually used to determine whether a relationship exists, while other measures (for example, Cramer's V) are employed to describe the strength of demonstrated relationships. The chi-squared test is one of the simplest and most useful statistical tools available to archeologists. This test shows the porbability that the distribution of the data could occur by chance if there is, in fact, no such patterning in the population. Because so much archeological data is collected with nominal scales and because classifications have so often been based on relationships between such variables, the chi-squared test of variable analysis is particularly important.

For example, suppose for a collection of burials the sex of the individual and the pottery type found in each burial are recorded as in table 5.2. It appears that there was a tendency to bury males with red pots. One needs to know, however, whether these observed frequencies are significantly different from what might occur by chance. The chi-squared test shows how much this set of frequencies differs from what would have been expected from chance association be-

Table 5.2.
Observed Frequencies

	Red Pottery	*Not Red Pottery*	Totals
Males	33	7	40
Females	12	8	20
Totals	45	15	60

Archeological Analysis

Table 5.3.
Expected Frequencies

	Red Pottery	Not Red Pottery	Totals
Males	30	10	40
Females	15	5	20
Totals	45	15	60

tween pottery type and sex in the burials. The expected values can be determined by assuming that because ⅔ (40/60) of the individuals were male and ¾ (45/60) of the pots were red, then—purely by chance—½ (⅔ × ¾ = ½) of all the burials would be of males buried with red pots. Thus, of 60 burials, one would expect 30 males to be buried with red pots purely by chance. The figures for the rest of table 5.3 are derived in the same way.

By comparing table 5.2 with table 5.3 one can see that the observed frequencies are not far different from the expected frequencies. The value of chi-squared is computed, and, by referring to an appropriate table, one can find that the observed distribution could be expected to occur about one time in nine (that is, in more than 10 percent of the cases) by chance alone.

Two things must be made clear. The larger the sample, the smaller the likelihood that any deviation from the expected distribution will be due to chance alone. If 600 burials had been found in exactly the same proportions as before, the distribution would be exhibited as in table 5.4. This distribution would occur only one time in 1,000 by chance alone.

Second, it should be noted that the chi-squared test shows nothing about the strength of the relationship between the variables. If the sample size is very large, any percentage deviation from ex-

Table 5.4.
Observed Frequencies

	Red Pottery	Not Red Pottery	Totals
Males	330	70	400
Females	120	80	200
Totals	450	150	600

pected values is much less likely than in a small sample. Thus, if even a small proportional deviation occurs, the likelihood that it is due to chance alone is very slight. There are situations in which a slight deviation is statistically significant, but the actual proportion of cases that deviate from the expected is so small that the relationship between the two variables may be unimportant. If the sample includes several thousand items, a deviation from the expected involving thirty items might be statistically significant. However, because the sample size is large, the percentage of items involved is so small that the situation would probably be culturally uninteresting. "Uninteresting," of course, is relative. In the above case something happened that is not likely due to chance, but relationships this weak can often be justifiably ignored. Of course, the deviation may be related to some other relationship between other variables that should be looked for. Suppose, for example, that of 1000 burials there are 30 more males (only 3 percent of the total) buried with red pots than expected. If one looks at the data again, one might find that of all the males buried with red pots 3 percent are deformed in some way, or are under 10 years of age, or are buried with exotic marine shells under their skulls. Then the statistically relevant deviation from chance discovered by comparing male burials and red pots could be justifiably inferred to be also culturally relevant. One might even want to look at the red pots that accompany the 30 odd males to see whether they differ in any way from the red pots accompanying the other (male and female) burials.

Statisticians traditionally consider a distribution significant if its chance of occurrence is less than one time in 20 (or 5 percent of the time). This is referred to as the ".05 level of significance." This is, of course, an arbitrary cutoff point. If hundreds of comparisons are made between large numbers of variables, as can now easily be done by computer, one will find that many statistical associations that are only "accidental" are significant by definition. In theory this presents no problem because one must always interpret any distribution: "No suggestion [is] made that any statistical operations [will] disclose the ultimate significance of the clusters described" (Spaulding 1954:392). Mere statistical significance does not supply meaning, no matter what the level of significance. In practice, one must decide whether or not what is statistically significant is also culturally significant on whatever substantive grounds are available. One may miss interesting and real relationships by ignoring all distributions that do not have a high statistical significance level. Conversely, if all low levels of statistical significance are taken to be culturally significant, then one is bound to include some that are due only to chance.

For example, during his study of Upper Paleolithic end scrapers, Sackett (1966) decided that the traditional .05 level would probably eliminate too many nonchance relationships because of the nature of the sample, so he chose a .10 level. Although he risked including some spurious relationships in his results, the gains were worth the additional analytical effort. This is an important point because there are many gaps between the behavior and selected debris of the people who once occupied a site and our description and interpretations based on the altered remains in the archeological record. Flint artifacts can be broken by subsequent weathering, and spatial distributions of artifacts can be modified by noncultural factors. This does not mean the data are unusable, but it does mean that statistical procedures often must be modified accordingly, as Sackett did in the present example.

Variable analysis requires prior defining of types. And in fact confirming the existence of "types" is not different from finding relationships among variables. Actually identifying specimens according to type, however, is a different matter and is discussed under case analysis below.

TYPES

The concept of types raises some of the most involved problems in archeology. The term *type* has been used for a long time and bears a large number of meanings. The term is common in the natural sciences, for example, biology, but archeologists and biologists often use it quite differently. Moreover, archeologists use the term explicitly in some situations (for example, for pottery types) and not in others (for example, for cultures). Some types are rigidly defined and others are informal generalizations. There is also the question of how close the artifact or culture types we define are to the groupings that were in the minds of the makers. Finally, in the last two decades there have been a number of attempts to use quantification procedures both to define types and to search for types.

This quantitative trend has the advantage of bringing into sharp focus what is being done, but so many *different* things were and are being done that numerous arguments and misunderstandings have resulted. It is beyond the scope of this chapter to discuss all aspects of the archeological concept of type, but we address those of the greatest relevance to scientific archeology.

There is an important fundamental distinction between two different kinds of types (Clarke 1968) that must be noted. A *monothetic* type is defined by attributes all of which all members of the type must possess. A pottery type is an example.

A *polythetic* type is defined by a family of attributes, no one of which need be possessed by all members of the type. Questions of how many of the family of attributes must be present for an item to be a member of a polythetic type, and whether there is any reason to classify objects polythetically at all, can be answered only for each particular situation.

It should be obvious that the more attributes one uses to define a type, the more likely it is that the type will be polythetic. And a great advantage of polythetic definition is that it allows one to accept and use the differences between members of the same type instead of ignoring these differences. Polythetic types are also more compatible with systemic analyses than are monothetic types.

Just as measures with interval scales result in more detailed information than do measures with nominal scales, classifications according to polythetic types accommodate more information than do classifications according to monothetic types. Nevertheless, monothetic types have been and continue to be valuable in archeology.

Most traditional archeological types were not originally explicitly defined. They are based on the implicit fundamental assumption that a type is a group or a cluster of objects more similar to one another with respect to two or more variables than to objects in other groups. This typological approach to data is not limited to artifacts but is widely applied to many ranges of material up to and including whole cultures (for example, Willey and Phillips 1958).

There has also been long-term discussion among archeologists about how a type is constituted and what a type really represents. Brew states the position that types are conceptual or nominal constructions made for analytical purposes:

> "Types" are not "found." The student does not "recognize" a type, he *makes* it and *puts* the object in it. Objects do not "belong" or "fall into" types, they are *placed* in types by the student. . . . No typological system is actually inherent in the material. . . . The classes are entities and realities only in the minds of students, they have no other existence. (Brew 1946:46).

For Brew, types do represent actual conjunctions of attributes in actual objects, but a type itself is merely a classificatory device determined by archeologists' interests and not by objects. Thus a class of objects for Brew is an arbitrary abstraction.

Spaulding holds the opposing view that types are determined by actual objects: "Classification into types is a process of discovery of combinations of attributes . . . not an arbitrary procedure of the classifier" (Spaulding 1953:305).

There is probably less disagreement here than first appears. Brew is thinking of how archeologists define types for special purposes, whereas Spaulding focuses on the fact that many types consist of "natural" groupings. Before discussing this issue, we review how typologies are developed.

One must sometimes categorize large collections of sherds, projectile points, and sites for purposes of description. Given a box full of projectile points, most archeologists will order them by size, shape, notch type, etc. The result will usually be several clusters of projectile points. There are likely to be a few borderline cases and a few complete oddballs. But the clusters do seem to be types that are or represent natural orderings of the objects. Other workers can arrive at more or less the same groupings independently, and there does seem to be a limit on the extent to which useful types can be arbitrarily constructed.

Regardless of one's position about the reality or naturalness of useful types, there is considerable agreement among archeologists about significant types, and Spaulding's view that objects determine types is widely held. However, one might make three "mistakes" in sorting artifacts into groupings—as described above—that are meant to be monothetic types. First, the "sample" may be sorted into "types" that are of no use in solving the problems in hand (a point elaborated below). Second, important but not so obvious aspects of the projectile points may be ignored. For example, raw material may not be taken into consideration. Third, even on the basis of the attributes originally used there may be further possible subdivisions of types that one does not see.

Spaulding advocates division into real types (see the following discussion about the validation of types). He cautions that failure to recognize real types or reliance on "nonreal" arbitrary types leads to identification of patterns other than those we should be searching for. That is, we should make sure that the subgroups into which we partition the study universe have characteristics that are at least potentially useful. Regardless of one's view about the reality of types, Spaulding's concern with utility is important. We need constantly to try to understand what we are dong, what assumptions we have made, and what the implications of these may be.

Unfortunately, there has been a tendency to use as a discovery procedure the mathematical technique Spaulding discusses as a means to check the validity of types. There is nothing wrong with this approach, and there are many materials for which it is appropriate. Frequently, however, use of an exhaustive mathematical search procedure for combinations of attributes involves ignoring the insight a researcher has gained from experience and may generate volumes of useless data.

Hill and Evans (1972) discuss many aspects of selecting and using monothetic types (we refer to one point of disagreement with them below; see also Taylor 1948:142; R. Watson 1976a). The particular attributes chosen to define a type are arbitrary in the sense that they are selected from a large number of available attributes, but once they are chosen, whether or not they define common or useful or "natural" conjunctions must be tested empirically. Such tests are made with basic statistical methods.

A type consists of two or more attributes in conjunction. To be useful a type must be more than just a nonrandom conjunction of attributes. That is, the presence of one attribute must be predictive for the presence or absence of one or more other attributes. And as remarked several times, the statistical significance of a type (an attribute cluster)—as determined by empirical tests—does not assure its cultural significance. Archeologists form types by putting together objects with similar attributes. These types almost always consist of nonrandom clusters of attributes. However, empirical checks must be made to confirm that the attributes are, in fact, associated nonrandomly. Thus, the crucial problem is that of making explicit the nonrandomness of the clusters. Typologists who work intuitively with untested types may be mistaken in their assessments of attribute distributions. For example, "black-on-red shell-tempered" may appear to be a useful pottery type for describing some potsherds, but a count of the total occurrences of black-on-red with shell temper might show that there is no real, statistically significant relationship between these attributes and that therefore "Black-on-red Shell-Tempered" is not a valid pottery type in this instance.

One way to exhibit the relationship between attributes is to use a two-by-two (or larger) table. Such a table is made by listing the mutually exclusive attributes of one variable along the left vertical line of a square, and the mutually exclusive attributes of another variable along the bottom horizontal line of the square. The inside of the square is then cross-lined vertically and horizontally to provide boxes or cells for each possible attribute combination. Then each object under study can be registered in the appropriate cell according to which attributes it possesses. Table 5.5 shows the variable "tempering" with two mutually exclusive attributes "shell-tempered" and "not shell-tempered," and the variable "pot design" with two mutually exclusive attributes "black-on-red" and "'not black-on-red." The numbers

Table 5.5.
Distribution of Black-on-Red and Shell-Tempered Pottery
(site 1) Showing Random Distribution of Attributes

	Shell-Tempered	*Not Shell-Tempered*	*Percent*
Black-on-red	26	25	51
Not black-on-red	22	27	49
Percent	48	52	100

in the four cells are sherd counts. The marginal totals are the total numbers of sherds that have each attribute. In this table the marginal totals are given in percentages.

The table shows that shell temper is no more likely to occur in black-on-red pottery than in non-black-on-red pottery. In this case the pottery is divided into four groups, with a resulting classification that does not show a significant relationship between tempering and design. Because there is no nonrandom association—that is, no clustering—among the attributes examined, no usable types have been isolated.

It might be asked whether the classification as it stands is not still useful in some way. Unfortunately, such classifications sometimes obscure rather than clarify meaningful changes and relationships between attributes and at best do not add to our understanding of the artifacts.

For example, suppose that the distribution shown in table 5.6 is found at another site. Given this distribution, one might claim that black-on-red shell-tempered is a useful pottery type—arbitrary or not—because the proportion of black-on-red shell-tempered pottery is markedly different between the two sites. However, these figures do not show any statistically significant clustering of the attribute "black-on-red" with the attribute "shell-tempered" at either site. The ratio of black-on-red sherds to non-black-on-red sherds and of shell-tempered to non-shell-tempered at site 1 are both approximately 50 percent; at site 2, they are approximately 80 percent. These differences are unrelated as far as any mathematical or statistical analysis shows. Therefore, because the attribute distributions at these two sites are

Table 5.6.
Distribution of Black-on-Red and Shell-Tempered Pottery
(site 2) Showing Random Distribution of Attributes

	Shell-Tempered	Not Shell-Tempered	Percent
Black-on-red	64	16	80
Not black-on-red	16	4	20
Percent	80	20	100

NOTE: While frequencies of attributes differ from those in table 5.5, there is no change in the relationship of the attributes.

Archeological Analysis 207

Table 5.7.
Distribution of Black-on-Red and Shell-Tempered Pottery
(site 3) Showing Random Distribution of Attributes

	Shell-Tempered	*Not Shell-Tempered*	*Percent*
Black-on-red	24	6	30
Not black-on-red	56	14	70
Percent	80	20	100

NOTE: While frequencies of attributes differ from those in tables 5.5 and 5.6, there is no change in the relationship of the attributes.

random, the differences in attribute frequencies between the two sites are probably not culturally significant.

The acceptance of black-on-red shell-tempered as a type here might conceal the real differences between the two sites: frequency of black-on-red pottery; and frequency of use of shell temper.

To take another example, assume that the frequencies given in table 5.7 are observed at site 3. Once more the frequencies of the two attributes at site 3 differ from their frequencies at sites 1 and 2, and thus the frequency of the spurious pottery type "black-on-red shell-tempered" is also different but the distribution of attributes is still random.

Black-on-red shell-tempered pottery occurs in approximately the same proportions at site 3 and site 1. On this basis, one might infer some similarity between these two sites. However, at site 3 the ratio of shell-tempering to non-shell-tempering is 80 percent, and black-on-red to not black-on-red is 20 percent. That is, both ratios are different from the ratios at site 1. By lumping the two unrelated variables "pot design" and "tempering" together, one may miss important relations of each of these variables to other variables.

As these examples indicate, one runs the risk of obscuring or completely missing real relationships if one uses analytical types that are not statistically significant. An analysis of black-on-red versus non-black-on-red pottery and a separate analysis of shell-tempered versus non-shell-tempered at the three sites would show all the statistically significant attribute distributions for each variable.

The point of the discussion so far is that, regardless of how or why we look for or find types, we can determine by statistical analyses whether or not they are nonrandom associations of attributes. Furthermore, if a type is not defined by a statistically significant cluster, then it is not a "real" or "natural" type. Although the attributes one chooses to measure should be relevant to the problem one is working on, the types defined by them should be statistically demonstrable if they are to be useful for cultural interpretation. That is, speaking very informally, types are usually culturally significant only if they consist of real conjunctions of attributes.

TYPES AND "MENTAL TEMPLATES"

A mental template is defined as follows: "The idea of the proper form of an object exists in the mind of the maker, and when this idea is expressed in tangible form in raw material, an artifact results. The idea is the mental template from which the craftsman makes the object" (Deetz 1967:45).

Suppose that an artifact type has been confirmed as "real" by analysis that shows that the conjunction of attributes defining it is statistically significant (that is, nonrandom). Does this type reflect "cultural reality"? That is, did the makers of this type of artifact have in mind just this type or "mental template" when they made the artifacts? Archeologists sometimes argue that they did. For example, Spaulding says,

> If small size and an expanded stem are closely associated in the collection of projectile points, then our best explanation for the association is that the makers reproduced a customary pattern—that they thought of the expanding stemmed and small projectile point as a definite sort of projectile point. Further, we are permitted to suspect that the special kind of projectile had a special function or range of functions and perhaps even that the makers had a special name for the type. (Spaulding 1960:76)

We agree that statistically significant types reflect patterned behavior, but these types may or may not correspond to mental templates. Patterned behavior can be the result of individual motor habits or other idiosyncratic behavior, or of culturally defined behavior. Mechanical contingencies may also be a factor; for example, of the

Archeological Analysis 209

materials available in a certain region, only obsidian may chip well enough for the manufacture of microlithic projectile points. The type "microlithic obsidian point" would then be statistically relevant and real, but the mental template of the makers may not have included raw material.

The eliciting of mental templates is an interesting problem, but the concept is hard to work with for two reasons. First of all, the content of the concept is not widely agreed upon. For example, are culturally appropriate behavior patterns that influence artifact form part of the mental template? And if so, must they be consciously recognized by the artifact makers themselves? Secondly, it is difficult both to devise ways to check whether or not artisans had a given hypothetical mental template (or any mental template at all) in mind and to incorporate mental templates into testable explanations.

Although it is difficult to confirm the existence of particular mental templates in the past, several researchers have turned their attention to the discovery of material products of individual craftsmen (Hill and Gunn 1977). Archeologists characteristically avoid descriptions and interpretation involving individuals by treating cultures and communities as their units of interpretation. However, most archeologists do agree that much of the behavior they are interested in discovering and explaining is the result of individual perceptions, intentions, decisions, and actions. Basketry techniques, pottery designs, and microvariations in the manufacture of lithics have been used to delineate the works of separate individuals within a culture or community. Some archeologists suggest that many models of exchange and organization can be adequately tested only when the distribution of the products of particular individuals is understood. While agreeing in principle with this position, Redman (1977) suggests that focusing research on the identification of works of specific individuals is not necessary for the formulation and testing of behavioral models. Rather, archeologists use new techniques of identification to delineate the smallest verifiable units of production. Whether these are individuals or small groups of closely interacting individuals is not critical because reference to these "analytical individuals" is adequate for devising and testing detailed models of exchange and organization.

In sum, searches for mental templates and, by extension, for individual craftsmen may be useful. But types not known to be past templates are also useful, and if we work with "analytic individuals," many detailed problems can be solved.

ATTRIBUTE SELECTION

For any array of objects, there is an extremely large number of attributes that can be used to order or sort the objects into types. One's choice of attributes should never be arbitrary but should depend on one's purpose. Once attributes are chosen, the types they define must be shown to be real in the sense that the attribute clusters are statistically significant.

Different problems require different intensities of typological analysis. For certain problems gross types based on only a few attributes are appropriate, whereas for other problems highly specified types based on many attributes may be necessary.

In testing a hypothesis concerning form and function of the rooms at Broken K Pueblo, Hill examines the pottery from all the rooms to see whether or not the postulated storage rooms contain more large, undecorated jars (known ethnographically as storage devices) than do the other rooms (Hill 1968). He checks this hypothesis using a gross pottery classification—"large-plainware-jars" versus "not-large-plainware-jars"—that can be applied with no reference to the standard Southwestern pottery types present at the site (St. Johns Polychrome, Tularosa Black-on-White, etc.).

Similarly, Deetz, in his study of Arikara ceramics, does not utilize traditional pottery types at all. He says, "Only attributes here designated as stylistic were chosen. For the present study, a stylistic attribute will be defined as one which results from a choice on the part of the manufacturer from a number of possibilities, made to produce a certain effect on the finished vessel" (Deetz 1965:46).

Deetz constructs a very detailed categorization scheme that—like Hill's gross pottery classification—is appropriate to his problem. He defines fifteen variables, such as surface finish (with such attributes as plain, brushed, simple stamped, etc.), profile (eighteen different vessel profiles are included), shoulder-neck angle (angular or curved), lip profile (square, pointed, braced, etc.), lip decoration technique (cord-impressed, tool-impressed, trailed, punctate, etc.).

Deetz uses more than 150 different attributes to type approximately 2,500 rim sherds from two sites. Analysis of the distributions of these attributes shows subtle differences in the styles characteristic of the various components represented by the sherd sample. Thus, Deetz, like Hill, finds traditional types unsuitable for his purposes and so devises an entirely new typology.

Another study demonstrating that typologies must be adjusted to problems is Wilmsen's pioneer work with Paleoindian flaked stone artifacts (1968). To study the functional variation and the probable uses of these artifacts, Wilmsen defines new types based on variables such as location of use, angle of edge, and direction of use marks. The resulting typology does not coincide with the traditional one, but by using it Wilmsen is able to make important generalizations concerning the functions of these artifacts.

Another example is Gunn's work with bifacially flaked stone tools from sites in the Great Basin (Gunn 1977). For purposes of his analysis, Gunn uses a classification of the scar patterns on these implements as delineated by laser diffraction. The different scar patterns are represented by histograms and are used by Gunn to define a typology for these bifacial tools that is quite different from any traditional chipped stone categorization scheme but that is appropriate to the problem.

These examples show how typologies are developed in response to specific problems and how the concept of relevant data is expanded. The same sherds can be used to determine basic cultural affiliations, particular craft specializations, intrasite social relationships, trade relationships, evidence for room function, and cooking group size.

Despite many examples such as the above of the relation between problems and typologies, Doran and Hodson (1975:101) argue that by avoiding redundancy of variables and using a little common sense one can establish a problem-independent attribute list definitive of any particular artifact category or type. While it is not completely clear how they reach this conclusion, it seems to stem from the idea that typology is merely description. They say, "It has been found in practice that a suitable descriptive level of item attributes has often been found" (1975:103). Much of their work is done with some form of numerical taxonomy, yet their concerns are primarily about cultural relationships. Therefore, while they present a number of techniques that are useful in certain situations, their general attempt to define absolute types seems misconceived.

TRADITIONAL TYPES VERSUS ANALYTIC TYPES

Given that one can formulate a wide variety of different types based on the same body of data depending on one's needs, why then do we continue to use highly standardized or traditional types? Hill and Evans (1972), along with some other archeologists, argue that the traditional types have very little utility. We take a middle-of-the-road position on this issue.

The vast majority of traditional types are probably real in the sense of being based on statistically significant attribute clusters, although many of them have not been tested. Traditional typologies that have been developed in places where very intensive work has been done are also likely to be more differentiated or subdivided than is necessary. Nevertheless, traditional types are usually based on attributes that many archeologists believe to be significant, and most of them probably are. For example, many traditional types have chronological significance. In general, they should be examined very carefully before being discarded.

On the other hand, to analyze one's data *only* in terms of traditional types would be to ignore some of the major advances in contemporary archeology. Site reports in which the ceramic analysis consists exclusively of frequency counts of standard Southwestern pottery types are inadequate. However, even if nothing else, traditional types are very useful as shorthand ways of indicating time and space distributions. A statement that a site or level contains St. Johns Polychrome, or Folsom points, or Acheulean hand-axes conveys a large amount of information very succinctly. As long as we realize that most traditional types have not been tested and that they do not represent all the cultural information that the assemblages carry, then they are useful.

Archeological Analysis

MULTIPLE VARIABLE ANALYSIS: LOG LINEAR METHODS FOR TESTING AND DISCOVERING TYPES

Our discussion about testing types is deliberately oversimplified. We discuss a situation in which only two variables, each with attributes, are considered. When there are more than two variables, the test is much more complicated than for the two-variable model. That is, the problem of testing a two-variable model is a special case of a more general problem.

The general problem is to determine whether or not the presence of a given variable is significantly related to the presence of other variables. How does one determine that a conjunction of attributes defines a real type? For example, a set of projectile points may be sorted according to these attributes: obsidian or other material, long or short, broken or complete. Suppose one of the resulting groups consists of obsidian, short, complete points. Is it a real type? Further analysis might show that the significant relation is not between obsidian and short but between short and complete because short points *regardless* of material are less likely to be broken than large points. This simple case illustrates the general problem. Discovering real associations is difficult and complicated. The most promising current method is the log linear technique (see Read 1974, and Dixon 1975). This technique is not yet used much in archeology so its potential and limitations cannot be evaluated. However, it is not logically different from the simple cases of type testing described here, and now that a "canned" program is available (Dixon 1975), log linear analysis may prove to be very useful.

It would appear that the log linear method is particularly well suited to the discovery of types. We can also look for types by entering numerous variables and attributes into a computer, and running hundreds of chi-squared tests on their possible relations. Unfortunately, this is an easy procedure to follow. "Unfortunately" because, although it is a good means to check for "missed" types, merely grinding out types without having some rationale for selecting variables and for suspecting that a particular combination of attributes is significant is of little utility. There are so many different variables that are relevant to any one question that great numbers of associations can be found. But a proliferation of types generated blindly is as likely to bury those most relevant to the problems at hand as to uncover them. And again, the discovery of a real type is not necessarily the discovery of a culturally significant relationship among attributes.

The use of log linear techniques seems to bridge the gap between monothetic and polythetic types and to provide insight into which variables are most important analytically. On the basis of this information we should be able to use some of the techniques discussed below to produce useful polythetic types as well as monothetic ones.

SUMMARY

Types are, have been, and will continue to be of great analytical importance in archeology. Certainly, however, not all or even most analysis needs to be done on the basis of types. Also, the use of traditional types as standard analytic units is not commensurate with the view that a data set contains a variety of information that can be extracted with a variety of different techniques. Nevertheless, traditional types do have important uses and should not be summarily dismissed. New analytical techniques in combination with well-developed problem orientations can revolutionize archeological typology.

Case Analysis

Case analysis is done on collections of cases and on individual cases. There must always be some independent criterion for grouping cases into collections, and sometimes the criterion is obvious. For example, the problem of determining whether room sizes in two pueblos are the same or not is posterior to the grouping of rooms into pueblos. This example is very simple, but it makes the point that some criteria are always present and necessary to establish a nonrandom collection. Statistical analysis (in this case the t test) can be carried out to determine whether or not the room size means for the two collections of rooms are significantly different. Similarly, we can ask about proportions between collections. Do the two pueblos have the

Archeological Analysis

same proportions of special function rooms? We can test for other kinds of differences between collections, such as comparison of standard deviations, and there are also techniques for making comparisons among more than two collections.

A special case of such comparisons is the determination of whether or not two sets of cases have the same distribution (for example, binominal, poisson, normal). It is often useful to compare a collection of observed cases with a theoretical set of cases. That is, one determines what a similar sized set of cases would be like if it had a poisson distribution, then compares this construct with the real data. Much of locational analysis, for example, consists of comparing collections of cases with theoretical distributions of one kind or another.

The above examples are of cases measured with interval scales. Similar comparisons can be made for collections of cases measured with ordinal and nominal scales, but because these scales elicit less information than do interval scales, the scope of the potential comparisons is somewhat narrower.

In this section we assume that some consistently applied criteria are used to sort cases into collections. Sometimes these criteria are very obvious, as in the case of pueblo rooms. Here the underlying assumption is that the pueblos themselves are different from each other. This is easy to check, but the criteria for differentiation of collections are usually more difficult to define or discern. For example, in defining a cultural boundary, we might have to test the hypothesis that two adjoining sites belong to two different collections. If no differences are found, we could conclude, for example, that (1) no cultural boundary exists (that is, the hypothesis is disconfirmed by the test), or (2) there is a boundary (perhaps we have independent evidence for this) but we have examined the wrong attributes for the cases, or (3) the two sites are really only one site. There are some techniques (such as discriminant function analysis) for determining whether cases have been correctly placed into categories once a sorting is completed. But we also need criteria for sorting cases into categories initially.

Individual case analysis is fairly common in archeological research. The search for patterning in individual cases is often a matter of looking for polythetic types. The situation is one in which there are few or no known criteria for sorting cases into collections in the first place. To find such criteria we begin by making pair-wise comparisons to assess the similarity between each possible pair of cases. Then, via a variety of techniques, this measure of similarity can be used to sort the original cases into groups or collections of cases. Alternatively, we can use the pair-wise comparison measures of similarity to order the cases in some manner without defining any groups or collections at all. This ordering procedure is usually called seriation.

The fundamental and initial step in individual case analysis is to make the initial pair-wise comparisons. This is done by defining or selecting some measure (coefficient) of association or similarity, which is then computed for each pair of cases. There are many different possible coefficients; which one is chosen depends on the kinds of variables used to describe the cases initially. These coefficients range from the generalized Euclidian distance measure for interval scales to coefficients for presence/absence (dichotomous nominal) data. See Sokal and Sneath (1963), and Doran and Hodson (1975) for a wide variety of possible indices. However, one may wish to develop a particular coefficient that is designed for a particular problem and a particular data set (see LeBlanc 1975).

In general, the role of coefficients in analysis is not well understood by archeologists. The use of different coefficients implies different assumptions about the data. One coefficient commonly employed by archeologists is the Brainerd-Robinson coefficient for frequency data. But other coefficients have been shown to work as well if not better on the same types of data (LeBlanc 1975).

The next step in case analysis is to put all the pair-wise comparisons into one big table called either a similarity matrix or a distance matrix. These two matrices are functionally equivalent, but a similarity matrix shows high values for cases that are most alike, and a distance matrix shows high values for cases that are most different.

Next, one tries to find some order or patterning in the matrix. The order found is, in part, determined by the order sought. One begins with a hypothesis about the order in the matrix. If we hypothesize and analyze for a linear order—that is, if we are not looking for clusters but wish to line the cases up into a linear similarity sequence—the result will be a seriation matrix. If, on the other hand, we hypothesize and analyze for clusters of cases, we can construct a tree diagram that summarizes relationships among the cases (one way of constructing such a diagram is by using "canned" computerized clustering programs such as those in the BMDP series [Dixon 1975] or SAS [Barr et al. 1979]). One can also make a plot in which the distances between the points on the plot represent the degrees of differences exhibited among the cases. This technique, called multidimensional scaling, requires the user to bound the clusters. A third method that is appropriate to some kinds of data is to use a factor analysis to generate factor scores. One then plots these scores to find clusters. As Cowgill (1968) and LeBlanc (1975) point out, although factor analysis and cluster analysis are based on different assumptions, they often give extremely similar results.

This approach amounts to testing hypotheses about the data. Carrying out a seriation, for example, means looking for a noncluster solution, regardless of the presence or absence of clusters in these data. As is the case with sampling, one cannot operate without at least an implicit hypothesis; one does not go on a presuppositionless search for patterning, and the method chosen prefigures the kinds of results obtained. Only certain kinds of outcomes are possible from each method. Furthermore, any *particular* hypothesis being tested by a cluster or seriation procedure is not necessarily the ultimate one to be investigated. For example, one may be seriating ceramics merely to help develop a chronology so that one can look at social organizational changes over time.

All these preliminary steps are part of the test of the main hypothesis that determines the coefficients or ordering methods to be used. Derived clusters are then used to test the main hypothesis. This is difficult because there are usually no confidence estimates to indicate how likely it is that the clusters are real. Thus, it is hard to judge how well the clusters fit those of the hypothesis.

In the light of the above discussion, consider again the typing of cases. The relationship among cases in a collection can be determined as above. All cases having a pattern of attributes as defined by a collective relationship are in the same class or category. If we find that wide lines and black paint are two attributes that tend to co-occur, then we put pots having such attributes into the same group.

The problem with this approach is that when we have more than two variables we often find that, although the attributes tend to co-occur, not all cases in a group have the same attributes. The resulting groups are real, but not all the cases within a group are exactly the same. Such groups are polythetic. A monothetic type is a special form of case clustering. In a polythetic *cluster of cases,* the cases are highly similar to each other but not necessarily identical; a monothetic *type* is the special situation when all the cases in a cluster are exactly the same for the variable under investigation. As the number of variables being considered increases, it becomes more and more difficult to find situations where any significant number of cases are exactly the same. In these situations case clusters or polythetic types are more common than monothetic types.

There is no difference between case and variable analysis in practice. This is largely because the values of pair-wise coefficients for individual cases are determined by the variables we chose. To the extent that these variables measure random noise, or are redundant, they adversely affect the similarity coefficients for pairs of individual cases. This is the primary disadvantage in using numerical taxonomy. A basic tenet of numerical taxonomy is that all variables are equally significant, but our search is for unequally relevant variables. One way to proceed is to do some variable analysis first, then on the basis of those results pick a subset of the original variables for analysis with the similarity coefficient. Methods such as factor analysis or multidimensional scaling are well suited to the task of preliminary variable analysis.

We sometimes need a rule or equation that shows how cases known to belong to particular groups can be separated by a given set of variables. For example, given five variables, how can we find a rule that will separate the cases into two groups known to be present? Discriminant function analysis can be used to do this. An equation or discriminant function can be developed so that, when new cases arise and we do not know to which group they belong, we can use the function to place them into the proper one. For example, if height and weight are used as variables, we can sort out collections of pygmies and Swedes. Not all collections can be sorted so easily, however. For instance, using height and weight we could not separate males from females so easily as Swedes from pygmies. Discriminant function analysis tells us how well the variables we have chosen actually separate the cases of one known collection from the cases of another known collection. The hypothesis is, "These variables will separate the cases into the known groups." A negative result may mean only that the wrong variables are being used as separation critieria. Unfortunately, discriminant function analysis requires interval data, and there are no common or well-known techniques for using this analysis on ordinal or nominal data.

Multidimensional Scaling (Proximity Analysis) and Factor and Cluster Analysis

These are generalized methods, each of which comprises numerous techniques of variable and case analysis. Each of the three methods can be used either for variables or for cases. Again, when they are used for case analysis, then one is often searching for polythetic types. As noted above, cluster analysis and multidimensional scaling (the latter is sometimes referred to as proximity analysis) are based on matrices of similarity coefficients. Thus, similarity coefficients derived from pair-wise comparisons of individual cases, like the Brainerd-Robinson coefficient, can constitute the basic information analyzed by these methods. However, the correlation coefficient r is also a kind of similarity coefficient. When the absolute value of r is high, the two variables are measuring closely related phenomena; when it is near zero, the measured phenomena are not so closely related. Thus, the correlation matrix (all possible pairs of r's for a set of variables) and the Brainerd-Robinson similarity matrix provide the same kinds of results insofar as multidimensional scaling and cluster analysis are concerned, and either may be used. Under the right conditions, this is also true for factor analysis, which can be used to find relationships among cases as well as among variables. Each of these methods is considered separately below. However, because a good discussion of them is already available (Cowgill 1968), only a few salient points need to be made here.

Factor Analysis

Factor analysis is a means of reducing a large number of variables to a smaller set of new variables (the factors) that carry essentially the same information but in a simpler or more interpretable manner. Factor analysis is used on interval data and is a means of finding the patterning that exists in a correlation matrix. In carrying out a factor analysis, we are assuming that a smaller set of variables, the factors, exists because several of the original variables are probably measuring the same phenomena, or because some variables are recording the effects of several different underlying phenomena at the same time. Expressing these facts with a small set of new variables—factors—enables one to simplify the representation of the empirical situation.

We give an example below to illustrate how a factor analysis may lead to insights that would not otherwise be obvious. We do this to demonstrate the use of factor analysis and also to show that mathematical techniques can produce information not otherwise discernible even when one is extremely familiar with the data. The moral is that, although mathematical analyses must be evaluated and interpreted, they are often the only way to find the patterning in a set of data.

The use of factor analysis to delineate tool kits from descriptive data on paleolithic flints provdes our example. (For a published account of a pioneer archeological use of this technique, see Binford and Binford 1966). Imagine five archeological floors, each one resulting from numerous activities being performed on it. Suppose further that a total of three different activities was carried out on these floors, each with a tool kit containing two types of tools. However, floor A may have been used five times for activity I, three times for activity II, and only once for activity III, and we would expect that these activities would be carried out in still different frequencies on each of the other floors. Furthermore, suppose that the tools were abandoned randomly on the floors (the worst of all possible situations, and, fortunately, not likely in reality). In such a situation one piece of tool kit I may lie next to tools belonging to kit III, and so on.

At first glance there appears to be no hope of ever discovering what

Archeological Analysis

tools originally belonged to which tool kit. If, however, we can assume that, for each activity, tools were discarded in constant ratios (we do not need to know what the ratios were), then we can extract information about the original composition of the tool kits. That is, for activity I we assume that tools I_1 and I_2 were abandoned in a fixed proportion to each other, etc.

Suppose data are collected as in table 5.8.

Notice that tools I_1 and I_2 occur in the ratio 1:2; tools II_1 and II_2 in the ratio 3:1; and tools III_1 and III_2 in the ratio 3:2. Thus, if one knows the count for one tool type of each pair, one can determine the counts for the other pair. This is equivalent to having a correlation coefficient of $r = 1$ between tool types I_1 and I_2, between II_1 and II_2, etc. Notice that one cannot use the numbers of tools in I_1 to predict much about tools in II_1, II_2, III_1, or III_2; hence, the correlations between tools of different kits are very low. Factor analysis using the correlation coefficients from these data would sort them into three groups or factors. Each factor would show the tools from one of the three kits.

If one tool were used in all three kits, the factor analysis would show this as well. This tool would be included in each factor and thus would be recognized as belonging to each kit. In reality, we would not expect the proportions between tool types to be perfect, and factor analysis does not, in fact, require perfect correlations. The point of this discussion is to show that by using factor analysis one can find patterns that are not apparent even from close inspection. It certainly is not obvious that one can determine the composition of the tool kits from tools randomly abandoned on floors.

Table 5.8.
Quantities of Tools in Each Tool Kit as Distributed on the Five Floors

Floor	Tool Kit					
	I_1	I_2	II_1	II_2	III_1	III_2
A	5	10	15	5	6	4
B	6	12	30	10	24	16
C	10	20	12	4	6	4
D	15	30	6	2	30	20
E	9	18	21	7	9	6

There are many other types of problems to which factor analysis is appropriate. However, the isolation of groups by means of factor analysis does not tell us what the groups represent. Interpretation of the factors is necessary. If all the tools in the example were used for the same task but there were changes in tool types over time, then we would still be able to find factors, but they would not represent different tool kits.

Besides this difficulty of interpreting factors, there is also the problem that factor solutions are not unique. A process called "rotation" is used to modify solutions, and different rotations produce somewhat different solutions. Different rotations are based on different assumptions about the data. For example, one can assume that the underlying factors that really account for the observed correlations in the original data are independent of one another. In graphical terms, this means that the factors would be graphed at right angles to one another, and hence they are called orthogonal factors. This kind of rotation is then an orthogonal rotation. The factors produced by an orthogonal rotation are usually quite different from those produced by other kinds of rotations. There is a tendency in many of the social sciences to use only orthogonal rotations. However, archeological research designs do not necessarily require one to assume independent factors, and thus it is not necessary to use orthogonal rotations exclusively. Research designs including possibly related factors are also feasible, and nonorthogonal rotations would be required in these cases. Because there are computer programs that permit either type of rotation (as well as variations not considered here), there is no a priori reason to use one type of rotation rather than another.

The kind of rotation used should be justified on the basis of the data being analyzed and the question being asked. Even after rotation, one must still interpret the factors and decide just what effects or causes they represent. In general, deciding what factors really measure is logically on the level of hypothesis formulation, and the explanation of the factors cannot be based solely on factor analysis. Instead, these explanations, like other hypotheses, must be tested by independent means. It is equally possible that, having already formulated a hypothesis, one could employ factor analysis as one means of testing this hypothesis.

Cluster Analysis and Multidimensional Scaling

Cluster analysis has an advantage over factor analysis in that it uses as input a similarity matrix, and as we have seen, such matrices can be constructed for ordinal and nominal data as well as for interval data. Cluster analysis generally puts cases (or variables) into hierarchical groups. There are a great number of computer programs for this because there are a great number of criteria for assigning cases to groups. In any clustering you must have a rule for adding cases to clusters and for deciding which additional clusters should be formed. Many programs such as the BMDP series offer various options, so it is easy to make different clusterings with different rules and then to compare the results.

An alternative to the use of clustering to form trees is to use techniques generally called proximity analysis, small space analysis, or multidimensional scaling. In this type of analysis the input is also a similarity matrix, but the analysis is quite different from clustering. In particular, the absolute size of the similarity coefficients is ignored, and the only information used is whether one similarity coefficient is larger or smaller than another (that is, the coefficients are treated as ordinal measures). This procedure is particularly well adapted to use by archeologists because it is usually unrealistic to assume that the coefficients in archeological similarity matrices really represent interval data. The outputs from multidimensional scaling programs are plots with distances between points on each plot representing degrees of difference between cases. A one-dimensional plot shows the cases on a line, that is, it is a seriation of the cases.

It should be obvious that these techniques are extremely useful for individual case analyses of large numbers of cases. The results of factor analysis, as well as those of cluster analysis and proximity analysis, can be used to generate hypotheses and also to test implications. In these cases we must be sure that the assumptions used in making the analyses are coordinate with the assumptions used in inferring implications from the hypothesis being tested.

Locational Analysis

One of these hypothesis-testing techniques is locational analysis. Many of the techniques and approaches to locational or spatial analysis are discussed by Hodder and Orton (1976; see also Smith 1976; and Fox and Smith 1982). Only a few brief points need to be made here. Basically, locational techniques involve comparing distributions of artifacts, sites, or other phenomena with theoretical distributions. These theoretical distributions can be probability distributions, such as poisson or binomial, or specially derived distributions, such as nearest neighbor coefficients or node frequencies. In some cases counts of artifacts or sites per grid unit are compared with expected counts. In these cases, spatial analysis is no different logically from comparing collections of cases as described above. A hypothesis that indicates a particular distribution is compared with the actual data. Here spatial analysis is different from testing for a normal distribution of projectile point lengths only in that the hypothesis concerns the locations of artifacts or features rather than their morphological characteristics.

In other forms of locational analysis, models based on locational theory and previous study are used to compare size and distribution of sites (or other phenomena). Depending on what is believed about site function (market center, frontier post, religious center, etc.), we expect different patterns of spacing, site size, and so on. In these situations we test for conformity, not to mathematical distributions, but to spatial patterns. It is often difficult to determine the degree of fit between the observed patterns and the hypothetical spatial patterns. Moreover, because the theoretical patterns are not probability distributions that can be computed in the abstract, locational patterns are evaluated by comparison with examples where actual relationships between type of site organization and site distributions are thought to be known. However, if actual relations do not fit the predicted distribution, it may be because the model (the theoretical distribution) is faulty. In particular, there is little reason to assume that there can be only one kind of spatial pattern for any given kind of organization; functional equivalents may exist. In effect the law-like generalizations used to explain particular distributions here are

Archeological Analysis 225

not very well confirmed. Hence, there is a reasonable degree of uncertainty involved in using them to explain particular cases or to derive hypotheses for testing. Obviously, however, archeologists constantly pose spatial questions about materials, from artifacts on a floor to sites in a region, so we are compelled to improve and to expand our ability to work with spatial distributions.

Computers and Archeology

Computers facilitate the application of all analytic techniques. They permit the use of highly sophisticated analyses on large bodies of many kinds of data. Hence, the use of computers is very important in archeology.

Computers can be used to help with at least four kinds of archeological tasks: (1) data storage and retrieval; (2) statistical and other analyses; (3) simulations; and (4) graphics. (This does not imply that there are no additional, specific tasks for which the computer is helpful; see Doran 1972 for other examples.)

Computers are indispensible for storage and retrieval of archeological data, although computerization of museum collections has progressed more rapidly than that of field data. Computerized methods can be used not only to store quantities of data but also to organize and retrieve particular data sets. Card indices are always limited to a few categories, but computerized data can be indexed for virtually unlimited kinds and quantities of categories. A museum collection can be computerized so that requests like "Produce a list of all obsidian points four centimeters long or longer" result in printed lists that include museum location for each item along with any other information asked for such as the name of the site where the point was found and the date it was collected. The utility of computerized data storage and retrieval is obviously great.

How computers can be used for archeological field data is far less clear. Several directors of excavation projects (for example, Irwin-Williams et al. 1975; Gaines 1974) have used computer hookups in the field. They have been able to send data via telephone to university computers and receive immediate data summaries and results of analytic programs. These field computer systems are still in the early stages of development. With today's mini minicomputers, some of their mechanical problems can be eliminated. However, the greatest problems do not center around hardware.

One problem is how to record the data fed into the computer from the field. If field recording forms are carefully designed, they can be directly transcribed into computer storage, but such forms require much standardization. Each category of data or data type that is to be recorded must be determined in advance of excavation, which means that the attributes defining each category must be established. Once this is done, various schemes can be used to code the data. Numeric codes for each attribute can be employed (for example, 1 = sandy clay, 2 = clayey sand), or strict technical vocabularies can be established for describing the data. But once coding techniques are worked out, the problem arises of fieldworkers feeling that they are restricted to answering a series of cut-and-dried questions and that they are thus not required to interpret what they find. Thus, much of the expertise and firsthand knowledge possessed by and gained on the dig by the actual excavators may be lost when rigid recording schemes are used.

Field computerization does require that raw data be recorded in computer compatible form. But if this is done, one should also require a detailed synthesis and interpretation of each excavation unit by the actual excavators. The raw data can be used to check these interpretations and to discover additional patterns not recognized by the excavators.

Adequate computerized analyses cannot be carried out on the basis of excavation notes alone. Detailed artifactual and bio-environmental data must be computerized as well. The time required to code these data is much greater than that required for excavation. For example, it took three hundred person-days to sort out and record just the lithic material from a survey recently completed by one of us (LeBlanc). The survey itself took only four hundred person-days, with three more person-days required to key punch the coded data into the computer. That is, analysis of the lithic material alone required nearly as much time as did the entire survey.

Another problem is that until representative collections are available—in other words, until the analysis is partially completed—it is

Archeological Analysis   227

impossible to choose variables and attributes. Then when they are chosen, computerized procedures tend to freeze recording categories at an early stage in the research. Field computerization thus tends to inhibit or destroy innovation at other levels.

Directors of long-term projects for which several field and analytical cycles have been completed may be in a position to use some computerized analysis concurrently with excavation, but at present the potential of a significant return from field computerization is low in relationship to its cost. Actual site reports by means of which one can evaluate results of field computerization are necessary. The computerization of field data after excavation is very useful, however, and here significant progress is being made.

Computers and Analysis

The use of computers for data manipulation and statistical analysis is far better developed than are their capacities for storage of raw archeological data. A wide range of programs is readily available and extremely easy to use. Of these "canned programs" or "statistical packages," three of the most common are the BMD series (especially useful is the BMDP series, Dixon 1975), Statistical Analysis System (SAS, Barr, Goodright, and Sall 1979), and the Statistical Package for the Social Sciences (SPSS, Nie et al. 1975). Of these packages SAS is the most versatile in handling data storage, retrieval, and reorganization; and SAS and the BMDP series programs are compatible. Use of these packages requires very little knowledge of computers, and results can be obtained with a few hours of effort. Expenses are low; today (1982) a factor analysis often costs less than a dollar. The main effort required to use these programs is coding and punching the raw data onto cards, although for data sets of only a few hundred cases this is no more than a few hours' work.

One problem with canned programs is that they are so cheap and easy to use that one can ask for far more analysis than one needs or can assimilate, so that one is swamped with results. Moreover, one's use of such programs is no better than one's understanding of the analytic and statistical techniques employed in them.

Besides these sets of programs, there are seriation and multidimensional scaling programs. These are not so widely available as the statistical packages, and often their use requires some computer expertise.

Computers can also be used for simulations. We discuss the role of simulation in hypothesis formulation and testing in chapter 2. The computerization of complex simulations requires that one be able to use a programming language. This is not generally true for other uses of computers, although the ability to write programs in such compiler languages as FORTRAN, for example, is convenient and useful for doing all kinds of computer work in almost all areas of computer application. Nevertheless, archeologists who have no knowledge of computer languages can still use many standard programs.

Using Analytical Techniques in Archeology

Hypotheses must be constructed in such a way that they can be tested by data and measurements that can be collected and taken in practical and standardized ways. Both research materials and recorded data should be considered to be open to new examinations and to a variety of codifications. No analysis or codification or interpretation should be considered final or complete. Survey and excavation data are rather viewed as a reservoir of information to be tapped as needed in response to research on specific problems. A detailed example follows.

How should one conceptualize a body of data consisting of painted pottery? One can ask, What are the basic design types? What do the motifs mean? Is some of the pottery more complex or better made than the rest? And so on. These questions can be framed as hypotheses, and then the analyses required to test them, or to answer the original questions, may necessitate procedures quite different from traditional ceramic analyses. First, terms must be defined so that measurements can be taken on the artifacts. How does one define *complexity* and *motif*, for example? Then if the traits in question can be measured straightforwardly, one can define types, motifs, or complex pottery designs according to obvious criteria. However, another worker might well define different but equally obvious types, motifs, and complex pottery designs. Thus, standardization is desirable both for communication and for comparative analysis.

Now suppose we are considering hypotheses not just about pottery types or motifs but about how they reflect cultural change. Suppose we ask, Does complexity increase with time? Or, Do certain vessel forms and motifs indicate status? These new questions require new conceptualizations or definitions of *complexity* and *motif* that impose new requirements on data needed to answer the questions.

New questions usually derive from implications of the original hypotheses. For example, *hypothesis:* Craft specialization increases with time. *Implication:* Complexity of painted designs increases with time. To test these hypotheses, one must collect and categorize appropriate data.

Now *complexity* or *motif* can be defined with explicit reference to the purpose of the data being collected.

The same general criteria apply here as do in defining variables and attributes. Definitions must lead to reproducible results. Definitions must describe attributes that show sufficient variability in the sample to be treated statistically. A direct use of such definitions in testing hypotheses is to ask, Do the data defined in this way exhibit any patterns (either obvious to inspection or elicited by analysis)? If not, we can conclude for our example that (1) there was no increase in complexity, that is, we reject the prediction inferred from the original hypothesis and thus have so far disconfirmed that hypothesis; or (2) the definition of complexity was inadequate. Then we could try again with another definition. In this way we make progress one way or another. Either we confirm or disconfirm an hypothesis or we reject a definition. In this situation definitions are evaluated by their results. If a definition is useful, then it is a good definition; if it is not useful, it is a bad definition for our purposes.

We stress that—as always—archeologists must rely on their basic archeological knowledge and expertise in constructing good definitions in the first place. Workers familiar with given data are often able to construct definitions that have high probabilities of being good (useful) ones.

Complexity can be defined in many ways. We could, for example, count the number of motifs per vessel, count the number of individual paint strokes per vessel, or measure the proportion of the vessel covered by paint. Each of these definitions of complexity makes interval scale measurements possible. While some of these measurements, such as motif count, would be relatively simple to make, others—such as the proportion of the vessel covered by paint—might be difficult and thus expensive to measure. These measures could also be reduced to oridinal scales or to dichotomous nominal scales.

These various measures of complexity are obviously useful or not depending on the pottery in question. Pottery made by people who use only a few motifs would not be complex if complexity is defined as a large number of motifs. But this pottery might be very complex in terms of number of different motif combinations. (Think, for example, of the variety of patterns possible with the use of only twenty-six different motifs.) As to proportion of pot covered with paint, those pots covered with a few, very broad bands of paint would generally not be considered complex even though the paint covers most of the vessel. Obviously, the definition of complexity must be appropriate to the nature of the material being studied.

For most samples of pottery one should be able to derive some workable definitions of complexity such that measurements can be made for either variable or case analysis. For variable analysis, we might investigate the relationship between complexity and time. We could use these same measurements to determine how homogeneous the design system is (that is, how similar the pots are to one another) and also to do case analysis.

In doing case analysis, we need to formulate a hypothesis that relates the case clusters as found to some other phenomenon, say, spatial distribution, of the pottery in question. For example, we might pose the hypothesis that the cases tend to cluster by valley but not by sites within valleys. A problem, question, or hypothesis is always necessary for determining which of the patterns that result from clustering the cases are significant. Merely clustering pots is not enough; a cluster—like factors in a factor analysis—must be interpreted. An explicitly stated problem or hypothesis is the first step in interpretation. Analysis of cases is the means both of relating problem or hypothesis to interpretation and of collecting the data to solve the problem or to test the hypothesis to further the interpretation.

Archeological Analysis 231

If complexity shows no correlation with time, then the specific hypothesis, Complexity *as defined by our measurement* increases with time, is so far disconfirmed. This does not mean that complexity as defined by some other measure does not increase with time. Similarly, if pottery types as defined do not cluster by valley, pottery types differently defined might be found to do so.

Similar comments might be made about definitions of design motifs and questions about their distribution, correlation, and so on. We would probably define these motifs on a nominal scale. That is, we would make up rules to place each design in one and only one motif category. The result would be a useful analytic variable. However, this procedure is believed by some archeologists to be arbitrary and capricious. For example, motifs may be overdifferentiated, that is, we may subdivide motifs that the makers conceived of as single motifs. In one sense, of course, our definitions are arbitrary, but they are not capricious. This procedure is in no way different from selecting attributes with which to define types. In each case we use our best archeological knowledge to select either the motifs or the attributes. We have no sure way of knowing whether our criteria are the same as past mental templates. But our purposes are not necessarily the same as those of the people of the past. We may want to learn what they thought, as far as is possible, but our criterion of "correctness" of definitions is their usefulness for our analytical purposes. If the motifs, as defined, show a pattern that is not random, then we have found something potentially useful. Other definitions of the motifs may show other useful patterns, and some may be the definitions the makers had in their minds.

Conclusion

In conclusion, we stress once more that there is a close relationship between the epistemological issues presented in chapter 1 and the actual doing of archeology. The concept of a research design and what it comprises as discussed in this chapter derives directly from chapter 1.

We make two points concerning analytical techniques and sampling. First, the more you know about your data, the more sophisticated and useful you can make your analyses. These techniques are very powerful and are potentially very productive for archeologists, but they are no better than the data they are used upon. The quality and usefulness of data depend on choices made by archeologists. But data and analytical results are not in themselves interpretations. Interpretation and understanding cannot be provided by data, analyses, or computers, but only by archeologists.

The second point is that the concepts of scales, variables, statistical significance, and so on presented here are employed by all who perform analyses whether they know it or not. When one compares artifacts in the most informal way one is measuring them on implicit scales and is implicitly computing similarity coefficients. Whether one does this by computer, with paper and pencil, or in one's head, the logical procedure is the same.

We do not think that analytical methods and techniques should become the main concerns of archeologists any more than we think one must use computers to do "scientific" analysis. However, scientific archeology cannot be done explicitly without some understanding of the basic principles of research design, hypothesis formulation and testing, data definition and collection, problem solving, and analysis.

CHAPTER SIX
Archeology and Society: Problems and Prospects

We have examined the foundations of scientific archeology as well as the theoretical framework and methods of excavation, analysis, and interpretation. In this concluding chapter we consider a series of topics arising from the relationship of archeology to modern society in the United States. We restrict our specific remarks to the United States because the majority of our combined experience as to academic training in archeology, publication in archeology, and long-term institutional support for archeology has been in the United States. We begin with a discussion of the reporting and publication of archeological data, and we pay particular attention to the problems that archeologists face (and must resolve) in these areas. Then, after consideration of the most pressing practical issues confronting professional archeologists in the United States at the present time—site preservation and contract archeology—we conclude with discussions of archeology conceived as social science and of the aims of archeology.

Publication of Archeological Reports

The widespread acceptance of regional, long-term, interdisciplinary projects as the norm for archeological research has created a series of difficult problems for the directors of such projects (see chapter 3), not least of which is that of publication. What format is best for publication of archeological reports has long been a matter of concern and discussion among archeologists, and recent research trends have much complicated previous difficulties.

Anyone setting out to publish the results of even a limited investigation must make basic decisions about how much emphasis is to be placed on the various components of the study: the goals or objectives of the work, the methods used, the basic data recovered by means of those methods, and the interpretation of the results. Now that all archeology is, to a greater or lesser degree, interdisciplinary or multidisciplinary, problems of balance in organizing the publication are much more complex than formerly. For example, not only must archeologists decide whether and how much of the raw artifactual and architectural data to publish, but also they must make this decision for all the data categories treated by all the collaborators. And, of course, whatever decisions are reached in those matters necessitate many others with respect to graphic and tabular material.

It is in the publication process that all the weaknesses and failings of any interdisciplinary project are most clearly demonstrated. These weaknesses usually stem from the communication problems referred to in chapter 3 and range from total default by one or more participants, through procrastination by one or several participants, to the submission of borderline or even unacceptable manuscripts. There is, or course, no quick or easy remedy for any of these personnel difficulties. The coordinators of even a relatively small interdisciplinary project must simply be prepared to face and to cope with such eventualities—for some or all of them will certainly occur—and to handle them on an individual, person-to-person basis. There is undoubtedly much truth in the statement that a successful archeologist must be as skilled in interpersonal relationships as he or she is in using a trowel or in analyzing potsherds.

However, there are some useful observations that can be made about other aspects of archeological publication. These center upon time lag and format (nature and content) of reports.

As well as interacting with and coordinating the varied personnel of an interdisciplinary project, directors of modern archeological investigations must publish a comprehensive report reasonably soon after completion of basic fieldwork and analyses. Unless the work is done on a contract budget and schedule—as a great deal of it is at present—it will take several years to obtain the most vital analytical results, integrate them, write them up, and publish them. In academic or "ivory tower" archeology, one must contend with varying work schedules imposed by the varying institutions where project participants are employed and with the vagaries of part-time (sometimes bootlegged) commitment to project goals. Not even a relatively generous NSF, NEH, or other foundation grant can pay for all of the time, expertise, and facilities required to carry out and publish a limited, modern archeological study, let alone a large, long-term one. Hence, a great deal of the work must be done on a volunteer basis, so strong sanctions are not easy to apply.

Contracted archeological research, on the other hand, must be promptly written up, and this is usually possible because of the negotiated budget and other explicit contract arrangements. However, the final report on contracted archeological work, prompt though it may be, is likely to be reproduced in only a few dozen copies and to be entombed quickly in corporation or agency files, remote from the usual professional publishing outlets (Schiffer and Gumerman 1977:xxi, 14). Some of this information is available though the National Technical Information Service (NTIS) and the new journal *American Archaeology* (formerly *Contract Abstracts and CRM Archaeology*). Schiffer and Gumerman (1977:14–15) and Dunnell (1982a:512–514) describe other procedures for facilitating access to this material, but obscurity and inaccessibility are still a common fate for a great many contract reports.

Contract archeology gives rise to another serious publication problem. These contract archeological reports contain immense quantities of data now accumulating every year in every one of the United States. Even were all these thousands of reports centrally stored and indexed instead of buried in obscure files, it would be an immense task to read and synthesize the information they contain on just one or two narrow topics. We are faced here with a crushing problem of information overload that may take decades to solve.

Another major problem for all archeologists is to decide what form of archeological report to use. Although basic content is usually clearly stipulated by the contracting agency, this difficulty is as severe for contract archeologists as for academic archeologists because contractors must reconcile a modern, problem-oriented research strategy with the requirements of the contracting agency, knowing that the agency will pay for—and wants to hear about—only that research most relevant to its activities. We do not discuss the situation of contract archeology further here because we take up some aspects of that topic in the next section and because there are several thoughtful and detailed discussions readily available (Dunnell 1982a; McGimsey and Davis 1977; Schiffer and Gumerman 1977; South 1977: ch. 9).

In presenting the results of a relatively complex, moderately long-term, interdisciplinary archeological project, should the aim be to publish large quantities of detailed description and primary data, or should the stress be on interpretation of these data? There are two extremes. On the one hand some reports emphasize description, detail, and measurements, with only a small percentage of the report given to interpretation of the materials described. On the other hand, a number of large, long-term projects have resulted in no overall reports at all. Instead, dissertations, theses, and papers have been focused on particular aspects of the work with book publication consisting mainly of collected papers—often the results of seminars or symposia—that emphasize results and problem orientation. But there is usually no integrated or unified corpus of primary, detailed information with which to evaluate the interpretations given. Achieving some balance between these two emphases is crucial for all archeologists.

However, there is a concern that goes beyond that of reporting for other professionals. As archeologists, we do not have the luxury of working and writing only for one another. It is also our responsibility to keep the general public informed of our results. Even researchers in the most esoteric branches of the natural sciences are occasionally required to justify their research in terms intelligible to interested laymen if they are to continue to get the large government grants vital to their work. Conveying the significance of archeological research results to the public has always been important, but is now crucial for a number of reasons:

Archeology and Society 237

    1. To obtain funding of modern, intensive, interdisciplinary research, because such funding is regularly available only from U.S. government agencies and these funds are not administered by archeologists. They are administered by U.S. government officials who are not ordinarily trained in archeology.
    2. To ensure that the level of government funding (NSF and NEH) for archeological research remains at a viable level. This means convincing the voting citizens of the United States and their congressional representatives that archeology is a good investment for U.S. tax money.
    3. To combat the appalling amount of casual vandalism of archeological sites by private citizens who are ignorant of the historical and cultural significance, fragility, and irreplaceability of archeological remains.

Thus, archeologists must perform two very different tasks in the publication of their research results. One is to convey new information to their peers as efficiently and comprehensively as possible; the other is to participate as effectively as possible in a public relations campaign to achieve the goals listed above. We do not believe that a single published document can satisfactorily fulfill both those functions. As an illustrative example, we consider briefly a report published by one of us, *Archeology of the Mammoth Cave Area* (Watson ed. 1974). A fellow archeologist and specialist in the same geographic and problem area said:

> One finds in this book a valuable catalog of data relevant to the cave and its environs which is both descriptive and comparative, and which makes important theoretical and methodological contributions.
>   The methodological contributions are particularly noteworthy. Most of the analysts have carefully outlined their specific approaches to the material remains, ranging from procedures for reconstituting paleofecal specimens to a valuable appendix in which various methodological (interpretive) difficulties encountered here in dealing with such material are specified and suggestions offered for obtaining meaningful and comparable analytical results.
>   This book is highly recommended for anyone interested in the aboriginal occupation and utilization of Midwestern caves as well as for those whose interest lies in the way in which archeological problems of subsistence, seasonality, and paleoecology can be approached in a multidisciplinary frame of reference. (Vickery 1976:937-938)

Whereas a reviewer who is not an archeologist but who is an intelligent, adult U.S. citizen and a caver said:

> This technical work has thirty-one chapters by various specialists and the editor, who wrote over half of them. The nonspecialist, even among archeologists, will not be interested in a lot of it, and cavers will be impressed chiefly by the lengths modern archeologists go to in pursuing their hobby (as it must be called, even though they get paid for it); six and a half chapters and the appendix are devoted to detailed analyses of paleofeces, which are just what the name suggests. . . . . Quite a bit of space is taken up by the obligatory for-the-record type of tables which will be of interest to exactly no one. . . . . A valuable work, one must assume. But at least three-quarters of the material in it will really be of interest to at most twenty-five people in the entire world. The only motivation for publishing all the details in book form must be to rip off libraries and other suckers (like me) who will buy anything. They belong in journal articles, and one suspects that most of them *have* been in articles. But the caver with a knack for browsing can glean some interesting information (the Indians practiced at least occasional cannibalism and how Little Alice became Little Al without a trip to Sweden) without getting too bogged down in the turds. (Mixon 1975)

As a matter of fact—as illustrated by the example below—a single professional report on a discrete piece of archeological research will probably not satisfy even the small circle of one's closest archeological peers. P.E.L. Smith reviewed an important and detailed archeological report by Frank Hole, Kent Flannery, and James Neely (1969) as follows:

> This book calls for a split-level review: as the exposition of an archeological approach with its subsequent hypotheses, and as a descriptive excavation report. It is a pity that in the process of illustrating how productive and stimulating an ecological approach can be in archeology the authors have written a rather less than satisfactory excavation report. Indeed, the defects shown here raise some important questions concerning archeological technique, theory, and strategy. The real trouble is that the report fails to present all the information one expects to find in a modern and final description of several important sites. Researchers who wish to consult it for certain kinds of information, or from viewpoints somewhat different from those the authors have considered important will find the work unnecessarily difficult or even impossible. (Smith 1970:708)

Smith approves of the theoretical orientation of the Hole, Flannery, and Neely report but, from his own point of view, finds definite shortcomings in it:

> Since archeologists must rely on very detailed descriptions and presentations of all the data observed which enter into the investigator's interpretations, it is necessary for final reports to be as exhaustive as is humanly possible. A colleague who has read this book argues that its defects are inherent in research which is oriented to a single approach. I don't agree with him. Much in this book is good, and the weaknesses were avoidable. (Smith 1970:708, 709)

Although we do not think the report that Hole, Flannery, and Neely have produced is as far from the standard of total publication as Smith does, we can use this example to make the following point: The Hole, Flannery, and Neely position fits that described here (chapter 4) in our discussion of relevant data, but—as Smith indicates—it does not produce results entirely satisfactory to archeologists with interests that differ from those of the investigators and who make different demands on the archeological record. On the other hand, a report full of detail describing artifactual categories traditionally believed to be of significance for comparative purposes is not entirely satisfactory to the needs and interests of problem-oriented archeologists, who may require information that is not even recognized as data by the excavator and hence is not recorded and published.

We suggest that all archeologists will soon be obligated to report their results in several different formats. A few workers have done this for some time, but it seems clear that in the near future every archeologist will have to employ systematically a carefully selected melange of publication outlets. There are at least three reasons why a multilevel publication strategy is essential:

First, comprehensive, detailed accounts of procedures, descriptions of techniques and equipment used, all data tables, and so on necessary for evaluating the interpretations must be accessible to the readers of the final report who are specialists in the topic and area being investigated. Traditionally, these data all appeared in book, or sometimes journal form, but this format is becoming so cumbersome and expensive that it cannot survive much longer. Microfiche recording of these detailed data is a currently feasible alternative, and some archeological materials have already been published in this way, beginning in the 1960s, when a microfiche "Archives of Archaeology" was begun (but did not survive). An entire report can be produced on microfiche, or the microcards can be used to carry detailed data tables, charts, or catalogs, much reducing the size of the printed text and the cost of the entire array of materials. Some archaeologists working in parts of the world remote from libraries carry their own basic reference libraries with them on microfiches. At least a few publishing outlets—British Archaeological Reports, HRAF Inc., and the UCLA Institute of Archaeology—are experimenting with inexpensive formats for data-heavy manuscripts.

Second, the major interpretative results must be widely accessible, not only to specialists and colleagues, but also to the general public.

This accessibility problem is solved by sending general articles to nonspecialist journals with nationwide circulation (such as *American Anthropologist, Archaeology,* and *Science*), to regional journals and newsletters (such as *Tennessee Anthropologist, Kentucky Archaeologist, Old World Archaeological Newsletter, Southeastern Archaeology, Wisconsin Archaeologist, Plains Anthropologist,* and *The Kiva*), to popular science journals *(Scientific American, Science 84, Natural History),* and to local newspapers and magazines. Papers read at a variety of national and regional meetings also help disseminate major results to interested people outside the immediate circle of concerned specialists.

Third, progress reports and final results of the work in nontechnical terminology must be accessible to the people within and near the research area. This objective partially overlaps with the second objective above, but we wish to emphasize the importance of good and abundant communication with the inhabitants of the study area. Not only is this ethically correct and desirable, but also it has a number of practical advantages. Local people are often the best source for finding sites and for getting information important to interpretations of a variety of data. In western Kentucky, for example, while investigating riverside shellmiddens, geoarcheologist Julie Stein (1980) obtained valuable information on the nature and rate of riverbank alteration—"slip-ins"—from some of the older farmers. Finally, vandalism of archeological sites—unfortunately a very common problem

Archeology and Society

in many parts of the world—cannot be controlled without the active cooperation of informed and concerned local residents.

One approach that has been applied successfully is the issuing of short annual or preliminary reports written for the nonspecialist, but also of use to specialists. Douglas Schwartz of the School of American Research in Santa Fe did this for the Arroyo Hondo project, an achievement that inspired LeBlanc to initiate a similar program for the Mimbres Foundation. Copies of the Mimbres report were placed on sale at cost throughout the community, thus increasing accessibility to the information by the regional population.

Publication is not the only way to disseminate information. A public openhouse held by a field project is perhaps the single best means to educate and repay the local public for its support of archeology.

Thus the general public's right to and need for increased access to archeological results leads to new professional canons. Because failure to behave in a responsible manner with respect to the public affects the future of all archeological work, professionalism must be judged by means of a standard that includes attention to popular as well as to professional reports of archeological concerns.

A separate point concerning archeological publication has to do with the format of presenting hypothesis testing. A number of authors of recent publications state separately and label the hypotheses and the implications from them that they are testing. This certainly makes diagrammatically explicit what is being done. However, failure to use this format is not unscientific. (In fact, few presentations in the natural sciences are in this form, as any issue of *Science* shows). Whether hypotheses and the implications draw from them are stated in tabular form in one place or discursively throughout a report, one must remember that their explicit statement does not constitute their confirmation. It is important to state the grounds on which hypotheses are constructed and to show how inferences are drawn from them, but this does not constitute their confirmation. Hypotheses and implications must be logically cogent, but their confirmation or disconfirmation depends on empirical tests, and it is the making and reporting of these tests that crucially makes archeological work explicitly scientific.

One final note on archeological publication should be included here, although it represents quite a different perspective from that taken in the previous discussion. As Zubrow (1981) makes clear, there are significant high-level constraints on archeological book publication having to do with the activities of the large corporations that control commercial publishing houses. Within this corporate world, there are very few outlets for technical archeological materials, and Zubrow believes a similar monopolizing trend characterizes the university presses. This means that—for these two important outlets—a very few people control content and format. On the other hand, there is rapidly increasing proliferation in the publication of primary archeological data by museums, universities, contracting firms, and other organizations, but these materials are usually rather limited in distribution.

Hence, there are some very serious problems with archeological publication at a number of different levels. These must be vigorously addressed soon if progress in the field is not to be severely hampered.

Site Preservation and Contract Archeology

Since the early 1970s, the closely related topics of site preservation and government funding for documentation of archeological materials endangered by federal construction projects have overwhelmingly dominated archeology in the United States. In the past, prehistoric and historic remains have often been disturbed or destroyed by large and small earthmoving or other construction work, but in the decades since World War II these activities have intensified to the point that, together with increasing vandalism of archeological sites, they will quite soon destroy whatever is left of the archeological record in the United States that is not specifically and carefully protected.

Two kinds of solutions have been applied to this problem at the national level. One is the successful lobbying by archeologists for legislation necessitating recovery of archeological information before federally financed construction can take place (the Archeological Conservation Act of 1974; see King, Hickman, and Berg 1977), and the enhanced protection of federally owned sites by the Archeological Resource Protection Act of 1979 (Public Law 96-95; see Michel 1981). The other is the formation of a private corporation, the Archaeological Conservancy, to acquire endangered sites and then to safeguard them in perpetuity (LeBlanc 1979).

Action at both private and public levels is essential because in the United States—in stark contrast to nearly every other nation on earth—there is no protection whatever for historic or prehistoric remains that happen to be on privately owned land. Such privately held cultural properties can be, and often are, disturbed or destroyed at the whim of the landowner. This fact together with the burgeoning art market for prehistoric objects, on the one hand, and the increasing pace of destructive alteration of the land surface, on the other, will obliterate the archeological record in the United States in the very near future if strong action is not taken soon.

The Archaeological Conservancy is the most successful attempt to date to save at least a few U.S. sites from devastation by privately directed forces. At the moment it offers the only means of protecting archeological remains on private land from locally based vandals who for profit, for recreation, or simply out of casual curiosity destroy hundreds of sites each year.

The Archeological Conservation Act, on the other hand, potentially protects only sites endangered by federally financed construction. The legislation necessitates survey and—if deemed necessary by the archeologists contracted to carry out the survey—excavation of any or all significant remains found. The impact of federally funded contract work on U.S. archeology is enormous; it is far beyond the scope of this chapter to discuss or to evaluate it in detail, but the situation has been briefly summarized by LeBlanc (1980) as follows (and see below, end of this section): Sums in the range of $100 million are now spent annually on U.S. contract archeology. An important commentary on the impact of this activity is the widespread concern that contracting as such is a grave threat to archeology as a discipline. One can take a negative stance and argue that contract bidding and science are inherently incompatible and that the constraints imposed by a series of bureaucratic agencies make contracting of marginal scientific value. Alternatively, one can take a more positive position and argue that the rapid increase in the amount of contracting work has outstripped both the bureaucracies' and the professionals' ability to handle the problems in the short run but that the rate of improvement at all levels is adequate to predict that in another few years a smoothly running, highly productive system will be in place.

The main point we wish to make here about contract archeology (also called public archeology, conservation archeology, and cultural resource management [CRM]) is that it need be no different from academic archeology with respect to problem orientation and construction of explicit research designs. In the pioneer era of what was originally called salvage archeology (1930s to 1960s), there was much room for doubt about its relevance to academic archeology and to the development of archeological theory (King 1971, 1977), but by the mid-1970s the situation was so much improved that some of the clearest published statements and exemplars of good archeological research design were coming out of contract work (Goodyear et al. 1978; see for example, Chapman 1973, 1975, and subsequent publications by the University of Tennessee and the Tennesssee Valley Authority on the archeology of Tellico Reservoir in the Little Tennessee River Valley; Faulkner and McCollough 1973 and subsequent publications by the University of Tennessee and the Tennessee Valley Authority on the archeology of Normandy Reservoir in the Duck River Valley; Price et al. 1975; Schiffer and Gumerman 1977: pts. 2, 3). Although there is no longer much uncertainty about the theoretical integration of contract and ivory tower archeology, it is worth quoting a statement of William Lipe's that resolves the theoretical issues in a nutshell:

> The implication of this is that problem orientations and research designs are as important in salvage as in academic research. Whereas the academic archaeologist ideally tries to find the site or sites where best to test his hypotheses, the salvage archaeologist is confronted with the sites and must develop his problem orientation in such a way as to make the most of the raw material. Of the two approaches, the latter seems intellectually the more challenging. In the long run, however, it does not matter in what sequence the problem, hypotheses, and data get together. What matters is that they are logically appropriate to one another and that significant results are obtained. (Lipe 1977:34)

Archeology and Society 245

British archeologists have also become engaged in considerable contract or "rescue" archeology, although on a smaller scale than in the United States. They, too, have expressed considerable concern with the nature of that work. A recent symposium on the problem sums up the British position:

> Let us assert then, that all rescue is research or it is nothing. And that all research in archeology must contribute to our understanding of early man, and offer explanations as well as descriptions. In saying "understanding" I mean first yours and mine, as archeologists. But then there must follow also the understanding of the public at large. (Darvill et al. 1978:)

Like many archeologists in the United States, these British scholars believe that there is no logical reason why rescue archeology cannot be scientific, and they argue that in Britain it must be scientific in practice as well as in theory.

The picture is not entirely rosy (and see Dunnell's comments below as well as various problems noted in chapter 4 here), but there is no question about the ability of contract archeologists to plan and carry out innovative, problem-oriented research. Although contract archeology usually necessitates working under tight deadlines and within spatial limits imposed from outside, and although contract archeologists nearly always face major problems when it comes to distribution of their reports, nevertheless there are advantages to contract work as noted above: multidisciplinary projects are relatively generously fundable, and submission of analytical results and of final manuscripts—being under contract—are enforceable.

Other advantages of contract archeology following from the relatively generous funding situation it enjoys include large-scale use of techniques (such as innovative sampling designs for site survey, delimitation, and excavation) that would be prohibitive in time and cost for most noncontract work. The use in Tennessee by the Tellico and Normandy projects of earthmoving equipment to expose large portions of deeply buried sites and the massive use of flotation techniques on those deposits are illustrative of this point (Chapman 1981, for example). Another advantage of the comprehensive areal coverage necessitated by many contract projects is the discovery of important settlement components that would probably have been missed otherwise (see, for example, Gumerman 1980:882).

Nevertheless, at least two well-informed observers believe that the actual gap between contract archeology and academic archeology is increasing, to the detriment of the whole field (Wendorf 1979; Dunnell 1979:446–449; 1980b:464–465; 1981:431–432, 435; 1982a:512–514). Wendorf fears that a dichotomy has developed in American archeology with the proliferation of what he sees as a low-level form of applied archeology as a result of massive infusion of federal money into contract work. Dunnell's concern is that contract archeology could have a decisively deleterious effect on the entire discipline.

> The rapid development of CRM has to a certain degree upset the normal progress of disciplinary development because it threatens to make permanent the condition of the discipline at a time in which rigidity is least warranted. (Dunnell 1979:449)
>
> The theoretical and metaphysical fumbling on the part of the new archaeology is characteristic of periods of development in all of the sciences. For this reason, the lack of integration between CRM and academic archaeology might not be viewed with much alarm. But Ptolemy did not have it within his power, let alone within his charge, to change the nature of the heavens and so the stars were still there for Copernicus to study. Archaeology is different. (Dunnell 1981:445)

Dunnell's point is well taken. If archeology is to progress, there must be innovation. But if contract archeology is to be done under "accepted practices" and only "established" procedures are to be funded, the potential for stifling innovation is great. As yet, however, this problem does not seem to have materialized. Innovation does take place in contract settings, and in fact such fears have encouraged noncontract funded archeologists to make extra efforts to be innovative.

The biggest apparent danger in contract archeology is the failure to produce publicly perceptible results commensurate with the costs. Such a failure will ultimately lead to a lack of trust in archeologists by the public and financing institutions to the overall detriment of the profession. So far, complaints about some examples of contract work have usually been focused on the quality of particular practitioners or of particular projects. Some problems of this sort are unavoidable. The more basic question, however, is whether contract archeology is inherently inefficient and wasteful. If one believes that cultures are systems and that a regional approach is the most effective way of studying them, and if one also believes that multistage sampling is the most effective approach to that study, then one may have to conclude that some forms of contract work are wasteful.

When areas are selected for survey and sites are selected for excavation on the basis of where impacts will occur rather than on the basis of what we need to know about particular cultural systems, then regional approaches to obtaining that knowledge are hampered. To the extent that each individual project is conceived of and financed as a discrete effort, one's ability to analyze materials and synthesize the results of different projects is also hampered. That is, inability to carry out the synthetic studies necessary to integrate extant contract work and inability to add survey areas and excavations to already extant samples means that the full potential of the materials recovered at great expense is not realized. Although not generated by any single contract project or any single funding agency, this problem is grave. Archeologists must explain to nonarcheologists the potential loss of information caused by these inherent limitations, and we must find solutions to these problems if we are to expect large-scale public support in the future.

We now leave the practical issues of archeological publication and antiquities legislation to return to more abstract theoretical issues about the nature and function of archeological research.

Archeology as Social Science

The main purpose of this book is to provide a synthesis of scientific procedure in archeology. We regard the recent emphasis on scientific method and explanation as the culmination of a long development within the field, going back at least as far as the first issue of *American Antiquity* and the advocacy of a deductive approach to archeology by Arthur C. Parker, first president of the Society for American Archaeology (Parker 1935). Some of the subsequent phases are shown in the writings of Julian H. Steward and Frank M. Setzler (1938), John W. Bennett (1943), Walter W. Taylor (1948), and Albert C. Spaulding (1953). However, this is not to say that we think all archeologists should and must be scientists. There is no more reason for all archeologists to be scientists than for all historians to be sociologists, psychologists, or anthropologists. But in its concern with human behavior, archeology is a social science, a part of general anthropology. One purpose in writing this book is to present what we take to be the most important characteristics of a model of archeology as a social science.

Social sciences are not logically different from other sciences. Anything that is empirically observable can be studied scientifically. Present human behavior is empirically observable, and the remains of past human behavior are empirically observable wherever the results of that behavior—cultural debris and its spatial distributions—are preserved. Thus archeological knowledge claims about past behavior are empirically grounded in present observations. Past behavior is objective in principle (that is, we could have observed it had we been there; it is not logically unobservable), but it is, of course, not now directly observable. A major goal of archeology is to infer past human behavior from its presently observable remains.

The hallmark of the physical sciences is the employment of controlled experiments. The subject matter of the social sciences—human behavior, past and present—is not easily amenable to experimental study, but human behavior can be studied effectively by making controlled observations. Experiments using models are also useful in archeology. With controlled observations and model experiments, and without the aid of actual experimentation on the subject matter itself, astronomy has become a mature, predictive science. Archeology has the advantage over astronomy to the extent that a variety of replicative and other actual experiments are possible in archeology.

Although social sciences are not logically different from other sciences, they are more difficult than the physical and many of the biological sciences. This is because, first, it is difficult or impossible, and often morally wrong to experiment with human subjects. Hence, controlled observations and investigations of various kinds of human behavior in many times and places are necessary to provide data for testing possible laws, explanations, and theories in the social sciences.

Second, there is a great deal of variation in both group and individual human behavior, more than in the behavior of any other animal, and certainly more than in atoms, molecules, and stars. This means that behavioral norms and their ranges of variation are more difficult to delimit for human beings than the behavioral norms of bees or hydrogen atoms, for example. This is in part because the range of variation in individual human behavior is so much greater than that of individual insects and atoms. Human beings, like mammals in general, are the result of a long period of positive evolutionary selection for behavioral adaptability rather than for behavioral specialization. This adaptability has led to the development of various cultures, which are forms of learned group and individual behavior that have evolved in much greater complexity in humans than in any other animal.

Anthropology as a social science is defined as that discipline whose practitioners are concerned with the explanation and prediction of human sociocultural behavior throughout time and space wherever human societies are or have been found. Archeologists are anthropologists who have developed techniques and skills to investigate past human behavior as it can be inferred from the archeological record. Archeologists as anthropologists and social scientists explain how the archeological record was emplaced, and also they use archeological data to derive and test generalizations and to construct theories about cultural processes that are represented in the archeological record.

For example, Longacre has investigated the interrelationship of social organization and economy in prehistoric eastern central Arizona, especially during a period of environmental stress (drought) (Longacre 1968:69). To test his hypotheses concerning this interrelationship, he had to be able to infer from the archeological record the social organization before, during, and after stress. As a first step in comprehending the social organization, he devised a distributional study of design elements (Longacre 1968, 1970) that has been widely discussed in the archeological literature (the most recent detailed analyses are those of Plog 1980 and Graves 1981). The results indicated to him, as one major conclusion, that the social organization at the time of occupation included postmarital residence of couples with or near the wife's female relatives. Although the substance of this conclusion has been challenged on a number of grounds, the approach is one that has the potential of explaining some of the particulars of the archeological record at the Carter Ranch site while also advancing the study of prehistoric cultural processes in that region.

Another example is provided by the research of David Thomas in Nevada (Thomas 1973, 1974, and see discussion in the simulation section of chapter 2 here). He is concerned about the accuracy of Julian Steward's reconstruction of aboriginal social organization and subsistence in the Great Basin area (Steward 1938). Steward's results (especially his inferences about the effects of subsistence type on social organization) are widely used by archeologists and other anthropologists, but the way of life he describes was extinct by 1860 at the latest. Hence, his informants told him about processes and beliefs they could not have experienced firsthand except as young children, and then only in a fragmentary or distorted way.

Steward's account can be tested only by means of archeology for there are no other records. Therefore Thomas draws implications from Steward's reconstruction—that is, he makes predictions about the nature and patterning of archeological debris that should be found in the home territory of the Great Basin Indians if Steward's account is correct—then he undertakes an archeological project to locate and examine the remains. Thomas finds archeological materials sufficiently similar to the predicted patterns that he believes that he has helped corroborate Steward's reconstruction. In so doing he not only secures descriptions and explanations of four thousand years of cultural history in a part of the Great Basin, but also he helps to confirm Steward's generalizations about the relationships between social organization and subsistence in that kind of environment (Steward 1949: chs. 3, 6, 7).

In many cases, the archeological record may not provide the best data for testing possible generalizations or explanations, even if the methods of testing have been worked out. Some problems may be solved more readily with the use of ethnographic, sociological, or historical data. For other problems, however, the archeological record may be extremely helpful or may furnish information available nowhere else. If a problem has to do with hunting-gathering groups, for example, use of archeological data about past hunters and gatherers in various parts of the world will add greatly to the set of data about living hunter-gatherers, which is extremely small (see discussion at the end of the next section).

Finally, there is a unique area that is exploitable by archeologists: Only archeological data can be used to help devise and test possible laws and theories about various aspects of prehistoric cultural change because archeological data contain the only records of long-term information about the technology, social and political organization, art forms, and so on of past nonliterate human societies. Historians can study only those aspects of societies that are covered by written records that have been preserved.

> Given the enormous time depth with which only archeology is prepared to deal, what can we learn of the changing relation between man, society, and culture on the one hand and environment on the other; what of the generalized cultural processes . . . which, because of the bearing of this time factor . . . can be examined in no other way. (Braidwood 1967:226)
>
> Archeologists are not merely passive consumers of anthropological knowledge. This is so because they also apply nonanthropological knowledge to their relics to produce plausible inferences as to relative and absolute age, ecological circumstances, and other relevant dimensions of cultural variation. In so doing, they contribute independent data to theories of sequence of forms and rate of change of at least some aspects of customary behavior. The chronological data are clues to the identification of antecedent and consequent conditions in slow-moving cultural transformations. (Spaulding 1968:37–38)

Evolutionary Theory and Archeology: The Formulation of Robert C. Dunnell

An approach different from that advocated by Braidwood and Spaulding has been presented by Robert C. Dunnell, who believes that further progress in archeology depends on the conception and application of "a general theory capable of generating scientific explanations in an historical framework and integrating those explanations into a systematic, coherent body of knowledge" (Dunnell 1980b:83). He believes that this general theory is derivable from modern evolutionary biology. He makes a sharp distinction between the theory of biological evolution, which he calls "scientific evolution" or "Darwinian evolution," and "cultural evolution" of the various forms espoused by Herbert Spencer, Karl Marx, Lewis Henry Morgan, and Leslie White.

> The approach represented by cultural evolution is a social philosophy directly derived from the tradition of Herbert Spencer and the early anthropologists and is unrelated to Darwinian principles. As a philosophical rather than scientific approach to the explanation of variability by change, it is an inappropriate model for a scientific archaeology. On the other hand, modern evolutionary biology and Darwinian evolution do provide the elements of a suitable explanatory structure. Evolutionary biology cannot, however, be applied unamended and uncritically to cultural phenomena, be they ethnographic or archaeological. . . . If evolutionary theory is to be extended to the explanation of cultural phenomena, archaeology as a discipline will have to play a major role in its development. To a very real extent, the application of evolutionary concepts to sociocultural phenomena may depend upon the development of archaeological theory in this mold and not the reverse. (Dunnell 1980b:37–38)

While it is not our purpose to argue the point here, and while at least Spencer and Marx certainly do have social philosophies, their versions of cultural evolution like those of Morgan and White are not unscientific. For example, Spencer's "social Darwinism"—the most metaphysical of the four—can be separated from a scientific theory of Spencerian cultural evolution that is empirically testable. Marx's theories have been tested and modified. Morgan and White offer their theories as models. A scientific theory of evolution is not necessarily true, and a cultural theory of evolution is not necessarily unscientific.

Dunnell does not spell out exactly what development of archeological theory based on evolutionary biology would entail, but it would necessitate application of evolutionary mechanisms such as natural selection to cultural transmission. However, Dunnell questions the adequacy of genetic transmission and selection at the level of individuals for both biological and cultural evolution:

> *If a given trait is heritable to a measurable degree* (the mechanism of inheritance need not be known) *and if it also affects the fitness of organisms possessing the trait to some measurable degree* (recognizing the possibility of neutral or stylistic traits), *then the trait must be subject to natural selection* and will be fixed in populations in accord with the biological model. Biologists' definitional insistence on a genetic basis for human behavioral traits seems no more warranted than the anthropological insistence on special mechanisms unique to culture. . . . A dogmatic insistence on genetic transmission and selection limited to the scale of [the] individual, simply because both appear to be true of nonhuman and simple human societies, will doom evolutionary explanations of cultural phenomena to an early and unjustified death. (Dunnell 1980b:63, 66; stress is Dunnell's)

To implement interpretation of the archeological record in terms of scientific evolution, Dunnell—following Lewontin (1974)—calls for a change in the philosophical or ontological conception of archeological subject matter. The subject of investigation must be seen as empirical variability; such variability must be seen as historically continuous; and change must be viewed as selective rather than transformational. For cultural evolutionists the subject of investigation (culture) is typological; it is discontinuous with nature and biology; and change is transformational.

We cannot go into the detailed discussion here that Dunnell's distinction between what he takes to be an acceptable theory of "scientific evolution" and unacceptable metaphysical theories of "cultural evolution" merits. However, one reason that theories of biological evolution stress continuity of genetic transmission and some theories of cultural evolution do not is that biological traits are carried in genes while cultural traits are not known to be. Evolutionary theories are merely metaphysical or philosophical in the pejorative sense of being empirically untestable as long as no possible mechanism is hypothesized for carrying, transmitting, and modifying traits. The excitement in biology today comes from the possibility that empirically accessible molecular mechanisms can be used to explain biological evolution. And sociobiologists argue that some cultural traits and changes also are genetically based.

Dunnell appears to be ignoring or dismissing molecular biology. And he seems to be suggesting that the subjects of cultural evolution are not individual human beings but collective entities such as societies or institutions or motifs that persist and change through time beyond the life or existence of the individual entities that make them up. Without sorting various meanings of *superorganic*, we do agree that archeologists should consider collective entities as well as individual entities (indeed, most of the methods of analysis we describe in this book are for this purpose). And these collective entities do change through time. The question is whether or not cultural change is similar enough to biological evolution to be explained by a theory derived from that of biological evolution. Our point now is that mere similarity of *form* of change is not enough. The *mechanisms* of change must be similar, too. Dunnell offers the concept of natural selection. But in biology, natural selection is explained on the level of individuals. Dunnell thinks that this stress on genetic mechanisms is narrowly dogmatic, but the fact is that no other mechanisms of explanation have stood the test of empirical investigation. What alternative hypothetical mechanisms are available? As yet Dunnell has offered no explanatory mechanisms for either biological or cultural evolution alternative to genetic transmission and selection at the level of individuals.

Dunnell concludes by stating that archeologists want the kinds of explanations only scientific evolution can provide and that archeological evolutionary theory will have to be constructed by applying modified biological evolutionary theory to ethnographic data about artifact frequencies and distributions. He stresses the significance of functional versus stylistic attributes and artifacts (only those in the functional category would be subject to selection) and says that stylistic aspects of the archeological record are not directly subject to selection, so require explanation in cultural terms alone. Elsewhere he says, "Explanations of stylistic phenomena will be found in stochastic processes and devices such as Markov Chains" (Dunnell 1978b:200).

In another publication, Dunnell (1978a) provides an example of the way in which functional classes of archeological materials might be defined. But the result is an attribute analysis of use wear on stone tools which is difficult to generalize and fit into the scientific evolutionary model he proposes for all the archeological record of the human past. In other words, even if one were to agree with him on theoretical grounds, one would still be at something of a loss to understand how to implement Dunnell's recommendations. He appears to be offering a metaphysical ground for analytic techniques that they do not need, and to the extent that this is what he does—and it is not clear—he enters the ranks of those he calls unscientific cultural evolutionists. Much of the practice of Morgan, Spencer, and White is scientific; it is just that their different theories and results are or may be—like anyone's—wrong in various ways.

Another major ambiguity emerges from Dunnell's comments on the relationship of archeology to anthropology, and the nature of the ethnographic record. In his discussions of cultural evolution in anthropology, and of the reconstructionist approach (that is, viewing the archeological record as an incomplete ethnographic record and interpreting it via inferences based on sociocultural anthropology), there is a separatist theme (Dunnell 1980b:37–38, 46–47, 64, 84–85; 1978b:194–195; 1978a:41–49). That is, he seems to be urging archeologists to remove from before their eyes the lenses of sociocultural anthropology in order to see the archeological record on its own terms, rather than viewing it as impoverished sociocultural data that must be "reconstructed" before it can be understood. However, he does speak of settlement and subsistence patterns (Dunnell 1978a:67) and these are not primitive concepts embedded in the "hard phenomena of the archaeological record." They are anthropological notions derived from ethnographic accounts. Again, in his example of a functional stone tool classification, Dunnell does not use reconstructionist labels ("ax," "knife," etc.) for the classes he devises, but he does choose attributes on the basis of ethnographic data or information derived from experimental archeology (identification of hafting devices, the nature and importance of edge-wear and edge-angle). In three archeological situations, Dunnell finds such classes to covary with environmental features (microtopography, or character of the matrix), a result he regards as confirming the general hypothesis that *"functional classes ought to correlate directly with other evidence of activity character"* (Dunnell 1978a:60; original emphasis). Barring ambiguities about site formation processes that may have affected the contexts in question, including the classic uncertainty as to whether or not even close correlation means causation, this is perhaps the case. But one does not come away from this discussion with a clear understanding of exactly how his approach differs in practice from a reconstructionist one.

With respect to ethnoarcheology, Dunnell (1978a:67) stresses that archeological methods must be applied to ethnographic materials rather than the reverse, which is certainly a productive technique (examples include Rathje 1978; Nelson 1981; Kramer 1982). But he seems to have a very narrow view and a negative opinion of ethnographic analogy in general, like that expressed by R. Gould (1980: ch. 2; Dunnell 1978a:66–67; 1978b:194–195; see Watson 1982; Gould and Watson 1982, and discussion below). Yet, as indicated above, clearly anything we say about archeological materials is ultimately an argument from analogy. We could not even comprehend such a concept as "an archeological record" were we not analogizing from contemporary observations of, and knowledge about, discard and loss behavior by human beings, and about taphonomy, bioturbation, and other archeological site formation processes.

In sum, Dunnell's comments on archeological theory are provocative but inconclusive.

In addition to Dunnell, three philosophers of science and another archeologist have taken an active interest in the issue of grand archeological theory and are making major contributions to the literature. Alison Wylie's 1981 dissertation, "Positivism and the New Archaeology," is briefly discussed in chapter 1 here. Another book devoted to philosophy and archeology has just appeared (Salmon 1982), and *Archaeology and the Methodology of Science* by Marsha Hanen and Jane Kelley is forthcoming. All of the above merit the careful attention of archeologists.

We next take up some of the points raised earlier about site formation processes, ethnographic analogy, and ethnoarcheology.

Site Formation Processes

As noted in chapter 1, there is the potential for development of a body of specifically archeological theory (or minitheory) centering on natural and cultural site formation processes. Willey and Sabloff (1980:249–254) call the study of these two processes "lower-level interpretation," as distinct from "middle-level interpretation" or "middle-range theory" (see below).

Because archeologists infer past human behavior from altered material remains of human activity, it is important to know as much as possible about the processes of emplacement and of modification of these materials. Although this concern has been present in some form since the origins of archeology as a discipline, it has recently come to the fore in response to what Dunnell calls "the reconstructionist paradigm" during the 1960s and 1970s discussions about archeological method and theory. Some of the first new archeologists followed quite literally claims made by Binford (1962) and others about the behavioral reality behind the archeological record and believed that that behavioral reality is fairly readily and directly accessible. That is, they act as though there is a one-to-one correlation between artifact or attribute patterning on the one hand and the behavioral patterning that characterizes the past human group being investigated on the other. Among others, Michael Stanislawski (1969a, b), Phil Weigand (1969), and Michael Schiffer (1972, 1976) call attention to the complex variety of factors and forces that actually intervene between the use of materials or objects within a functioning society and their incorporation into the archeological record after a society abandons a particular location or dies out. A number of archeologists now devote large amounts of research time to the study of what Schiffer calls cultural and natural transforms, the cultural and natural mechanisms that alter materials before, during, and after their entry into the archeological record (David 1972; DeBoer and Lathrup 1979; Wood and Johnson 1978; McIntosh 1974; Murray 1980; Stein 1980, 1983; Kent 1981).

Archeologists are also concerned to document the behavioral contexts of artifacts, artifact-complexes, and architectural features produced and used in specific living societies (Leone 1973; Yellen 1977; Binford 1978b; Rathje 1978, 1979; Watson 1979a; Gould 1980; Longacre 1981; Kramer 1982). This information can then be used to interpret archeological remains of past societies. The theoretical and methodological issues relevant to this intepretive process are indicated below.

Geoarcheology and taphonomy (Gifford 1981; Gladfelter 1981) are the most important subdisciplines in the study of the natural transformational processes that result in archeological sites. The study of cultural transformational processes and of behavioral contexts for archeologically relevant materials falls under the broad heading of ethnoarcheology (Donnan and Clewlow 1974; Ingersoll, Yellen, and MacDonald 1977; Stiles 1977; Gould 1978; Kramer 1979; Watson 1979a, 1979b; Gould and Watson 1982).

Although there are not many detailed investigations of geoarcheological site formation processes, there are a few good examples, such as Farrand (1975) and Stein (1980). Farrand and Stein use numerous geological (especially sedimentological) techniques to answer basic questions about how natural deposits were built up and about how the original deposits were altered during and after the prehistoric occupations at a limestone rockshelter containing archeological materials dating between 22,000 and 34,000 years ago (Farrand), and at a riverside shellmound 4,000 to 5,000 years old (Stein). Stein delineates the results of faunalturbation (disturbance of various kinds by small animals that lived in or near the site from prehistoric times to the present). Farrand draws paleoclimatological implications from the ancient sediments in the rockshelter to describe major differences between the climate at Abri Pataud during Upper Paleolithic times and now.

Ethnoarcheologists use published and unpublished ethnographic material including archival objects in museums and elsewhere, photographs, and documentation; data resulting from experiments; and information deliberately sought from living societies to answer general and specific questions about the archeological record and the relationships of human behavior to material culture. Ethnoarcheology is currently popular and it is believed by some to be the answer to nearly all the difficulties archeologists have in understanding the archeological record. An ethnoarcheological approach does open highly productive lines of research and can provide an abundance of possible answers to questions about archeological materials, but it is not the ultimate solution to all problems of archeological interpretation.

Ethnographic Analogy and Ethnoarcheology

Archeologists must always rely, directly or indirectly, on information derived from present materials to understand remains of past activities and events. If the dynamics of present cultural systems were as well understood as the dynamics of present fluvial systems, for example, we would be able to understand the traces of ancient cultural systems exposed at archeological sites as readily as geologists understand the traces of ancient rivers exposed in road cuts or backhoe trenches. Geologists use what Alison Wylie (1980) calls "a principle of generic similarity" to interpret the geological record. Processes observed in the present are thus used to gain understanding of processes operative in the past.

Cultural systems are much more complex than geological systems, but this does not support the argument that the principle of generic similarity cannot be used to understand past cultural systems. The problem is that human behavior is so variable and that cultural systems differ from one another in so many significant ways that they are similar only at levels of generality well above the levels of detail that archeologists want to understand and explain. Nevertheless, detailed comparisons are sometimes possible. And probabilistic or stochastic generalizations about site formation processes and about the relationships between human sociocultural behavior and material culture are very useful.

So what are the grounds on which archeologists support statements about past cultural systems? The basic principle of all archeological interpretation is analogical. All archeological materials are understood in some part by analogy with items, events, activities, and processes observable in the present. Strict generic similarities are important when an archeological study includes geological materials like chert and obsidian, or biological materials like pollen and certain species of gastropods or pelecypods. For the interpretation of materials such as painted designs on pottery, archeologists implicitly or explicitly use analogies and generalizations drawn from their observations and from ethnographic literature. If there is little or no relevant information, or if the available information is inadequate in other ways, archeologists may design research projects involving fieldwork in a living society (for instance, Binford 1978b; Watson 1979a; Longacre 1981), or the carrying out of a series of experiments (Coles 1979), or both, to obtain data for use in interpretation by analogy.

To explain specific parts of the archeological record or some class of archeological remains common in the records of various times and places, archeologists often use simple, straightforward form-function analogies (for example, Ochsenschlager 1974). For more complicated cases they often construct detailed analogies (usually called models) using both social scientific and natural scientific information (for example, Gould 1980:ch. 6; Jochim 1976). Natural scientific processes themselves suggest analogical models, and in particular our knowledge of biological systems is useful in interpreting past human behavior and in understanding past cultural systems. Obviously interpretations of past human beliefs are based in large part on our knowledge of psychology, sociology, anthropology, and history.

These hypothetical interpretations in the form of analogical models are tested by analyses of the archeological materials under investigation to determine whether or not the remains do represent the past activities and events proposed. (Here, again, it is necessary to understand site formation processes). Often the interpretive procedure ends with the statement of an analogy if it fits the archeological data reasonably well or can be modified until it does. But this is seldom adequate for confirming a hypothesis. To complete the testing process, one should use a wide variety of means to try to disconfirm the hypothesis and to form and test as many alternate ones as can be argued to be plausible, accepting a hypothesis only if it survives all such tests.

Analogies, whether simple form-function parallels or complex ecologically based systems models, and regardless of their source (direct historical or general comparative), should be tested in a covering law framework. However, acceptance of any analogy or hypothesis requires an inductive leap. This is true because, even though we may have tested and tried the hypothesis in every manner possible, we

Archeology and Society 261

cannot know with deductive certainty that the archeological patterns we are trying to explain could not have been produced in still another way (see Salmon 1976; Wylie 1980; and chapter 1 here).

Analogies, like any other hypotheses, can be constructed on the basis of any plausible data, but archeologists working in areas of the world where some forms of cultural continuity are strong (like the Near East or parts of Africa or Mexico) have what is usually regarded as an advantage in being able to use a direct historical or folk culture approach (cf. Watson 1979a). That is, they can observe very old living systems of material culture that are still functioning as they did in antiquity. A favorite example for the Near East is construction of coursed mud walls (puddled adobe; *tauf* in Arabic, *chineh* in Persian). The archeological remains of this kind of mud architecture are especially difficult to identify, but archeologists can greatly increase their abilities both to identify it and to understand it by watching and recording how present-day villagers build *tauf* houses and by studying the details of decay processes acting on abandoned houses of this kind. Hence, archeologists doing prehistory in areas of the world where old traditions are extant can collect much detailed data useful for interpreting archeological remains by analogy (McIntosh 1974, 1977; Kramer 1982; Watson 1979a).

Archeologists are sometimes called to task for doing ethnoarcheology (Binford 1968a:12–14; Dunnell 1980a:467–471; Freeman 1968; see also Schiffer 1978). There are two basic criticisms. One is leveled by those who are opposed to much if any deliberate use of ethnographic analogy because, these critics believe, such use will bias and distort one's views of the prehistoric materials so that one will try to force them into categories derived from modern ethnography. We have already noted that such a position is ultimately indefensible because nothing can be said about prehistoric people that is not based— directly or indirectly, and usually both—on observations of living people or other modern phenomena. Use of such information does not mean that our knowledge of the past is entirely constrained by exactly what societies observable in the present do. We can reason systematically from data about the present in combination with generalizations and theories based on them, and on our understanding of other present-day physical phenomena, to the past societies of prehistory. We do this by constructing analogical models for interpreting past societies that are in many ways different in detail and social structure from observed living societies. That is, archeologists do not argue that past cultures are exactly similar to present ones. Analogies are not often made between complete societies or between complete parts of societies, and sometimes analogies are not even made between complete artifacts. What archeologists obtain from observation of present societies are the elements from which models specific to past societies can be constructed and tested. There are no living cultures exactly like the Sumerian, but by putting together parts of what we know about various past and present cultures, archeologists can—with this general analogical method—construct testable models with which to come to much confirmed understanding of the ancient Sumerians. These points have been argued repeatedly (Gould and Watson 1982; Watson 1979a: introduction, 1979b, 1982; Wylie 1980, 1982b, in press).

The second criticism is much more important and deserves further discussion. In the references cited above, Binford, Dunnell, and Schiffer are concerned that too much attention is being paid to the particularistic collection of data for rather parochial problems of archeological interpretation, while insufficient thought is being given to studies meant to advance knowledge about the general functioning of material culture systems.

Of course, archeologists working in places where whole or partial ancient technologies still function but are threatened should continue their particularistic documentations of these systems. It is probably fair to say, however, that the field of ethnoarcheology at present is dominated by a particularistic rather than a generalizing emphasis. Perhaps the challenge that Binford, Dunnell, and Schiffer issue should be taken up with the greatest vigor by those archeologists who work on prehistoric societies and topics (such as settlement-subsistence patterns of Paleolithic French caribou-hunters, or social and political organizations of Bronze Age European chiefdoms) that exclude them from use of the direct historical approach and force them to rely on its alternative, the general comparative approach (Levy 1982 provides a good example for Bronze Age Denmark, and Binford's books and his series of papers on the Nunamiut provide well-known examples relevant to prehistoric hunter-gathers like those of the European Upper Paleolithic).

In sum, we suggest the following generalized covering law procedures with respect to the use of ethnographic analogy:

If an archeologist is concerned about the accuracy of a specific interpretation based on ethnographic, ecological, or experimental information, or some combination of these, he or she should draw inferences from the hypothetical interpretation about what the archeological materials should contain and then check to see whether or not they do. Wylie (1980) suggests that one should also evaluate form-function analogies by using specific criteria of number and nature to test similarities in form between archeologically known traits or complexes and their proposed parallels. This should be done in a series of both archeological and ethnographic contexts independent of those central to the investigation. Wylie cites Curren (1977) as an example of this technique (and see also Bass 1967:52–83).

Such checking is somewhat tedious to do. We do not believe that any archeologist could or should check every single detail of interpretation. But such checking should certainly be done as carefully as possible for the most crucial or significant portions of all archeological interpretations.

Another use of analogy is to compare proposed interpretations with well-confirmed interpretations of the same general type. Although this is not a substitution for actual testing, it can be part of the process of confirmation. But is this not to reason in a circle, to confirm one interpretation by comparison with another similar one that is already confirmed and thus build up the body of interpretations of that type that can be used to support others, and so on? No, it is not a vicious process. It is just another example of the back-and-forth checking and modification of hypotheses discussed in chapter 1.

Middle-Range Theory

In several publications, Binford discusses what he calls middle-range theory (Binford 1977: introduction, 1978b:45, 486), a concept that, as he uses it—overlaps with ethnoarcheology in that ethnoarcheology is a major technique for obtaining the information needed to construct middle-range theories. Binford defines middle-range theory as the means whereby archeologists give dynamic meaning to the characteristics of the static archeological record. (See the comparison with Merton's use of "middle-range" in Salmon 1982:170, 177; see also Goodyear and Raab 1984). For example, Binford says that to investigate the archeological remains of a hunting-gathering society one needs a body of interpretive material (that is at least partially axiomatized) about the relevant activities of appropriate kinds of living hunting-gathering societies from which to derive understanding of the particular past society we are examining by means of its archeological record. Gould makes much the same point in his discussion of "living archeology" (Gould 1980).

Binford's statement that middle-range theory is necessary before archeologists can fully comprehend archeological materials is equivalent to saying that laws and models based upon ethnographic and experimental data are necessary for making interpretations of the archeological record. Broadly stated, this is certainly true and has been recognized repeatedly, but a question that has not been explicitly addressed in the current literature is how particular or specific these bodies of middle-range theory can or should be. Is one model necessary for Arctic hunter-gatherers (Binford 1978b) and another for desert hunter-gatherers (Gould 1980; Yellen 1977)? Is a body of middle-range theory about tribal horticulturists useful for interpreting the archeological remains of chiefdoms? Even if one decides that relatively broad, ethnoarchaeologically derived middle-range theories are adequate, one is still faced with the fact that there is no ethnographic access to many classes of societies that are quite well documented archeologically, such as the pristine civilizations of both the Old World (for example, Sumer and Old Kingdom Egypt) and the New World (for example, Chavin and Olmec developments), the earliest food-producing societies of the Old and New World such as Abu Hureyra, Çayönü, and Pre-Pottery Neolithic A Jericho in the Near East; Late Archaic communities in Kentucky and Tennessee; and those of Tehuacan and Tamalipas in Mexico), the Chaco Canyon and Mimbres Classic societies of the prehistoric Southwest, and the medieval entrepôts of Islamic North Africa. This does not mean, of course, that we cannot ever hope to understand how such societies originated and functioned. Although denied the possibility of obtaining specific comparative information from a series of closely analogous living societies, we can certainly understand them—sometimes in considerable detail—by using relevant data drawn from ethnography, ethnohistory, and a variety of other social sciences. Construction of analogical models for this purpose is discussed above. In fact, this entire issue reduces to the same basic points made in the previous discussion about ethnographic analogy and about direct historical versus general comparative analogies.

What is critical is the kind of relationship being investigated, not the specific source of the information. For example, Binford (1978b) is concerned not with all the general aspects of Arctic hunters but with the archeologically relevant aspects of relationships between human hunters and herds of large migratory mammals in an Arctic or sub-Arctic environment. Much of the behavior of societies that occupy extreme physical environments (such as the Nunamiut of the Alaskan Arctic, or the aborigines of the Western Desert in Australia) is narrowly constrained in many ways by those environments (problems and methods of food storage, for example, are very different in the Arctic from what they are in the tropics or the desert). Nevertheless, many of Binford's findings (the general strategies used for monitoring movements of the prey species; the general characteristics of residential versus special purpose sites; the nature and significance of kin and fictive kin to a nuclear family or small band living in a marginal environment) pertain in general to various kinds of hunting-gathering and foraging societies in a variety of physical environments. Our position that any kind of bridging argument between static archeological remains and the prehistoric adaptational systems that generated them is analogical has already been adequately stated.

In sum, the use of middle-range theory or any other form of ethnographic analogy is often very useful but is not in and of itself definitive. That is, there is no single or best way to obtain interpretive models. Different kinds of problems and different types of societies require different approaches. Ethnographic analogy and Binfordian middle-range theory certainly make up one very productive approach for many problems, but what is best is what is most widely and persistently useful.

The Aims of Prehistory

Given the immense amounts of data about past human behavior to which archeologists potentially have access, what should be the objectives of archeological research?

One major objective of archeological research should be the formulation and testing of theories and laws possibly explanatory of the human past and of human behavior in general. Some archeologists disagree with this and argue that the pursuit of general knowledge conflicts with, or is even antithetical to, collecting and describing archeological data. Old or traditional or culture-historical archeology has thus been characterized as particularist in contrast to generalist, new or processual, or scientific archeology (Flannery 1967, Trigger 1970, 1973; Watson 1973). The dichotomy is, of course, exaggerated, but it is fair to describe Americanist archeologists of the 1930s, 1940s, and 1950s as predominantly historicist and particularist (idiographic) in orientation, and the new archeologists of the 1960s as scientific and generalizing (nomothetic) in orientation. Therefore, as noted in chapter 1, a history versus science debate was staged among Americanist prehistoric archeologists, as it had been a decade earlier in physical anthropology (Washburn 1953), and at other times in other disciplines (Harvey 1969: preface; South 1977: ch. 1). The new archeologist revolution in Americanist prehistory is over; the field today has a general scientific orientation, if only in the sense that archeologists are careful to state the grounds of their knowledge claims, even when they deny that they are appealing to general covering laws.

It is also generally recognized today that these two approaches—particularizing and generalizing—are not mutually exclusive. On the contrary, they are necessarily complementary. Without reference to generalizations about human behavior, not even the most doctrinaire of particularists could compose a narrative or history about an individual human being or a human group; no historian can explain the past without persistent (if only implicit)) appeal to such generalizations. In order to explain particulars one must have theories and general laws that subsume them. And, conversely, the main practical justification for constructing and testing theories is to find confirmed lawlike generalizations for use in understanding, explaining, and predicting human behavior and cultural processes. The acquisition of knowledge about anything requires continuous interaction between generalizing (nomothetic) and particularizing (idiographic) procedures of investigation and interpretation.

Although there are, within any science, individual researchers more interested in constructing theories and in formulating and testing possible general laws than in applying them (and vice versa), the goal of any science is to develop theories, laws, and possible laws for use in understanding its subject matter.

The archeological remains of prehistory provide a primary data base for deriving and testing generalizations about cultural processes and the evolution of human behavior over very long time periods. Prehistoric remains are also an independent source of data for testing theories and possible laws derived from observations of living societies today. Nevertheless, the question of which (if either) emphasis—nomothetic or idiographic—should dominate prehistory continues to be discussed and probably cannot be permanently resolved. For arguments on both sides of the issue see Hawkes (1968), Isaac (1971), Trigger (1970), Watson (1973), and Watson, LeBlanc, and Redman (1971:165-172).

As noted above, similar conflicts are present in other fields. In fact, this is probably one of the oldest debates in human intellectual history. Temperament, training, and interest play large roles in the choices individual archeologists make. With our general view of scientific archeology as consisting of necessarily integrated particularist and generalist procedures, we—of course—recommend balance. Leibniz expressed the situation very well nearly three hundred years ago in a letter to Simon Foucher: "Those who like to go into scientific detail scorn abstract and general inquiries, and those who work on fundamental principles rarely go into particulars. For my part, I have an equally high regard for both general and particular investigations" (Gerhardt 1875:401).

Differences between particularists and generalists are sometimes intensified by practical or pragmatic matters, two of which are especially significant. First, differences in training and in personal aptitude nearly always incline an individual researcher more in one direction than another (particularistic or generalizing). Such individual characteristics may be reinforced by simplistic caricaturizations such as the following: "New Archeologists go into the field with preconceived ideas (they call them hypotheses) about what they are going to find, and therefore they miss a lot of data and distort the rest" versus "Traditional archeologists have many implicit ideas about what they expect to find, but they are unclear about them and operate intuitively, therefore their results cannot be evaluated or trusted." Archeologists who actually believe one of these two statements will probably find compromise difficult if not impossible, but we hope that careful reading of this book will help them see that few if any contemporary Americanist archeologists actually occupy either of these extremes.

Second, in the actual world of archeological site excavation, a particularistic archeologist primarily interested in pottery and architecture because they yield the most cultural-historical information may not keep or even notice the chipped stone debitage or the rodent bone from excavated units and thus will destroy data that are of major importance for some other kinds of problems. Meanwhile, a generalist archeologist primarily concerned with formulating and testing cultural processual laws relating to site functions, distributions, and environmental settings may not publish or even record sherd counts for traditional pottery types, information vital to the cultural historian.

These examples are exaggerated, but only mildly; it is indeed very difficult to strike a fair balance even when trying hard to do so (see Smith's review of Hole, Flannery, and Neely [1969] and the general discussion of archaeological publishing strategies in the first section of this chapter).

To ameliorate the inevitable tension between nomothetic and idiographic archeologists, it is important for everyone to keep in mind that both emphases are logically and pragmatically essential. Although most individual archeologists are probably more comfortable and more skilled at one of these research orientations than the other, all archeologists should develop at least a basic competence in both and, above all, should recognize the contributions of both. It is difficult to do archeology, no matter where it is practiced: in the field, in the laboratory, in the classroom, or in the study. To do justice to the potential of our discipline we need to stress excellence in an increasingly wide variety of both particularist and generalist research skills; we need fair and open discussion of crucial theoretical and methodological issues; and we need mutual exchange of data and other information between and among both idiographically and nomothetically oriented archeologists.

Ideational Archeology

We cannot leave the topic of the aims of archeology without making reference to a relatively recent development that is variously referred to as cognitive archeology, ideational archeology, and, most recently, structuralist archeology. Published examples are increasing (see, for instance, Marshack 1972, 1981; Kehoe and Kehoe 1974; Fairservis 1975; Flannery and Marcus 1976; Hall 1976, 1977; Fritz 1978; Hodder 1982), and this approach is commonly thought to be an alternative to (if not actually opposed to) the materialist emphasis of most contemporary archeologists (Hall 1977). Some proponents are interested in what might be described as paleocognition or paleo-belief systems. One of their major points seems to be that we do a disservice to potential interpretations of past societies represented by the archeological record when we try to understand them from a narrowly functionalistic or purely utilitarian viewpoint while completely ignoring the "moral order" of these groups. It is surely true that the members of those vanished societies themselves were often more explicitly concerned with moral order than with technology and subsistence and viewed the universe from an ideological perspective rather than from, say, a strictly utilitarian one.

As we argue above, considerable understanding of past and present cultures can be gained by using categories of analysis that do not necessarily coincide with the mental templates of the bearers of these cultures. And as all anthropologists know, the categories of people's belief systems, ideologies, and moral orders often conceal important cultural relations. However, archeologists must keep in mind that beliefs have influenced the behavior of human beings from their first appearance in the geological past to the present day. It follows that some—potentially a great many, at least since the appearance of biologically modern humans—archeologically revealed phenomena may not be adequately explicable without considering the beliefs of their creators (see Wylie 1982, and Gould's statements about eco-utilitarian explanations in Gould and Watson 1982; Levy 1982 provides an example of an ethnoarcheological approach to the study of religious ritual and social stratification in a prehistoric society).

Mark Leone (1982b) provides an excellent summary of current attempts by archeologists to discover the beliefs of past peoples. He sorts these studies into three main categories: (1) those using structuralist and cognitive approaches; (2) those derived from the materialist and neoevolutionary (in the sense of cultural evolution) school of Leslie White; and (3) those based on various Marxist approaches. Leone believes that structuralist results are the most impressive but that the materialist approach—which he views as an extension of new archeology—offers important potential. We present below brief summaries of examples illustrating each of Leone's three categories.

Although the spectacular Upper Paleolithic decorated caves of southern France and northern Spain have been the subject of study and discussion since the end of the nineteenth century, André Leroi-Gourhan is the first to collate a large amount of systematically collected empirical data on these caves in support of a new interpretation. He personally studied 66 painted caves and used already published information for 44 others, the total of 110 comprising all known examples in Franco-Cantabria. He began the process of documenting the nature and quantities of motifs and their distributions in 1956, publishing the results in 1967.

At approximately the same time, an independent study of the decorated caves was made by Annette Laming-Emperaire, who arrived at conclusions rather similar to those of Leroi-Gourhan. They conclude that the cave-wall pictures are real compositions and not just haphazard agglomerations, that the different kinds of animals represented are deliberately placed in the compositions and in specific parts of the cave, and that different animals have different symbolic significance. In addition, at various Upper Paleolithic sites, horses, ibexes, and cervids are engraved on "male" artifacts: spears, harpoons, spear-throwers, and arrow shaft straighteners. And in the cave paintings, representations of male human figures seem to be associated with horses, ibexes, and stags, while females go with bison, aurochs, and mammoth.

Thus, Leroi-Gourhan is able to come to some novel conclusions about the world view of the cave painters. He hopes to convince scholars that these Upper Paleolithic people conceived their world in a dualistic manner organized by or ordered around male and female principles or deities.

> Without overly forcing the evidence, we can view the whole of paleolithic figurative art as the expression of ideas concerning the natural and the supernatural organization of the living world (the two might have been one in paleolithic thought). . . . To gain a dynamic understanding of the cave representations, one would still have to integrate into this framework the symbolism of the spear and the wound. Taken as symbols of sexual union and death, the spear and the wound would then be integrated into a cycle of life's renewal, the actors in which would form two parallel and complementary series: man/horse/spear, and woman/bison/wound. (Leroi-Gourhan 1967:174)

Alexander Marshack (1972, 1981) has also made a careful study of Upper Paleolithic (and later) art and symbolism. His conclusions differ from Leroi-Gourhan's in that he believes the creators of the cave paintings were concerned not so much with relatively overt sexual symbolism, but rather with the basic rhythms of the natural world: gestation, birth, maturation, and death of human and non-human animals; seasonal changes in plant and animal populations; and astronomical processes and progressions such as the waxing and waning of the moon.

Another example of ideational or cognitive archeology is the work of Robert Hall (1976, 1977), who uses historic and ethnographic information to make inferences about symbolic systems possibly functioning in prehistoric societies of the New World. Hall's concern is to help redress the heavy emphasis on materialist interpretations of the archeological record in the Eastern Woodlands of North America. He says he wants to provide an alternative to "archeological 'econothink' ":

> The prelude to understanding and the route to explanation for much of
> the evidence of prehistory may lie partly in viewing this data from a
> more anthropocentric perspective and with empathy, beginning with
> what we already know of the Indians of the Eastern United States in
> historic times and the manner in which their beliefs, values, and diverse
> economic activities interrelated. There are few bases for making pan-
> continental comparisons in United States prehistory. One is the ecolog-
> ical approach emphasizing technology and environmental adaptation.
> . . . One cannot ignore the influence of geography, but there is much
> to be gained also by giving due attention to the cognitive core of cul-
> tures. Cognitive archaeology begins with the assumption that we can-
> not really interpret prehistory without making a conscious attempt to
> understand the nature of humans as symbol-using social animals affec-
> tively involved in a perceived world that they have helped to create.
> (Hall 1977:515)

Flannery and Marcus (1976) follow a rather different tack in examining Zapotec archeology from a cognitive perspective. They use
ecological analysis to make inferences about the cognitive realm.
Drawing on early Spanish accounts of social and religious organization in Oaxaca for knowledge of Zapotec cosmology, society, and
ancient agricultural practices, they show how a complex, sophisticated ideology reinforces an equally sophisticated system of irrigation cultivation.

Some of Leone's own publications are excellent examples of his third
category: Marxist approaches to the archeological record (Leone 1981,
1982a). Leone's major concern is about how archeologists and others
with direct access to primary evidence about the past use that evidence to construct descriptions of a past that fits their culturally prescribed ideas. By and large this is an unconscious process. That is,
these interpreters of the past are not usually aware of the nature and
depth of their ideological biases and hence tend to construct pictures
of the past—to a greater or lesser extent—in the image provided by
their own enculturated perspectives. Leone finds especially graphic
examples of this process in the "living museum" exhibits now so
popular in the United States. Colonial Williamsburg in Virginia and
Shakertown near Lexington, Kentucky, are prototypical examples.

The living history museum of Shakertown consists of two dozen original stone, brick, and wood buildings dating from the second quarter of the nineteenth century.

> The houses, workshops, and outbuildings are each used to display a particular part of Shaker life and as one tours each, Williamsburg fashion, one learns about sleeping and cooking, worship and furniture, a bit of history, some dates, laundry and seeds [a major activity of the Shakers was selling garden seeds], water works and bathing. All the information is accurate, although somewhat fragmented because the displays are by nature limited to rooms and buildings and it is up to you to walk between them all. It is fair to say that one gets the overall impression that the Shakers were admirable but must have believed in some quite peculiar things [they were celibate, lived in three large families but with a sharp segregation of men from women, participated in religious dancing and singing—men and women separately—etc.]. This minor conflict is resolved in favor of Shaker efficiency. (Leone 1981:303)

Leone goes on to describe how the Shakertown Museum unintentionally hides Shaker history while imposing present-day Midwestern U.S. ideology on the Shaker material.

> The dual process is what Marx called ideology and, when operating in an outdoor history or archaeological museum, creates an ideotechnic artifact. Lewis Binford defined but never isolated this class of artifacts. He never found them because his theory of culture, use of sociocultural levels of integration, and emphasis on culture process show an underdeveloped concept of ideology, a problem that could be corrected by a more thorough integration of Marxist theory into the new archaeology.
> Once outdoor presentations that use archaeological knowledge and collections are seen as ideotechnic, the way to treat them becomes substantially more clear. For instead of being warehouses of artifacts needing further analysis or as neutral masses of potential information, such museum presentations can be seen as fully operating parts of modern American culture, and when we see the presentations of the artifacts as the true artifacts, then we, as archaeologists, can treat the ideotechnic item the way we would any item. It can be a clue to the ideological part of our own society, in this case our conception and use of the past and its relationship to the present. (Leone 1981:305–306)

In sum, cognitive archeologists focus on the fact that human beings do not live by bread alone, but always, everywhere (at least since the Middle Pleistocene) have had complete, sometimes all-engrossing ritual and belief systems. Some elements of these belief systems are recorded in archeological remains. Leroi-Gourhan's work on cave paintings is one of the earliest examples of cognitive archeology. In a sense, he is doing a kind of historic archeology, if one extends the usual definition of historic archeology as covering peoples with written records to covering peoples who left symbolic representations of any sort. If archeological material is recognizably primarily and deliberately symbolic—as many grave goods are, for example—then interpretations of past belief systems are possible. Temples, shrines, and so on also provide evidence of past belief systems. Materials that are most probably symbolic thus provide the best data for inferring past belief systems. One thing cognitive archeologists do is decipher past symbol systems.

But past belief systems can be inferred also from materials that past peoples did not intend to be primarily symbolic. One can infer beliefs, for example, from evidence of all-male and all-female work areas and dwellings. From this viewpoint, the presence of a projectile point in the skeleton of an extinct bison is evidence that past peoples believed numerous things about stone, bison, and their own abilities. This is, of course, to integrate cognitive archeology with the rest of archeology. The goals of cognitive archeologists are not new. With the general aid of ethnographic analogy, with innovative techniques, and with careful testing of hypotheses, cognitive archeologists may provide some of the most exciting results of scientific archeology.

Conclusion

Our primary assumption is that archeology is a science like other sciences. Archeologists are primarily concerned to understand and explain particular past events and processes and also to use archeological knowledge to formulate and test theories about human social and cultural behavior in general. We discuss what we believe to be the most important methods and techniques for doing scientific archeology. We do not provide detailed instructions but offer only a general guide.

If archeologists agree that one important goal of their research is explanation of past events and processes, then we must next agree on what we mean by explanation. If we agree that explanation means implicitly or explicitly showing how particular events and processes are covered by general theories and laws, then we must agree on how to test and confirm or disconfirm these theories and laws. Once we do this we can proceed to use the archeological record to explain particular events in human prehistory, to understand processual aspects of human behavior, and to interpret culture and cultural processes. We can describe the lifeways of the human past. These are not easy things to do because archeology is one of the most complicated and difficult of all sciences. This is because human behavior is so complex and because past societies are only incompletely recorded in archeological remains.

The foundations of scientific archeology were laid by previous generations of archeologists such as Sir Mortimer Wheeler and A. V. Kidder, who established basic standards of excavation and recording techniques; Walter W. Taylor, who stressed the importance of the cultural context of archeological materials; Albert C. Spaulding, who urged the explicit use of scientific method and the adoption of efficient, standardized statistical techniques by archeologists; and Robert J. Braidwood, who directed the first modern, long-term and large-scale, ecologically oriented interdisciplinary projects devoted to acquiring primary data about the most important turning point in the human career—the beginnnings of food production. It is the task of succeeding generations of archeologists to build a structure worthy of these foundations.

References

Adams, Robert M. 1960a. "Early Civilizations, Subsistence, and Environment." In C. Kraeling and R. Adams, eds., *City Invincible*, pp. 269–295. Chicago: University of Chicago Press.
——1960b. "Factors Influencing the Rise of Civilization in the Alluvium: Illustrated by Mesopotamia." In C. Kraeling and R. Adams, eds., *City Invincible*, pp. 24–34. Chicago: University of Chicago Press.
——1965. *Land Behind Baghdad: A History of Settlement on the Diyala Plains*. Chicago: University of Chicago Press.
——1966. *The Evolution of Urban Society: Early Mesopotamia and Pre-Hispanic Mexico*. Chicago: Aldine.
——1968. "Archaeological Research Strategies: Past and Present." *Science* 160:1187–1192.
——1974. "Anthropological Perspectives on Ancient Trade." *Current Anthropology* 15:239–258.
——1981. *Heartland of Cities*. Chicago: University of Chicago Press.
Adams, Robert McC. and Hans Nissen. 1972. *The Uruk Countryside: The Natural Setting of Urban Societies*. Chicago: University of Chicago Press.
Ahler, Stanley A. 1976. "Sedimentary Processes at Rodgers Shelter." In W. R. Wood and R. B. McMillan, eds., *Prehistoric Man and His Environments*. pp. 123–139. New York: Academic Press.
Ammerman, Albert J. and L. L. Cavelli-Sforza. 1973. "A Population Model for the Diffusion of Early Farming in Europe." In C. Renfrew, ed., *The Explanation of Culture Change: Models in Prehistory*, pp. 343–357. London: Duckworth.
——1979. "The Wave of Advance Model for the Spread of Agriculture in Europe." In C. Renfrew and K. Cooke, eds., *Transformations: Mathematical Approaches to Cultural Change*. pp. 275–294. New York: Academic Press.
Ammerman, Albert J., Diane P. Gifford, and Albertus Voorrips. 1978. "Towards an Evaluation of Sampling Strategies: Simulated Excavations of a Kenyan Pastoralist Site." In I. Hodder, ed., *Simulation Studies in Archaeology*, pp. 123–132. Cambridge: Cambridge University Press.
Ammerman, Albert J., C. Matessi, and L. L. Cavelli-Sforza. 1978. "Some New Approaches to the Study of Obsidian Trade in the Mediterranean and

Adjacent Areas." In I. Hodder, ed., *The Spatial Organization of Culture*, pp. 179–196. London: Duckworth.

Asch, David L. and Nancy B. Asch. 1980. "Early Agriculture in West Central Illinois: Context Development, and Consequences." Paper prepared for School of American Research advanced seminar, "The Origins of Plant Husbandry in North America," March 2–8, 1980. Santa Fe, New Mexico.

Ascher, Robert. 1961. "Analogy in Archaeological Interpretation." *Science* 163:133–138.

——1962. "Ethnography for Archaeology: A Case from the Seri Indians." *Ethnology* 1:360–369.

Ascher, Robert and Charles H. Fairbanks. 1971. "Excavation of a Slave Cabin: Georgia, U.S.A." *Historical Archaeology* 5:3–17.

Babbage, Charles. 1838. *The Ninth Bridgewater Treatise*. London: John Murray.

Bamforth, Douglas B. and Albert C. Spaulding. 1982. "Human Behavior, Explanation, Archaeology, History, and Science." *Journal of Anthropological Archaeology* 1:179–195.

Barr, Anthony J., James H. Goodnight, and John P. Sall. 1979. *SAS User's Guide*. Raleigh, N.C.: SAS Institute.

Barth, Fredrik. 1956. "Ecologic Relationships of Ethnic Groups in Swat, North Pakistan." *American Anthropologist* 58:1079–1089.

——1961. *Nomads of South Persia: The Basseri Tribe of the Khamseh Confederacy*. Oslo: Oslo University Press.

Bass, George F. 1967. *Cape Gelidonya: A Bronze Age Shipwreck*. Transactions of the American Philosophical Society, n.s., vol. 57. Philadelphia: American Philosophical Society.

Bates, Marston. 1953. "Human Ecology." In A. L. Kroeber, ed., *Anthropology Today*, pp. 700–713. Chicago: University of Chicago Press.

Bayard, Donn T. 1969. "Science, Theory and Reality in the 'New Archaeology.'" *American Antiquity* 34:376–384.

Bell, James A. 1981. "Scientific Method and the Formulation of Testable Computer Simulation Models." In J. Sabloff, ed., *Simulations in Archaeology*, pp. 51–64. Albuquerque: University of New Mexico Press.

Bennett, John W. 1943. "Recent Developments in the Functional Interpretation of Archaeological Data." *American Antiquity* 9:208–219.

——1976. *The Ecological Transition*. New York: Pergamon Press.

Berlinski, David. 1976. *On Systems Analysis: An Essay Concerning the Limitations of Some Mathematical Methods in the Social, Political, and Biological Sciences*. Cambridge: MIT Press.

Binford, Lewis R. 1962. "Archaeology as Anthropology." *American Antiquity* 28:217–225.

——1964. "A Consideration of Archaeological Research Design." *American Antiquity* 29:425–441.

———1965. "Archaeological Systematics and the Study of Cultural Process."*American Antiquity* 31:203–210.
———1967. "Comment on 'Major Aspects of the Interrelationship of Archaeology and Ethnology,' by K. C. Chang." *Current Anthropology* 8:234–235.
———1968a. "Archeological Perspectives." In S. Binford and L. Binford, eds., *New Perspectives in Archeology*, pp. 5–32. Chicago: Aldine.
———1968b. "Post-Pleistocene Adaptations." In S. Binford and L. Binford., eds., *New Perspectives in Archeology*, pp. 313–341. Chicago: Aldine.
———1972. *An Archaeological Perspective*. New York: Seminar Press.
———1978a. "Dimensional Analysis of Behavior and Site Structure: Learning from an Eskimo Hunting Stand." *American Antiquity* 43:330–361.
———1978b. *Nunamiut Ethnoarchaeology*. New York: Academic Press.
Binford, Lewis R., ed. 1977. *For Theory Building in Archaeology*. New York: Academic Press.
Binford, Lewis R. and Sally R. Binford. 1966. "A Preliminary Analysis of Functional Variability in the Mousterian of Levallois Facies." In J. Desmond Clark and F. C. Howell, eds., *Recent Studies in Paleoanthropology*. *American Anthropologist* Special Publication 68(2):238–295.
Binford, Sally R. and Lewis R. Binford, eds. 1968. *New Perspectives in Archeology*. Chicago: Aldine.
Birkby, Walter H. 1973. "Discontinuous Morphological Traits of the Skull as Population Markers in the Prehistoric Southwest." Ph.D. dissertation, University of Arizona.
Blalock, Hubert M., Jr. 1972. *Social Statistics*. New York: McGraw-Hill.
Braidwood, Robert J. 1967. "Archaeology: An Introduction." *Encyclopedia Britannica* 2:225–227.
Braidwood, R. J., Bruce Howe, et al. 1960. *Prehistoric Investigations in Iraqi Kurdistan*. Studies in Ancient Oriental Civilization, no. 31. Chicago: University of Chicago Press.
Braidwood, Robert J., Linda Braidwood, Bruce Howe, Charles Reed, and Patty Jo Watson, eds. 1983. *Prehistoric Archeology Along the Zagros Flanks*. Oriental Institute Publication, no. 105. Chicago: Oriental Institute.
Brew, J. O. 1946. "The Archaeology of Alkali Ridge, Southeastern Utah." Papers of the Peabody Museum of American Archaeology and Ethnology, vol. 21. Cambridge: Harvard University.
Brodbeck, May. 1962. "Explanation, Prediction, and 'Imperfect' Knowledge." In H. Feigl and G. Maxwell, eds., *Minnesota Studies in the Philosophy of Science* 3:231–272. Minneapolis: University of Minnesota Press.
Browman, David L. 1981. "Isotopic Discrimination and Correction Factors in Radiocarbon Dating." *Advances in Archaeological Method and Theory* 4:241–295.
Brown, James and Stuart Struever. 1973. "The Organization of Archaeolog-

ical Research: An Illinois Example." In C. Redman, ed., *Research and Theory in Current Archaeology*, pp. 261–280. New York: Wiley.

Brown, M. B., ed. 1977. *BMDP-77: Biomedical Computer Programs, P-Series*. Los Angeles: University of California Press.

Brown, Robert. 1963. *Explanation in Social Science*. Chicago: Aldine.

Buck, R. C. 1956. "On the Logic of General Behavior Systems Theory." In H. Feigl and M. Scriven, eds., *Minnesota Studies in the Philosophy of Science* 1:223–238. Minneapolis: University of Minnesota Press.

Buikstra, Jane E. 1976. "Hopewell in the Lower Illinois Valley: A Regional Approach to the Study of Human Biological Variability and Prehistoric Behavior." Northwestern University Archaeological Program Scientific Papers, no. 2. Evanston, Ill.: Northwestern University.

Butzer, Karl. 1975. "The 'Ecological' Approach to Prehistory: Are We Really Trying?" *American Antiquity* 40:106–111.

—— 1978. "Toward an Integrated, Contextual Approach in Archaeology." *Journal of Archaeological Science* 5:191–193.

—— 1980. "Context in Archaeology: An Alternative Perspective." *Journal of Field Archaeology* 7:417–422.

—— 1982. *Archaeology as Human Ecology*. Cambridge: Cambridge University Press.

Caldwell, Joseph R. and Robert L. Hall, eds. 1964. *Hopewellian Studies*. Illinois State Museum Scientific Papers 12. Springfield, Ill.: Illinois State Museum.

Callahan, Errett, ed. 1976. *Experimental Archaeology Papers No. 4: The Pamunkey Project, Phases I and II*. Student Papers from the Department of Sociology and Anthropology. Richmond: Virginia Commonwealth University.

Cannon, Walter B. 1939. *The Wisdom of the Body*. New York: Norton.

Caws, Peter. 1965. *The Philosophy of Science: A Systematic Account*. Princeton: Van Nostrand.

—— 1969. "The Structure of Discovery." *Science* 166:1375–1380.

Chadwick, A. J. 1978. "A Computer Simulation of Mycenaean Settlement." In I. Hodder, ed., *Simulation Studies in Archaeology*, pp. 47–57. Cambridge: Cambridge University Press.

Chamberlin, T. C. 1890. "The Method of Multiple Working Hypotheses." *Science* O. S. 15:92–96. Reprinted in *Science* 148:754–759 (1965).

Chang, K. C., ed. 1967. *Settlement Archaeology*. Palo Alto, Calif.: National Press Books.

Chapman, Jefferson. 1973. "The Icehouse Bottom Site, 40 MR 23." Report of Investigations, no. 13. Knoxville: Department of Anthropology, University of Tennessee.

—— 1975. "The Rose Island Site and the Bifurcate Point Tradition." Report of Investigations, no. 14. Knoxville: Department of Anthropology, University of Tennessee.

—— 1981. "The Bacon Bend and Iddins Sites: The Late Archaic Period in the Lower Little Tennessee River Valley." Report of Investigations, no. 31. *The Tennessee Valley Authority Publications in Anthropology*, no. 25. Knoxville: TVA.

Chapman, Jefferson and Andrea Brewer Shea. 1981. "The Archeobotanical Record: Early Archaic Period to Contact in the Lower Little Tennessee River Valley." *Tennessee Anthropologist* 6(1):61–84.

Chomko, Stephen and Gary W. Crawford. 1978. "Plant Husbandry in Prehistoric Eastern North America: New Evidence for Its Development." *American Antiquity* 43:405–408.

Clark, Geoffrey A. 1969. "A Preliminary Analysis of Burial Clusters at the Grasshopper Site, East-Central Arizona." *The Kiva* 35:57–86.

Clark, J. Desmond. 1969. *Kalambo Falls Prehistoric Site*, vol. 1. Cambridge: Cambridge University Press.

Clark, John Grahame D. 1952. *Prehistoric Europe: The Economic Basis*. London: Methuen.

—— 1954. *Excavations at Star Carr: An Early Mesolithic Site at Seamer near Scarborough, Yorkshire*. Cambridge: Cambridge University Press.

Clarke, David L. 1968. *Analytical Archaeology*. London: Methuen.

—— 1973. "Archaeology: The Loss of Innocence." *Antiquity* 47:6–18.

Clarke, David L. ed. 1972. *Models in Archaeology*. London: Methuen.

Coles, John. 1979. *Experimental Archaeology*. London: Academic Press.

Collingwood, R. G. 1946. *The Idea of History*. New York: Oxford University Press.

Cooke, Kenneth L. 1979. "Mathematical Approaches to Culture Change." In C. Renfrew and K. L. Cooke, eds., *Transformations: Mathematical Approaches to Culture Change*, pp. 3–44. New York: Academic Press.

Cooke, Kenneth and Colin Renfrew. 1979. "An Experiment on the Simulation of Culture Change." In C. Renfrew and K. Cooke, eds., *Transformations: Mathematical Approaches to Culture Change*, pp. 327–348. New York: Academic Press.

Cowan, C. Wesley. 1981. "The Cloudsplitter Rockshelter, Menifee County, Kentucky: A Preliminary Report." *Southeastern Archaeological Conference Bulletin* 24:6–76.

Cowgill, George L. 1968. "Archaeological Applications of Factor, Cluster, and Proximity Analysis." *American Antiquity* 33:367–375.

Crawford, Gary W. 1982. "Late Archaic Plant Remains from West-Central Kentucky: A Summary." *Midcontinental Journal of Archaeology* 7:204–224.

Crumley, Carole. 1979. "Three Locational Models: An Epistemological Assessment for Anthropology and Archaeology." *Advances in Archaeological Method and Theory* 2:141–173.

Curren, Cailup B. 1977. "Potential Interpretations of 'Stone Gorget' Function." *American Antiquity* 42:97–101.

Daniels, S.G.H. 1972. "Research Design Models." In D. Clarke, ed., *Models in Archaeology*, pp. 201–229. London: Methuen.

Darvill, T. C., M. Parker Pearson, R. W. Smith, and R. M. Thomas, eds. 1978. *New Approaches to Our Past: An Archaeological Forum*. Southampton: University of Southampton.

David, Nicholas. 1972. "On the Life Span of Pottery, Type Frequencies, and Archaeological Inference." *American Antiquity* 37:141–142.

DeBoer, Warren R. and Donald W. Lathrup. 1979. "The Making and Breaking of Shipibo-Conibo Ceramics." In C. Kramer, ed., *Ethnoarchaeology: Implications of Ethnography for Archaeology*, pp. 102–138. New York: Columbia University Press.

Deetz, James. 1965. *The Dynamics of Stylistic Change in Arikara Ceramics*. Illinois Studies in Anthropology, no. 4. Urbana: University of Illinois Press.

—— 1967. *Invitation to Archaeology*. Garden City, N.Y.: American Museum of Natural History, Natural History Press.

de Lumley, Henry. 1969. "A Paleolithic Camp at Nice." *Scientific American* 220 (5):42–50.

Deming, William E. 1950. *Some Theory of Sampling*. New York: Wiley.

Dixon, W. J., ed. 1975. *BMDP: Biomedical Computer Programs*. Berkeley: University of California Press.

Donnan, C. B. and C. W. Clewlow, Jr., eds. 1974. *Ethnoarchaeology*. University of California, Los Angeles, Institute of Archaeology Monograph, no. 4. Los Angeles: University of California.

Doran, J. E. 1970. "Systems Theory, Computer Simulations and Archaeology." *World Archaeology* (3):289–298.

—— 1972. "Computer Models as Tools for Archaeological Hypothesis Formulation." In D. Clarke, ed., *Models in Archaeology*, pp. 425–451. London: Methuen.

Doran, J. E. and F. R. Hodson. 1975. *Mathematics and Computers in Archaeology*. Cambridge: Harvard University Press.

Dray, William. 1957. *Laws and Explanation in History*. Oxford: Oxford University Press.

—— 1964. *Philosophy of History*. Englewood Cliffs, N.J.: Prentice-Hall.

Dunnell, Robert C. 1978a. "Archaeological Potential of Anthropological and Scientific Models of Function." In R. Dunnell and E. Hall, Jr., eds., *Archaeological Essays in Honor of Irving B. Rouse*, pp. 41–73. The Hague: Mouton.

—— 1978b. "Style and Function: A Fundamental Dichotomy." *American Antiquity* 43:192–202.

—— 1979. "Trends in Current Americanist Archaeology." *American Journal of Archaeology* 83:437–449.

—— 1980a. "Americanist Archaeology: The 1979 Contribution." *American Journal of Archaeology* 84:463–478.

—— 1980b. "Evolutionary Theory and Archaeology." *Advances in Archaeological Theory and Method* 3:35–99.
—— 1981. "Americanist Archaeology: The 1980 Literature." *American Journal of Archaeology* 85:429–445.
——1982a. "Americanist Archaeological Literature: 1981." *American Journal of Archaeology* 86:509–529.
—— 1982b. "Science, Social Science, and Common Sense: The Agonizing Dilemma of Modern Archaeology." *Journal of Anthropological Research* 38:1–25.
Durham, William H. 1976. "The Adaptive Significance of Cultural Behavior." *Human Ecology* 4:89–121.
Dye, David H. and Katherine M. Moore. 1978. "Recovery Systems for Subsistence Data: Water Screening and Water Flotation." *Tennessee Anthropologist* 3:59–69.
Earle, Timothy K. and Jonathon E. Ericson. 1977. *Exchange Systems in Prehistory.* New York: Academic Press.
Elliot, Kevin, D. Ellman, and Ian Hodder. 1978. "The Simulation of Neolithic Ax Dispersal in Britain." In I. Hodder, ed., *Simulation Studies in Archaeology*, pp. 79–87. Cambridge: Cambridge University Press.
Evans, J. G. and S. Limbrey. 1974. "The Experimental Earthwork on Morden Bog, Wareham, Dorset, England: 1963 to 1972." *Proceedings of the Prehistoric Society* 40:170–202.
Fairservis, Walter A., Jr. 1975. *The Threshold of Civilization: An Experiment in Prehistory.* New York: Scribners.
Farrand, William R. 1975. "Sediment Analysis of a Prehistoric Rockshelter: The Abri Pataud." *Quaternary Research* 5:1–26.
Faulkner, Charles H. and Major C. R. McCollough. 1973. "Introductory Report of the Normandy Reservoir Salvage Project: Environmental Setting, Typology, and Survey." Report of Investigations, no. 11, Normandy Archaeological Project, vol. 1. Knoxville: Department of Anthropology, University of Tennessee.
Feigl, H. and May Brodbeck, eds. 1953. *Readings in the Philosophy of Science.* New York: Appleton-Century-Crofts.
Flannery, Kent V. 1967. "Culture History v. Culture Process: A Debate in American Archaeology." *Scientific American* 217:119–122.
—— 1968. "Archaeological Systems Theory and Early Mesoamerica." In B. Meggers, ed., *Anthropological Archaeology in the Americas*, pp. 67–87. Washington, D.C.: Anthropological Society of Washington.
—— 1972. "The Cultural Evolution of Civilizations." *Annual Review of Ecology and Systematics* 3:399–426.
—— 1973. "Archaeology with a Capital 'S.' " In C. Redman, ed., *Research and Theory in Current Archaeology*, pp. 47–53. New York: Wiley.
Flannery, Kent V. and Joyce Marcus. 1976. "Formative Oaxaca and the Zapotec Cosmos." *American Scientist* 64:374–383.

Flannery, Kent V., ed. 1976. *The Early Mesoamerican Village*. New York: Academic Press.

Fowler, Don D. 1982. "Cultural Resources Management." *Advances in Archaeological Method and Theory* 5:1–50.

Fox, Richard and Carol A. Smith, eds. 1982. "The Evolution and Diversity of Urban Systems." *Comparative Urban Research* vol. 9, no. 1.

Freeman, L. G., Jr. 1968. "A Theoretical Framework for Interpreting Archeological Materials." In R. Lee and I. DeVore, eds. *Man the Hunter*, pp. 262–267. Chicago: Aldine.

Fritz, John. 1978. "Paleopsychology Today." In Charles L. Redman et al., eds., *Social Archaeology: Beyond Subsistence and Dating*, pp. 37–59. New York: Academic Press.

Gaines, Sylvia W. 1974. "Computer Use at an Archaeological Field Location." *American Antiquity* 39(3):454–462.

Gerhardt, C. J., ed. 1875. *Die Philosophischen Schrifter von Gottfried Wilhelm Leibniz*. Vol. 1 Berlin: Weidmannsche.

Gifford, Diane. 1978. "Ethnoarchaeological Observations of Natural Processes Affecting Cultural Materials." In R. Gould, ed., *Explorations in Ethnoarchaeology*, pp. 77–101. Albuquerque: University of New Mexico Press.

—— 1981. "Taphonomy and Paleoecology: A Critical Review of Archaeology's Sister Disciplines." *Advances in Archaeological Method and Theory* 4:365–438.

Gladfelter, Bruce G. 1981. "Developments and Directions in Geoarchaeology." *Advances in Archaeological Method and Theory* 4:343–364.

Goodyear, Albert and Mark Raab. 1984. "A Review of Middle-Range Theory in Archaeology." *American Antiquity* 49:255–268.

Goodyear, Albert C., L. Mark Raab, and Timothy C. Klinger. 1978. The Status of Archaeological Research Design in Cultural Resource Management." *American Antiquity* 43:159–173.

Gould, Richard A., ed. 1978. *Explorations in Ethnoarchaeology*. Albuquerque: University of New Mexico Press.

—— 1980. *Living Archaeology*. Cambridge: Cambridge University Press.

Gould, Richard A. and Patty Jo Watson. 1982. "A Dialogue on the Meaning and Use of Analogy in Ethnoarchaeological Reasoning." *Journal of Anthropological Archaeology* 1:355–381.

Graves, Michael. 1981. "Ethnoarchaeology of Kalinga Ceramic Design. "Ph.D. dissertation, University of Arizona.

Gumerman, George J. 1980. "Review of *Discovering Past Behavior: Experiments in the Archaeology of the American Southwest*." *American Anthropologist* 82:881–882.

Gunn, Joel. 1977. "Idiosyncratic Chipping Style as a Demographic Indicator: A Proposed Application to the South Hills Region of Idaho and Utah."

In J. Hill and J. Gunn, eds., *The Individual in Prehistory*, pp. 167–204. New York: Academic Press.
Haggett, Peter. 1965. *Locational Analysis in Human Geography*. London: Edward Arnold.
Hall, A. D. and R. E. Fagen. 1956. "Definition of a System." *General Systems* 1:18–28.
Hall, Robert L. 1976. "Ghosts, Water Barriers, Corn and Sacred Enclosures in the Eastern Woodlands." *American Antiquity* 41:360–364.
―― 1977. "An Anthropocentric Perspective for Eastern United States Prehistory." *American Antiquity* 42:499–518.
Hanen, Marsha and Jane Kelley. Forthcoming. *Archaeology and the Methodology of Science*. New York: Academic Press.
Hanson, Norwood R. 1958. *Patterns of Discovery*. Cambridge: Cambridge University Press.
Harary, Frank, Robert Z. Norman, and Dorwin Cartwright. 1965. *Structural Models: An Introduction to the Theory of Directed Graphs*. New York: Wiley.
Hardesty, Donald L. 1980. "The Use of General Ecological Principles in Archaeology." *Advances in Archaeological Method and Theory* 3:157–187.
Harlan, Jack. 1967. "A Wild Wheat Harvest in Turkey." *Archaeology* 20:197–201
Harvey, David. 1969. *Explanation in Geography*. London: Edward Arnold.
Hawkes, Jaquetta. 1968. "The Proper Study of Mankind." *Antiquity* 42:255–262.
Helm, June. 1962. "The Ecological Approach in Anthropology." *American Journal of Sociology* 67:630–639.
Hempel, Carl G. 1942. "The Function of General Laws in History." *The Journal of Philosophy* 39:35–48. Reprinted in Hempel 1965:231–243.
―― 1959. "The Logic of Functional Analysis." In L. Gross, ed., *Symposium on Sociological Theory*, pp. 271–307. New York: Harper & Row. Reprinted in Hempel 1965:297–330.
―― 1963. "Explanation and Prediction by Covering Laws." In B. Baumrin, ed., *Philosophy of Science: The Deleware Seminar*. Vol. 1, 1961–1962, pp. 107–133. New York: Wiley.
―― 1965. *Aspects of Scientific Explanation, and Other Essays in the Philosophy of Science*. New York: Free Press.
――1966. *Philosophy of Natural Science*. Englewood Cliffs, N.J.: Prentice-Hall.
Hempel, Carl G. and Paul Oppenheim. 1953. "The Logic of Explanation." In H. Feigl and M. Brodbeck, eds., *Readings in the Philosophy of Science*, pp. 319–352. New York: Appleton-Century-Crofts. Originally published in *Philosophy of Science* 15:135–175 (1948).
Hester, T. R. and R. F. Heizer. 1973. "Bibliography of Archaeology I: Experiments, Lithic Technology and Petrography. Addison-Wesley Modules 29. Reading, Mass.: Addison-Wesley.

Hill, James N. 1966. "A Prehistoric Community in Eastern Arizona." *Southwestern Journal of Anthropology* 22:9–30.

—— 1968. "Broken K Pueblo: Patterns of Form and Function." In S. Binford and L. Binford, eds., *New Perspectives in Archeology*, pp. 103–142. Chicago: Aldine.

—— 1972. "The Methodological Debate in Contemporary Archaeology: A Model." In D. Clarke, ed., *Models in Archaeology*, pp. 61–107. London: Methuen.

—— 1977. "Systems Theory and the Explanation of Change." In J. Hill, ed., *Explanation of Prehistoric Change*, pp. 59–103. Albuquerque: University of New Mexico Press.

Hill, James N. and Robert K. Evans. 1972. "A Model for Classification and Typology." In D. Clarke, ed., *Models in Archaeology*, pp. 231–273. London: Methuen.

Hill, James N. and Joel Gunn, eds. 1977. *The Individual in Prehistory: Studies of Variability in Style in Prehistoric Technologies*. New York: Academic Press.

Hodder, Ian and Clive Orton. 1976. *Spatial Analysis in Archaeology*. Cambridge: Cambridge University Press.

Hodder, Ian, ed. 1978. *Simulation Studies in Archaeology*. Cambridge: Cambridge University Press.

—— 1982. *Symbolic and Structural Archaeology*. Cambridge: Cambridge University Press.

Hodder, Ian, Glynn Isaac, and Norman Hammond, eds. 1981. *Pattern of the Past: Studies in Honor of David Clarke*. Cambridge: Cambridge University Press.

Hole, Frank. 1977. *Studies in the Archaeological History of the Deh Luran Plain: The Excavation of Chagha Sifid*. Memoirs of the Museum of Anthropology, no. 9. Ann Arbor: University of Michigan.

—— 1978. "Pastoral Nomadism in Western Iran." In R. Gould, ed., *Explorations in Ethnoarchaeology*, pp. 127–167. Albuquerque: University of New Mexico Press.

—— 1979. "Rediscovering the Past in the Present: Ethnoarchaeology in Luristan, Iran." In C. Kramer, ed., *Ethnoarchaeology: The Implications of Ethnography for Archaeology*, pp. 192–218. New York: Columbia University Press.

Hole, Frank and Kent V. Flannery. 1967. "The Prehistory of Southwestern Iran: A Preliminary Report." *Proceedings of the Prehistoric Society* 33:147–206.

Hole, Frank, Kent V. Flannery, and James A. Neely. 1969. *Prehistory and Human Ecology of the Deh Luran Plain*. Memoirs of the Museum of Anthropology, no. 1. Ann Arbor: University of Michigan.

Hole, Frank and Robert F. Heizer. 1969. *An Introduction to Prehistoric Archaeology*. 2d ed. New York: Holt, Rinehart and Winston.

——— 1973. *An Introduction to Prehistoric Archaeology.* 3d ed. New York: Holt, Rinehart and Winston.
Hoos, Ida R. 1972. *Systems Analysis in Public Policy: A Critique.* Berkeley: University of California Press.
Hosler, D. H., J. H. Sabloff, and D. Runge. 1977. "Simulation Model Development: A Case Study of the Classic Maya Collapse." In N. Hammond, ed., *Social Process in Maya Prehistory,* pp. 553–590. London: Academic Press.
Hume, David. 1739. *A Treatise of Human Nature.* See Selby-Bigge 1888.
——— 1777. *An Enquiry Concerning Human Understanding.* See Selby-Bigge 1902.
Huntington, Ellsworth. 1907. *The Pulse of Asia.* Boston: Houghton Mifflin.
——— 1915. *Civilization and Climate.* New Haven: Yale University Press.
——— 1945. *Mainsprings of Civilization.* New York: Wiley.
Huss-Ashmore, Rebecca, Alan H. Goodman, and George J. Armelegos. 1982. "Nutritional Inference from Paleopathology." *Advances in Archaeological Method and Theory* 5:395–474.
Ingersoll, Daniel, John Yellen, and William MacDonald, eds. 1977. *Experimental Archaeology.* New York: Columbia University Press.
Irwin-Williams, Cynthia, Rex Adams, Paddy C. Johnson, Ann Bennett, E. Pierre Morenon, and Gordon Alan Davis. 1975. "Salmon Ruin Archaeological Investigations." Archaeological Completion Report Series, no. 8. Washington, D.C.: National Park Service.
Isaac, Glynn. 1971. "Whither Archaeology?" *Antiquity* 45:123–129.
Iversen, Johannes. 1956. "Forest Clearance in the Stone Age." *Scientific American* 194:36–41.
Jacobsen, Thomas W. 1973. "Excavations in the Franchthi Cave, 1969–1971." *Hesperia* 42:45–88, 253–283.
——— 1981. "Franchthi Cave and the Beginning of Settled Village Life in Greece." *Hesperia* 50:303–319.
Jennings, Jesse D. 1966. "Glen Canyon: A Summary." University of Utah Anthropological Papers, no. 81. Glen Canyon Series, no. 31. Salt Lake City: University of Utah.
Jewell, P. A. and G. W. Dimbleby. 1966. "The Experimental Earthwork on Overton Down, Wiltshire, England: The First Four Years." *Proceedings of the Prehistoric Society* 32:313–342.
Jochim, Michael A. 1976. *Hunter-Gatherer Subsistence and Settlement: A Predictive Model.* New York: Academic Press.
——— 1979. "Breaking Down the System: Recent Ecological Approaches in Archaeology." *Advances in Archaeological Method and Theory* 2:77–117.
Johanson, Donald and Maitland Edey. 1981. *Lucy.* New York: Simon and Schuster.
Johnson, Gregory A. 1977. "Aspects of Regional Analysis in Archaeology." *Annual Review of Anthropology* 6:479–508.
——— 1978. "Information Source and the Development of Decision Making

Organizations." In C. Redman et al., eds., *Social Archaeology*, pp. 87–112. New York: Academic Press.
Kay, Marvin, Frances B. King, and Christine K. Robinson. 1980. "Cucurbits and Phillips Spring: New Evidence and Interpretations." *American Antiquity* 45:806–822.
Kehoe, Alice B. and Thomas F. Kehoe. 1974. "Cognitive Models for Archaeological Interpretation." *American Antiquity* 38:150–154.
Kent, Susan. 1981. "The Dog: An Archaeologist's Best Friend or Worst Enemy—the Spatial Distribution of Faunal Remains," *Journal of Field Archaeology* 8:367–372.
Kidder, Alfred V. 1937. "The Development of Maya Research." *Proceedings of the Second General Assembly, Pan American Institute of Geography and History, 1935*, pp. 218–235. U.S. Department of State Conference Series, no. 28. Washington, D.C.: Government Printing Office.
King, Leslie J. 1969. *Statistical Analysis in Geography*. Englewood Cliffs, N.J.: Prentice-Hall.
King, Thomas F. 1971. "A Conflict of Values in American Archaeology." *American Antiquity* 36:255–262.
—— 1977. "Resolving a Conflict of Values in American Archaeology." In M. Schiffer and G. Gumerman, eds., *Conservation Archaeology*, pp. 87–105. New York: Academic Press.
King, Thomas F., P. P. Hickman, and G. C. Berg. 1977. *Cultural Resource Management: An Anthropological Approach*. New York: Academic Press.
Kleindienst, Maxine R. and Patty Jo Watson. 1956. "Action Archaeology: The Archaeological Inventory of a Living Community." *Anthropology Tomorrow* 5:75–78.
Kluckhohn, Clyde. 1939. "The Place of Theory in Anthropological Studies." *Philosophy of Science* 6:328–344.
—— 1940. "The Conceptual Structure in Middle American Studies." In C. Hay et al., eds., *The Maya and Their Neighbors*, pp. 41–51. New York: Dover.
Kohl, P. L. 1981. "Materialist Approaches in Prehistory." *Annual Reviews in Anthropology* 10:89–118.
Kolstoe, Ralph H. 1969. *Introduction to Statistics for the Behavioral Sciences*. Homewood, Ill.: Dorsey Press.
Kramer, Carol. 1980. "Estimating Prehistoric Populations: An Ethnoarchaeological Approach." In *L'Archeologie de l'Iraq: Perspectives et limites de l'interpretations anthropologiques des documents*, pp. 315–334. Colloques internationaux du CNRS, no. 580. Paris: Centre National de Recherche Scientifique.
—— 1982. *Village Ethnoarchaeology: Rural Iran in Archaeological Perspective*. New York: Academic Press.
Kramer, Carol, ed. 1979. *Ethnoarchaeology: Implications of Ethnography for Archaeology*. New York: Columbia University Press.

Kuhn, Thomas S. 1962. *The Structure of Scientific Revolutions.* International Encyclopedia of Unified Science. Vol. 2, no. 2. Chicago: University of Chicago Press.
—— 1970a. "Postscript-1969." in T. Kuhn., 1970c:174–210.
—— 1970b. "Reflections on My Critics." In I. Lakatos and A. Musgrave, eds., *Criticism and the Growth of Knowledge,* pp. 231–278. Cambridge: Cambridge University Press.
—— 1970c. "The Structure of Scientific Revolutions." *International Encyclopedia of Unified Science.* 2d ed. Vol. 2, no. 2. Chicago: University of Chicago Press.
—— 1974. "Second Thoughts on Paradigms." In F. Suppe, ed., *The Structure of Scientific Theories,* pp. 459–482. Urbana: University of Illinois Press. Reprinted in Kuhn 1977:293–315.
—— 1977. *The Essential Tension.* Chicago: University of Chicago Press.
Leach, Edmond R. 1954. *Political Systems of Highland Burma: A Study of Kachin Social Structure.* Cambridge: Harvard University Press.
Leaf, Garry R. 1973. "Review of *Explanation in Archeology* by Patty Jo Watson, Steven LeBlanc, and Charles L. Redman." *Plains Anthropologist* 18:350–351.
LeBlanc, Steven A. 1971. "An Addition to Naroll's Suggested Floor Area and Settlement Population Relationship." *American Antiquity* 36:210–211.
—— 1973. "Two Points of Logic Concerning Data, Hypotheses, General Laws, and Systems." In C. Redman, ed., *Research and Theory in Current Archaeology,* pp. 199–214. New York: Wiley.
—— 1975. "Micro-Seriation: A Method for Fine Chronologic Differentiation." *American Antiquity* 40:22–38.
—— 1979. "A Proposal for an Archaeological Conservancy." *Journal of Field Archaeology* 6:360–365.
—— 1980. Review of T. K. King, *The Archeological Survey: Methods and Uses;* Darvill, Perason, Smith, and Thomas, eds., *New Approaches to Our Past: An Archaeological Forum;* F. Plog, ed., *An Analytic Approach to Cultural Management: The Little Colorado Planning Unit,* in *American Antiquity* 45(1):212–214.
—— 1983. *The Mimbres People.* London: Thames and Hudson.
Lehman, Hugh. 1972. "Statistical Explanation." *Philosophy of Science* 39:500–506.
Leone, Mark P. 1973. "Archaeology as the Science of Technology: Mormon Town Plans and Fences." In C. Redman, ed., *Research and Theory in Current Archaeology,* pp. 125–150. New York: Wiley.
—— 1981. "The Relationship Between Artifacts and the Public in Outdoor History Museums." *Annals of the New York Academy of Sciences* 376:301–314.
—— 1982a. "Childe's Offspring." In I. Hodder, ed., *Symbolic and Structural Archaeology,* pp. 179–184. Cambridge: Cambridge University Press.

—— 1982b. "Some Opinions About Recovering Mind." *American Antiquity* 47:742–760.

—— 1983. "Land and Water, Urban Life, and Boats: Underwater Reconnaissance in Chesapeake Bay." In R. Gould, ed., *Shipwreck Anthropology*, pp. 173–188. School of American Research Advanced Seminar Series. Albuquerque: University of New Mexico Press.

Leroi-Gourhan, André. 1967. *Treasures of Prehistoric Art*. New York: Abrams.

Levy, Janet E. 1982. *Social and Religious Organization in Bronze Age Denmark*. British Archaeological Reports, International Series, no. 124. Oxford: BAR.

Lewontin, R. C. 1974. *The Genetic Basis of Evolutionary Change*. New York: Columbia University Press.

Lipe, William D. 1977. "A Conservation Model for American Archaeology." In M. Schiffer and G. Gumerman, eds., *Conservation Archaeology*, pp. 19–42. New York: Academic Press.

Longacre, William A. 1968. "Some Aspects of Prehistoric Society in East-Central Arizona." In S. Binford and L. Binford, eds., *New Perspectives in Archeology*, pp. 89–102. Chicago: Aldine.

—— 1970. "Archaeology as Anthropology; A Case Study." Anthropological Papers of the University of Arizona, no. 17. Tucson: University of Arizona Press.

—— 1975. "Population Dynamics at the Grasshopper Pueblo, Arizona." In A. Swedlund, ed., *Population Studies in Archaeology and Biological Anthropology: A Symposium*, pp. 71–76. SAA Memoir, no. 40. Washington, D.C.: American Anthropological Association.

—— 1981. "Kalinga Pottery: An Ethnoarchaeological Study." In I. Hodder, G. Isaac, and N. Hammond, eds., *Pattern of the Past*, pp. 49–66. Cambridge: Cambridge University Press.

Low, Gilbert W. 1981. "Using System Dynamics to Simulate the Past." In J. Sabloff, ed., *Simulations in Archaeology*, pp. 249–282. Albuquerque: University of New Mexico Press.

Lyman, R. Lee. 1982. "Archaeofaunas and Subsistence Studies." *Advances in Archaeological Method and Theory* 5:331–393.

Lyon, Patricia. 1970. "Differential Bone Destruction: An Ethnographic Example." *American Antiquity* 35:213–215.

MacNeish, Richard S. 1964. "Ancient Mesoamerican Civilization." *Science* 143:531–537.

—— 1967. "A Summary of the Subsistence." In D. S. Byers, ed., *The Prehistory of the Tehuacan Valley, vol. 1, Environment and Subsistence*, pp. 290–310. Austin: University of Texas Press.

Marquardt, William H. and Patty Jo Watson. 1979. "Shell Midden Formation and Deformation: A Case Study." Paper presented in the symposium, "Natural and Cultural Processes in the Formation of an Archaic Shell

References

Midden on the Green River, Kentucky," at the Thirty-Sixth Annual Meeting of the Southeastern Archaeological Conference, Atlanta.
—— 1983. "The Shell Mound Archaic of Western Kentucky." In J. Phillips and J. Brown, eds., *Archaic Hunters and Gatherers in the American Midwest*, pp. 323–339. New York: Academic Press.
Marshack, Alexander. 1972. *The Roots of Civilization*. New York: McGraw-Hill.
—— 1981. "Epipaleolithic, Early Neolithic Iconography: A Cognitive, Comparative Analysis of the Lepenski Vir/Vlasac Iconography and Symbolism, Its Roots and Later Influence." Paper presented at the international symposium, "The Culture of Lepenski Vir and the Problems of the Formation of Neolithic Cultures in Southeastern and Central Europe," Romisch-Germanisches Museum, Cologne, February 18–25.
Martin, Paul S. and H. E. Wright, Jr., eds. 1967. *Pleistocene Extinctions: A Search for a Cause*. New Haven: Yale University Press.
Maruyama, Magoroh. 1963. "The Second Cybernetics: Deviation-Amplifying Mutual Causal Processes." *American Scientist* 51:164–179.
McDonald, William A. and George Rapp, Jr., eds. 1972. *The Minnesota Messenia Expedition*. Minneapolis: University of Minnesota Press.
McGimsey, Charles R., III. 1972. *Public Archaeology*. New York: Seminar Press.
McGimsey, C. R., III and Hester A. Davis. 1977. *The Management of Archaeological Resources: The Airlie House Report*. Washington, D.C.: Society for American Archaeology.
McIntosh, Roderick J. 1974. "Archaeology and Mud Wall Decay in a West African Village." *World Archaeology* 6:154–171.
—— 1977. "The Excavation of Mud Structures: An Experiment from West Africa." *World Archaeology* 9:185–199.
McMillan, R. Bruce. 1976. "The Dynamics of Cultural and Environmental Change at Rodgers Shelter, Missouri." In W. R. Wood and R. B. McMillan, eds., *Prehistoric Man and His Environments*, pp. 211–232. New York: Academic Press.
Meehan, Eugene. 1968. *Explanation in Social Science: A System Paradigm*. Homewood, Ill.: Dorsey Press.
Michel, Mark P. 1981. "Preserving America's Prehistoric Heritage." *Archaeology* 34(2):61–63.
Miksicek, Charles. 1975. "A Preliminary Examination of the Cibola Botanical Remains." Paper presented at the Fortieth Annual Meeting of the Society for American Archaeology, May.
Minnis, Paul E. 1978. "Paleoethnobotanical Indicators of Prehistoric Environmental Disturbance: A Case Study." In R. Ford, ed., *The Nature and Status of Ethnobotany*, pp. 347–366. Anthropological Papers, no. 67. Ann Arbor: University of Michigan Museum of Anthropology.
Minnis, Paul E. and Steven A. LeBlanc. 1976. "An Efficient, Inexpensive Arid Lands Flotation System." *American Antiquity* 41:491–493.

Mixon, Bill. 1975. Review of P. J. Watson, ed., *Archaeology of the Mammoth Cave Area.* In *The Windy City Speleonews* 15 (1):15.

Monks, Gregory G. 1981. "Seasonality Studies." *Advances in Archaeological Method and Theory* 4:177–240.

Mueller, James W., ed. 1975. *Sampling in Archaeology.* Tucson: University of Arizona Press.

Murray, Priscilla. 1980. "Discard Location: The Ethnographic Data." *American Antiquity* 45:490–502.

Nagel, E. 1961. *The Structure of Science: Problems in the Logic of Scientific Explanation.* New York: Harcourt, Brace, and World.

Nance, Jack D. 1980. "Non-Site Sampling in the Lower Cumberland River Valley, Kentucky." *Midcontinental Journal of Archaeology* 5:123–135

Nelson, Ben A. 1981. Ethnoarchaeology and Paleodemography: A Test of Turner and Lofgren's Hypothesis." *Journal of Anthropological Research* 37:107–129.

Nie, Norman H., C. Hadlai Hull, Jean G. Jenkins, Karin Steinbremmer, and Dale H. Bent. 1975. *Statistical Package for the Social Sciences.* 2d ed. New York: McGraw-Hill.

Oakeshott, Michael. 1933. *Experience and Its Modes.* London: Cambridge University Press.

Ochsenschlager, E. L. 1974. "Modern Potters at Al-Hiba, with Some Reflections on the Excavated Early Dynastic Pottery." In C. Donnan and C. Clewlow, eds., *Ethnoarchaeology,* pp. 149–157. Los Angeles: University of California, Institute of Archaeology.

Odner, K. 1972. "Ethno-Historic and Ecological Settings for Economic and Social Models of an Iron Age Society: Valldalen, Norway." In David L. Clarke, ed., *Models in Archaeology,* pp. 623–651. London: Methuen.

Odum, E. P. 1953. *Fundamentals of Ecology.* Philadelphia: Saunders.

—— 1963. *Ecology.* New York: Holt, Rinehart and Winston.

O'Shea, John M. 1978. "A Simulation of Pawnee Site Development." In I. Hodder, ed., *Simulation Studies in Archaeology,* pp. 39–46. Cambridge: Cambridge University Press.

Parker, Arthur C. 1935. "Editorials." *American Antiquity* 1:2–3.

Parmalee, Paul W., R. Bruce McMillan, and Frances B. King. 1976. "Changing Subsistence Patterns at Rodgers Shelter." In W. R. Wood and R. B. McMillan, eds., *Prehistoric Man and His Environments,* pp. 141–161. New York: Academic Press.

Pearsall, Deborah H. 1982. "Phytolith Analysis: Applications of a New Paleoethnobotanical Technique in Archaeology." *American Anthropologist* 84:862–871.

Piggott, Stuart. 1965. *Ancient Europe, from the Beginnings of Agriculture to Classical Antiquity: A Survey.* Chicago: Aldine.

Plog, Fred T. 1975. "Systems Theory in Archaeological Research." *Annual Review of Anthropology* 4:207–224.

References

Plog, Stephen. 1976. "Relative Efficiencies of Sampling Techniques for Archaeological Surveys." In K. Flannery, ed., *The Early Mesoamerican Village*, pp. 136–158. New York: Academic Press.

—— 1980. *Stylistic Variation in Prehistoric Ceramics: Design Analysis in the American Southwest*. Cambridge: Cambridge University Press.

Plog, Stephen, Fred Plog, and Walter Wait. 1978. "Decision Making in Modern Surveys." *Advances in Archaeological Method and Theory* 1:383–421.

Popper, Karl. 1959. *The Logic of Scientific Discovery*. New York: Basic Books.

Price, James E., Cynthia R. Price, J. Cottier, S. Harris, and J. House. 1975. *An Assessment of the Cultural Resources of the Little Black Watershed*. Columbia: University of Missouri.

Radcliffe-Brown, A. R. 1940. "On Joking Relationships." *Africa* 13:195–210.

Ragir, S. 1967. "A Review of Technologies for Archaeological Sampling." In Robert F. Heizer and J. A. Graham, eds., *A Guide to Field Methods in Archaeology: Approaches to the Anthropology of the Dead*, pp. 181–197. Palo Alto, Calif.: National Press.

Rapoport, Anatol. 1968. "Foreword." In W. Buckley, ed., *Modern Systems Research for the Behavioral Scientist*, pp. xiii–xxii. Chicago: Aldine.

Rapp, George, Jr. and John A. Gifford. 1982. "Archaeological Geology." *American Scientist* 70:45–53.

Rathje, William L. 1975. "The Last Tango in Mayapan: A Tentative Trajectory of Production-Distribution Systems." In J. Sabloff and C. Lamberg-Karlovsky, eds., *Ancient Civilization and Trade*, pp. 409–448. Albuquerque: University of New Mexico Press.

—— 1978. "Archaeological Ethnography . . . Because Sometimes It is Better to Give than to Receive." In R. Gould, ed., *Explorations in Ethnoarchaeology*, pp. 49–75. Albuquerque: University of New Mexico Press.

—— 1979. "Modern Material Culture Studies." *Advances in Archaeological Method and Theory* 1:1–37.

Read, Dwight W. 1974. "Some Comments on Typologies in Archaeology and an Outline of a Methodology." *American Antiquity* 39:216–242.

Read, Dwight W. and Steven A. LeBlanc. 1978. "Descriptive Statements, Covering Laws, and Theories in Archaeology." *Current Anthropology* 19:307–312.

Redman, Charles L. 1973. "Multistage Fieldwork and Analytical Techniques." *American Antiquity* 38:61–79.

—— 1974. *Archaeological Sampling Strategies*. Addison-Wesley Module No. 55. Reading, Mass.: Addison-Wesley.

—— 1977. "The 'Analytical Individual' and Prehistoric Style Variability." In J. Hill and J. Gunn, eds., *The Individual in Prehistory*, pp. 41–53. New York: Academic Press.

Redman, Charles L., Mary Jane Berman, Edward V. Curtin, William T. Langhorne, Jr., Nina M. Versaggi, and Jeffrey C. Wanser, eds. 1978. *Social Archaeology: Beyond Subsistence and Dating*. New York: Academic Press.

Renfrew, Colin. 1969. "Trade and Culture Process in European Prehistory." *Current Anthropology* 10:151–169.
—— 1972. *The Emergence of Civilization: The Cyclades and the Aegean in the Third Millennium B.C.* London: Methuen.
—— 1979. "Systems Collapse as Social Transformation: Catastrophe and Anastrophe in Early State Societies." In C. Renfrew and K. Cooke, eds., *Transformations: Mathematical Approaches to Culture Change,* pp. 481–506. New York: Academic Press.
—— 1981. "The Simulator as Demiurge." In Sabloff, ed., *Simulations in Archaeology,* pp. 283–306. Albuquerque: University of New Mexico Press.
Renfrew, Colin and Kenneth L. Cooke, eds. 1979. *Transformations: Mathematical Approaches to Culture Change.* New York: Academic Press.
Renfrew, Colin and Tim Poston. 1979. "Discontinuities in the Endogenous Change of Settlement Pattern." In C. Renfrew and K. Cooke, eds., *Transformations: Mathematical Approaches to Culture Change,* pp. 437–462. New York: Academic Press.
Rescher, Nicholas. 1970. *Scientific Explanation.* New York: Free Press.
Roper, Donna C. 1979. "The Method and Theory of Site Catchment Analysis: A Review." *Advances in Archaeological Method and Theory* 2:119–140.
Rovner, Irwin. 1983. "Plant Phytolith Analysis: Major Advances in Archaeobotanical Research." *Advances in Archaeological Method and Theory* 6:225–266.
Rudner, Richard S. 1966. *Philosophy of Social Science.* Englewood Cliffs, N.J.: Prentice-Hall.
Runnels, Curtis N. 1981. "A Diachronic Study and Economic Analysis of Millstones from the Argolid, Greece." Ph.D. dissertation, Indiana University.
Sabloff, Jeremy A. and C. C. Lamberg-Karlovsky. 1975. *Ancient Civilization and Trade.* Albuquerque: University of New Mexico Press.
Sabloff, Jeremy A., ed. 1981. *Simulations in Archaeology.* Albuquerque: University of New Mexico Press.
Sackett, James R. 1966. "Quantitative Analysis of Upper Paleolithic Stone Tools." In J. Desmond Clark and F. Howell, eds., *Recent Studies in Paleoanthropology. American Anthropologist* Special Publication 68 (2):356–394.
Sahlins, Marshall. 1972. *Stone Age Economics.* Chicago: Aldine-Atherton.
Salmon, Merrilee. 1975. "Confirmation and Explanation in Archaeology." *American Antiquity* 40:459–464.
—— 1976. "Deductive' Versus 'Inductive' Archaeology." *American Antiquity* 41:376–381.
—— 1978. "What Can Systems Theory Do for Archaeology?" *American Antiquity* 43:174–183.
—— 1982. *Philosophy and Archaeology.* New York: Academic Press.
Salmon, Merrilee H. and Wesley C. Salmon. 1979. "Alternative Models of Scientific Explanation." *American Anthropologist* 81:61–74.

Salmon, Wesley C. 1967. *The Foundations of Scientific Inference.* Pittsburgh: University of Pittsburgh Press.
—— 1971a. "Postscript 1971." In W. Salmon, *Statistical Explanation and Statistical Relevence,* pp. 105–110. Pittsburgh: University of Pittsburgh Press.
—— 1971b. "Statistical Explanation." In W. Salmon, *Statistical Explanation and Statistical Relevance,* pp. 29–87. Pittsburgh: University of Pittsburgh Press.
—— 1971c. *Statistical Explanation and Statistical Relevance.* Pittsburgh: University of Pittsburgh Press.
—— 1973. "Reply to Lehman." *Philosophy of Science* 40:397–402.
—— 1975a. "Reply to Comments." In S. Körner, ed., *Explanation,* pp. 160–184. Oxford: Blackwell.
—— 1975b. "Theoretical Explanation." In S. Körner, ed., *Explanation,* pp. 118–145. Oxford: Blackwell.
—— 1977. "A Third Dogma of Empiricism." In R. Butts and J. Hintikka, eds., *Basic Problems in Methodology and Linguistics,* pp. 149–166. Dordrecht: D. Reidel.
Schacht, Robert M. 1981. "Estimating Past Population Trends." *Annual Review of Anthropology* 10:119–140.
Schiffer, Michael B. 1972. "Archaeological Context and Systematic Context." *American Antiquity* 37:156–165.
—— 1976. *Behavioral Archaeology.* New York: Academic Press.
—— 1978. "Methodological Issues in Ethnoarchaeology." In R. Gould, ed. *Explorations in Ethnoarchaeology,* pp. 229–247. School of American Research Advanced Seminar Series. Albuquerque: University of New Mexico Press.
Schiffer, Michael and George J. Gumerman, eds. 1977. *Conservation Archaeology: A Guide for Cultural Resource Management Studies.* New York: Academic Press.
Schiffer, Michael and John House, comps. 1975. *The Cache River Archaeological Project: An Experiment in Contract Archaeology.* Arkansas Archaeological Survey, Research Series, no. 8. Fayetteville.
Schoenwetter, James A. 1981. "Prologue to a Contextual Archaeology." *Journal of Archaeological Science* 8:367–379.
Scriven, Michael. 1962. "Explanations, Predictions, and Laws." In H. Feigl and G. Maxwell, eds., *Minnesota Studies in the Philosophy of Science III,* pp. 170–230. Minneapolis: University of Minnesota Press.
Selby-Bigge, L. A., ed. 1888. *A Treatise of Human Nature by David Hume.* Reprinted from the original edition (1739). Oxford: Clarendon Press.
—— 1902. *Enquiries Concerning the Human Understanding and Concerning the Principles of Morals by David Hume.* Reprinted from the posthumous edition (1777). 2d ed. Oxford: Clarendon Press.
Shapere, Dudley. 1971. "The Paradigm Concept." *Science* 172:706–709.
Smith, Carol A. 1982a. "Modern and Premodern Urban Primacy." *Comparative Urban Research* 9:79–96.

—— 1982b. "Placing Formal Geographical Models Into Cultural Contexts: The Anthropological Study of Urban Systems." *Comparative Urban Research* 9:50–59.

Smith, Carol A., ed. 1976. *Regional Analysis*. 2 vols. New York: Academic Press.

Smith, P. E. L. 1970. "Ecological Archaeology in Iran." Review of Frank Hole, Kent. V. Flannery, and James A. Neely, *Prehistory and Human Ecology of the Deh Luran Plain*. *Science* 168:707–709.

Sokal, R. R. and P. H. A. Sneath. 1963. *Principles of Numerical Taxonomy*. San Francisco: Freeman. Revised 1973 as *Numerical Taxonomy*.

South, Stanley. 1977. *Method and Theory in Historical Archaeology*. New York: Academic Press.

Spaulding, Albert C. 1953. "Statistical Techniques for the Discovery of Artifact Types." *American Antiquity* 18:305–313.

—— 1954. Reply to Ford, "Comment on A. C. Spaulding, 'Statistical Techniques for the Discovery of Artifact Types.'" *American Antiquity* 19:391–393.

—— 1960. "Statistical Description and Comparison of Artifact Assemblages." In R. F. Heizer and S. F. Cook, eds., *The Application of Quantitative Methods in Archaeology*, pp. 60–83. Viking Fund Publications in Anthropology, no. 28. New York: Wenner-Green Foundation for Anthropological Research.

—— 1968. "Explanation in Archaeology." In S. Binford and L. Binford, eds., *New Perspectives in Archaeology*, pp. 33–39. Chicago: Aldine.

Stanislawski, Michael B. 1969a. "The Ethnoarchaeology of Hopi Pottery-Making." *Plateau* 42:27–33.

—— 1969b. "What Good Is a Broken Pot?" *Southwestern Lore* 35:11–18.

Stein, Julie K. 1980. "Geoarchaeology of the Green River Shell Mounds, Kentucky." Ph.D. dissertation, University of Minnesota.

—— 1983. "Earthworm Activity: A Source of Potential Disturbance of Archaeological Sediments." *American Antiquity* 48:277–289.

Steward, Julian H. 1938. "Basin-Plateau Aboriginal Sociopolitical Groups." *Bureau of American Ethnology Bulletin* 120.

—— 1949. "Cultural Causality and Law: A Trial Formulation of the Development of Early Civilizations." *American Anthropologist* 51:1–27.

—— 1955. *Theory of Culture Change: The Methodology of Multilinear Evolution*. Urbana: University of Illinois Press.

Steward, Julian H. and F. M. Setzler. 1938. "Function and Configuration in Archaeology." *American Antiquity* 4:4–10.

Stiles, D. 1977. "Ethnoarchaeology: A Discussion of Methods and Applications." *Man* 12:87–103.

Struever, Stuart. 1968a. "Problems, Methods and Organization: A Disparity in the Growth of Archaeology." In B. Meggers, ed., *Anthropological Ar-*

chaeology in the Americas pp. 131–151. Washington, D.C.: Anthropological Society of Washington.

—— 1968b. "Woodland Subsistence-Settlement Systems in the Lower Illinois Valley." In S. Binford and L. Binford, eds., *New Perspectives in Archaeology*, pp. 285–314. Chicago: Aldine.

—— 1971. "Comments on Archaeological Data Requirements and Research Strategy." *American Antiquity* 36:9–19.

—— 1978. "The Northwestern Archaeological Program." In J. Rick, *Heat-Altered Cherts of the Lower Illinois Valley* pp. iii–v, and inside back cover. Prehistoric Records, no. 2. Evanston, Ill.: Northwestern Archaeological Program.

Tainter, Joseph A. 1978. "Mortuary Practices and the Study of Prehistoric Social Systems." *Advances in Archaeological Method and Theory* 1:105–141.

Taylor, Walter W. 1948. *A Study of Archaeology*. American Anthropological Association Memoir, no. 69. Carbondale: Southern Illinois University Press, 1967.

Taylor, Walter W., ed. 1957. *The Identification of Non-Artifactual Remains from Archaeological Sites*. Publication #565. Washington D.C.: National Research Council.

Thomas, David H. 1972. "A Computer Simulation Model of Great Basin Shoshonean Subsistence and Settlement Patterns." In D. Clarke, ed., *Models in Archaeology*, pp. 671–704. London: Methuen.

—— 1973. "An Empirical Test of Steward's Model for Great Basin Settlement Patterns." *American Antiquity* 38: 115–176.

—— 1974. "An Archaeological Perspective on Shoshonean Bands." *American Anthropologist* 76:11–23.

Trigger, Bruce G. 1968. *Beyond History: The Methods of Prehistory*. New York: Holt, Rinehart and Winston.

—— 1970. "Aims in Prehistoric Archaeology." *Antiquity* 44:26–37.

—— 1973. "The Future of Archaeology Is the Past." In C. Redman, ed., *Research and Theory in Current Archaeology*, pp. 95–111. New York: Wiley.

Tringham, Ruth, Glenn Cooper, George Odell, Barbara Voytek, and Anne Whitman. 1974. "Experimentation in the Formation of Edge Damage: A New Approach to Lithic Analysis." *Journal of Field Archaeology* 1:186–196.

Tuggle, D., A. H. Townsend, and T. Riley. 1972. "Laws, Systems, and Research Designs." *American Antiquity* 37:3–12.

Vayda, A. P. 1969. "Introduction," In A. P. Vayda, ed., *Environment and Cultural Behavior: Ecological Studies in Cultural Anthropology*. New York: Natural History Press.

Vickery, Kent. 1976. Review of Patty Jo Watson, ed., *Archaeology of the Mammoth Cave Area*. In *American Anthropologist* 78:937–938.

Vita-Finzi, C. and E. S. Higgs. 1970. "Prehistoric Economy in the Mount

Carmel Area of Palestine: Site Catchment Analysis." *Proceedings of the Prehistoric Society* 36:1–37.

Wagner, Gail E. 1982. "Testing Flotation Recovery Rates." *American Antiquity* 47:127–132.

Washburn, Sherwood L. 1953. "The Strategy of Physical Anthropology." In A. Kroeber, ed., *Anthropology Today,* pp. 714–727. Chicago: University of Chicago Press.

Wasserman, Gerald D. 1981. "On the Nature of the Theory of Evolution." *Philosophy of Science* 48:416–437.

Watson, James D. 1968. *The Double Helix: A Personal Account of the Discovery of the Structure of DNA.* New York: Atheneum.

Watson, Patty Jo. 1973. "The Future of Archaeology in Anthropology: Culture History and Social Science." In C. Redman, ed., *Research and Theory in Current Archaeology,* pp. 113–124. New York: Wiley.

—— 1974a. "Prehistoric Horticulturists." In P. Watson, ed., *Archaeology of the Mammoth Cave Area,* pp. 233–238. New York: Academic Press.

—— 1974b. "Theory in Archaeology: The New Criticism." Paper presented at the Thirty-Ninth Annual Meeting of the Society for American Archaeology, Washington, D.C., May 2–4.

—— 1976. "In Pursuit of Prehistoric Subsistence: A Comparative Account of Some Contemporary Flotation Techniques." *Midcontinental Journal of Archaeology* 1:77–100.

—— 1977. "Central Kentucky Karst Archaeology Project." In *Cave Research Foundation Annual Report, 1976,* pp. 46–47.

—— 1978. "Cave Research Foundation Archaeological Project and Shellmound Archaeological Project, 1977." In *Cave Research Foundation Annual Report, 1977,* pp. 40–45.

—— 1979a. *Archaeological Ethnography in Western Iran.* Viking Fund Publications in Anthropology, no. 57. Tucson: University of Arizona Press.

—— 1979b. "The Idea of Ethnoarchaeology: Notes and Comments." In C. Kramer, ed., *Ethnoarchaeology: Implications of Ethnology for Archaeology,* pp. 277–287. New York: Columbia University Press.

—— 1980. "The Impact of Early Horticulture in the Upland Drainages of the Midwest and Midsouth." Paper prepared for School of American Research advanced seminar, "The Origins of Plant Husbandry in North America," March 2–8. Santa Fe, New Mexico.

—— 1982. Review of R. A. Gould, *Living Archaeology.* In *American Antiquity* 47:445–448.

Watson, Patty Jo et al. 1969. *The Prehistory of Salts Cave, Kentucky.* Report of Investigations, no. 16. Springfield: Illinois State Museum.

Watson, Patty Jo, Steven A. LeBlanc, and Charles L. Redman. 1971. *Explanation in Archeology: An Explicitly Scientific Approach.* New York: Columbia University Press.

Watson, Patty Jo, ed. 1974. *Archeology of the Mammoth Cave Area.* New York: Academic Press.
Watson, Richard A. 1976a. "Inference in Archaeology." *American Antiquity* 41:58–66.
—— 1976b. "Laws, Systems, Certainty, and Particularities." *American Anthropologist* 78:341–344.
Watson, Richard A. and Patty Jo Watson. 1969. *Man and Nature: Anthropological Essay in Human Ecology.* New York: Harcourt, Brace and World.
Weigand, Phil C. 1969. *Modern Huichol Ceramics.* Carbondale: Southern Illinois University Press.
Weiner, J. S., K. P. Oakley, and W. E. Le Gros Clark. 1953. "The Solution of the Piltdown Problem." *Bulletin of the British Museum (Natural History) Geology* 2(3):141–146.
Weiner, J. S., W. E. Le Gros Clark, K. P. Oakley, G. F. Claringbull, M. H. Hey, F. H. Edmunds, S. H. U. Bowie, C. F. Davidson, C. F. M. Fryd, A. D. Baynes-Cope, A. E. A. Werner, and R. J. Plesters. 1955. "Further Contributions to the Solution of the Piltdown Problem." *Bulletin of the British Museum (Natural History) Geology* 2(6):228–287.
Wendorf, Fred. 1979. "Changing Values in Archaeology." *American Antiquity* 44:641–643.
Wenke, Robert J. 1981. "Explaining the Evolution of Cultural Complexity: A Review." *Advances in Archaeological Method and Theory* 4:79–127.
White, Leslie A. 1959. *The Evolution of Culture: The Development of Civilization to the Fall of Rome.* New York: McGraw-Hill.
Wildesen, Leslie E. 1982. "The Study of Impacts on Archaeological Sites." *Advances in Archaeological Method and Theory* 5:51–96.
Willey, Gordon R. 1953. *Prehistoric Settlement Patterns in Viru Valley, Peru.* Bureau of American Ethnology Bulletin 155. Washington, D.C., Smithsonian Institution.
—— 1956. *Prehistoric Settlement Patterns in the New World.* Viking Fund Publications in Anthropology, no. 23. New York: Wenner-Gren Foundation for Anthropological Research.
Willey, Gordon R. and Philip Phillips. 1958. *Method and Theory in American Archaeology.* Chicago: University of Chicago Press.
Willey, Gordon R. and Jeremy A. Sabloff. 1980. *A History of American Archaeology.* 2d ed. San Francisco: Freeman.
Willey, Gordon R. and D. B. Shimkin. 1973. "The Maya Collapse: A Summary View." In T. P. Culbert, ed., *The Maya Collapse,* pp. 457–503. Albuquerque: University of New Mexico Press.
Wilmsen, Edwin N. 1968. "Functional Analysis of Flaked Stone Artifacts." *American Antiquity* 33:156–161.
Winters, Howard D. 1968. "Value Systems and Trade Cycles of the Late Ar-

chaic in the Midwest." In S. Binford and L. Binford, eds., *New Perspectives in Archeology*, pp. 175–221. Chicago: Aldine.
Wiseman, James. 1980. "Archaeology in the Future: An Evolving Discipline." *American Journal of Archaeology* 84:279–285.
Wittfogel, Karl A. 1957. *Oriental Despotism: A Comparative Study of Total Power.* New Haven: Yale University Press.
Wobst, Martin. 1977. "Stylistic Behavior and Information Exchange." In C. Cleland, ed., *Papers for the Director*, pp. 317–342. Anthropological Papers, no. 61. Ann Arbor: University of Michigan Museum of Anthropology.
Wood, W. Raymond and Donald L. Johnson. 1978. "A Survey of Disturbance Processes in Archaeological Site Formation." *Advances in Archaeological Method and Theory* 1:315–381.
Wood, W. Raymond and R. Bruce McMillan. 1976. *Prehistoric Man and His Environments: A Case Study in the Ozark Highland.* New York: Academic Press.
Wright, Gary. 1969. "Obsidian Analysis and Prehistoric Near Eastern Trade: 7500 to 3500 B.C." Anthropological Papers, no. 37. Ann Arbor: University of Michigan Museum of Anthropology.
Wright, Henry T. 1977. "Recent Research on the Origin of the State." *Annual Review of Anthropology* 6:379–397.
Wright, Henry T. and G. A. Johnson. 1975. "Population, Exchange, and Early State Formation in Southwestern Iran." *American Anthropologist* 77:267–289.
Wright, Henry T. and Melinda Zeder. 1977. "The Simulation of a Linear Exchange System Under Equilibrium Conditions." In T. Earle and J. Ericson, eds., *Exchange Systems in Prehistory*, pp. 233–253. New York: Academic Press.
Wylie, M. Alison. 1980. "Analogical Inference in Archaeology." Paper presented at the Forty-Sixth Annual Meeting of the Society for American Archaeology, Philadelphia.
—— 1981. "Positivism and the New Archaeology." Ph.D. dissertation, State University of New York, Binghamton.
—— 1982a. "Epistemological Issues Raised by a Structuralist Archaeology." In I. Hodder, ed., *Structuralist and Symbolic Archaeology*, pp. 39–46. Cambridge: Cambridge University Press.
—— 1982b. " 'What's in a Word?': An Analogy by Any Other Name Is Just as Analogical." *Journal of Anthropological Archaeology* 1:382–401.
—— in press. "The Reaction Against Analogy." In M. Schiffer, ed., *Advances in Archaeological Method and Theory*, vol. 8. New York: Academic Press.
—— forthcoming. *Conceptual Tensions in American New Archaeology: Philosophical Dialogue and Archaeological Practice.* New York: Academic Press.
Yarnell, Richard A. 1974. "Plant Food and Cultivation of the Salts Cavers."

In P. Watson, ed., *Archeology of the Mammoth Cave Area*, pp. 113–122. New York: Academic Press.

—— 1978. "Domestication of Sunflower and Sumpweed in Eastern North America." In R. Ford, ed., *The Nature and Status of Ethnobotany*, pp. 289–299. Anthropological Papers, no. 67. Ann Arbor: University of Michigan Museum of Anthropology.

Yellen, John E. 1977. *Archaeological Approaches to the Present: Models for Reconstructing the Past.* New York: Academic Press.

Zubrow, Ezra. 1981. "The Centralization and Cost of Archaeological Information." *American Antiquity* 46:443–446.

Zucchi, Alberta. 1973. "Prehistoric Human Occupation of the Western Venezuelan Llanos." *American Antiquity* 8(2):182–190.

Name Index

Adams, Robert McC., 50, 165, 167
Ammerman, Albert, 90, 91

Babbage, Charles, 156
Barth, Fredrik, 122
Bates, Marston, 119
Bell, James A., 101, 103
Bennett, John, 121, 248
Berg, G. C., 133
Binford, Lewis, viii, 1, 42, 43, 67, 69, 117, 121, 124, 125, 126, 156, 157, 257, 262, 263, 264, 265
Birkby, Walter, 165
Blalock, Hubert, 188
Braidwood, Robert J., 116, 124, 251, 275
Brew, J. O., 203
Brown, Robert, ix
Butzer, Karl, 121, 135

Cavelli-Sforza, L. L., 90, 91
Chadwick, A. J., 88, 91
Clark, J. D., 164
Clarke, Grahame, 115, 162, 167
Clarke, David, 46, 67, 68, 69
Collingwood, R. G., 28, 30, 31, 35, 62
Cooke, Kenneth, 67, 83, 87, 92, 93, 94, 99, 103
Cowgill, George, xiii, 217
Curren, Cailup B., 263
Cutler, Hugh, 131

Daniels, S. G. H., 169
Dawson, Charles, 18
Deetz, James, 164, 167, 210, 211
de Lumley, Henry, 164
Dewey, John, 16, 17
Doran, J. E., 192, 211, 216

Dray, William, 3, 15, 28, 29, 30, 31, 32, 33, 34, 35, 40, 62
Dunnell, Robert, xiii, 235, 245, 246, 251-56, 257, 262
Durham, William, 121

Edey, Maitland, 57
Evans, R., 204, 212

Fagen, R. E., 68
Farrand, William, 258
Flannery, Kent, 43, 44, 67, 68, 70, 76, 117, 164, 238, 239, 272
Foucher, Simon, 267
Fowler, Don D., 133

Gifford, Diane, 90, 166
Gould, Richard A., 256, 264
Gumerman, George, 133, 235
Gunn, Joel, 211

Hall, A. D., 68
Hall, Robert, 271, 272
Hanen, Marsha, 256
Hardesty, Donald, 121
Harlan, Jack, 125, 126, 140
Hawkes, Jaquetta, 267
Helm, June, 119, 121
Hempel, Carl G., 3, 4, 11, 14, 15, 16, 18, 21, 22, 25, 26, 28, 29, 30, 31, 105-8, 109
Hickman, P. P., 133
Hill, James N., 50, 83, 144, 164, 204, 210, 211, 212
Hodder, Ian, 90, 224
Hodson, F. R., 192, 211, 216
Hole, Frank, 67, 116, 164, 238, 239
Hosler, D. H., 95, 96, 98

House, John, 133
Hume, David, 4, 5, 6, 12, 22, 23
Huntington, Ellsworth, 120

Irwin-Williams, Cynthia, 133
Isaac, Glynn, 267

Jennings, Jesse D., 116
Jochim, Michael A., 121
Johanson, Donald, 57

Kelley, Jane, 256
Kidder, Alfred V., 116, 275
King, Thomas F., 133
Kolstoe, Ralph H., 188
Kuhn, Thomas, 36-40

Laming-Emperaire, Annette, 270
Leach, Edmond R., 121
Leaf, Garry R., 188
LeBlanc, Steven A., 67, 71, 133, 217, 241, 243, 267
Leibniz, Wilhelm, 267
Leone, Mark, xiii, 270-73
Leroi-Gourhan, André, 270-71, 274
Lewontin, R. C., 253
Lipe, William D., 133, 244
Longacre, William, 126, 164, 249
Low, Gilbert, 84

MacNeish, Richard S., 116
Malinowski, Bronislaw, 68, 105
Marcus, Joyce, 68, 272
Marshack, Alexander, 271
Maruyama, Magoroh, 72
Marx, Karl, 252
Matessi, C., 90
McGimsey, Charles R., 133
McMillan, Bruce, 127, 128, 129
Meehan, Eugene, 70
Miksicek, Charles, 144
Mixon, Bill, 238
Morgan, Lewis Henry, 252

Neely, James, 164, 238, 239

Oakeshott, Michael, 28, 29, 35
Oppenheim, Paul, 29

Orton, Clive, 90, 224
O'Shea, John M., 88

Parker, Arthur C., 247
Plog, Fred T., 67
Plog, Stephen, 89
Popper, Karl, 3, 12

Radcliffe-Brown, A. R., 68, 105
Redman, Charles L., 67, 209, 267
Renfrew, Colin, 83, 84, 87, 90, 92, 93, 94, 95, 99, 103, 109
Riley, T., 67, 70
Rudner, Richard S., 3
Runge, D., 95, 96, 98

Sabloff, Jeremy, 67, 95, 96, 98, 257
Sackett, James R., 201
Salmon, Merrilee, ix, xiii, 3, 12, 13, 25, 26, 71, 105, 108, 109
Salmon, Wesley, ix, xiii, 3, 6, 15, 21, 23, 24, 27, 49, 108, 109
Schiffer, Michael, 133, 235, 257, 262
Schwartz, Douglas, 241
Scriven, Michael, 26
Setzler, Frank M., 248
Shimkin, Dimitri, 95
Smith, P. E. L., 238, 239
Sneath, P. H. A., 216
Sokal, R. R., 216
South, Stanley, 164
Spaulding, Albert C., 192, 203, 204, 208, 248, 251, 275
Spencer, Herbert, 252
Stanislawski, Michael, 257
Stein, Julie, 240, 258
Steward, Julian H., 44, 50, 91, 121, 248, 250
Struever, Stuart, 67, 69, 117, 133, 167

Taylor, Walter W., viii, 1, 59, 68, 167, 248, 275
Thomas, David H., 87, 91, 92, 250
Townsend, A. H., 67, 70, 91
Trigger, Bruce G., 267
Tuggle, D., 67, 70

Name Index

Venn, John, ix
Vickery, Kent, 237
Voorrips, Albertus, 90

Wagner, Gail, 171
Watson, James D., 57
Watson, Patty Jo, 67, 121, 267
Watson, Richard A., xiii, 121
Weigand, Phil C., 257
Weiner, J. S., 17, 18
Wendorf, Fred, 246
Wheeler, Sir Mortimer, 167, 275
White, Leslie, 119, 252, 270

Wildesen, Leslie, 133
Willey, Gordon R., 95, 257
Wilmsen, Edwin, 211
Wittfogel, Karl A., 50
Wood, Raymond, 127
Wright, Henry, 87, 90
Wylie, M. Alison, 58-61, 256, 259, 263

Yellen, John, 12, 166

Zeder, Melinda, 87, 90
Zubrow, Ezra, 242

Subject Index

Activity area, 164, 220-21
Analytical individual, 209
Archaeological Conservancy, 243
Archeological Conservation Act, x, 132, 133, 242-43
Archeological record, 156-60, 256, 275
Archeological theory, 15, 27, 41, 45-47, 52-53, 56, 66, 131, 251-52
Archeology, vii; aims of, 266-69; anthropological, vii, 1, 67, 249; classical, vii, 47; conservation or contract, x, xi, 133, 134, 168, 188, 233, 235-36; historical, 47, 274; humanistically oriented, vii; ideational (cognitive, structuralist), 269-74; new, viii, xi, 15, 58-60, 266; "post-processual" (see also ideational), xi; prehistoric, vii, ix, 66; as science, 42-66, 129, 155, 232, 268, 275; as social science, vii, x, 1, 247-51
Attribute, 192
Axiomatization, 14, 34, 45, 46, 264

Bias, see Regular error
BMDP programs, 217, 223, 227
Brainerd-Robinson Coefficient, 216, 219
Bridgewater Treatise, 156
Broken K, 50, 210

Carter Ranch, 126, 250
Catastrophe theory, 77, 84, 102, 104, 110
Causal relevance, 21, 23
Causality, 22-23, 26-27, 33, 34
Çayönü, 180, 264
Certainty, 5, 6-7, 43, 261; see also Hume's problem of induction
Chi-squared test, 198-99

Computer simulation, 48, 85-102, 228; archeological examples of, 89-99
Confirmation or verification, 6, 11, 13, 16, 23, 33, 36, 38, 41, 43, 44, 45, 52, 53, 63-66, 95, 101-2, 129, 260, 263; see also Context of verification
Context of discovery, 16, 31, 35, 38, 65
Context of verification, 16, 31, 35, 38, 65; see also Confirmation
Covering law model, covering law approach, 7-10, 13, 15-25, 28-31, 33-34, 40-41, 61-65, 70, 102, 260, 263
Cultural history (culture history), 44, 51, 266, 268
Cultural process (culture process), vii, 44, 51, 69, 167, 250, 251, 267, 275
Cybernetics, 72, 105; see Systems theory

Deduction, deductive, 5, 16, 19, 22, 58, 59, 60, 143, 247, 261
Disciplinary matrix, 39; see also Paradigm

Ecofacts, 131, 132, 136, 143-44, 162, 163
Ecological niche, 122-23
Empirical generalization, 4, 11, 12
Empiricist, 58, 59, 61
Environmental determinism, 115, 120
Epistemological, 3, 58
Error, 169-75; see also Experimental error; Gross error; Random error; Regular error
Ethnoarcheology, 47, 256, 258, 259-65, 270
Ethnographic analogy, 47, 160, 256, 259-65, 274
Experimental error, 171-72, 175
Explanandum, 16, 21, 23
Explanans, 16, 21

Explanation, 4, 7-53, 275; CL, 7-10, 15-25, 28-31, 33-34, 41, 70-71, 110, 275; D-N, 16-18, 27, 28, 33, 58, 62, 108-10; D-S, 18-19, 27, 28, 62, 108-10; I-S, 19-20, 21, 28, 33, 62, 108-10; S-R, 21-25, 62, 108-10; causal, 22, 23, 33, 34; continuous series model, 29, 30; eco-utilitarian, 270; functional, 105-11, 124, 129; historical, 27-36; rational, see *Verstehen*; systems, 70-71, 124; theoretical, 27; *Verstehen* (empathic), 30, 62

Factor analysis, 158, 217, 219-23, 230
Falsification, 12, 260
Feedback, 71; negative, 72-73, 94, 103; positive, 74-75, 96, 103
Flotation, 55, 136-37, 139, 141, 146, 158, 161, 167, 171
Flow chart, 70, 80, 81, 82, 96
Functionalism, 68, 105-11

General law, see Law; Lawlike genealization
General systems theory, 102-5
Generalizing, 31, 63, 64, 262, 266, 267; see also Nomothetic
Georarcheology, 140, 258
Girikihaciyan, 180-82, 195
Glen Canyon, 116
Gross error, 169-70

Homeostatic, 74-75; see also Systems theory
Hume's problem of induction, 4, 5, 12, 22
Hypothesis/ hypotheses, 3, 4, 6, 7-13, 36, 39, 43, 44-58, 60, 63, 268; formulation, 44-53, 84, 222-23; multiple working hypotheses, 128; post hoc, 56-57; scope, 48-49, 50; testing, 39, 49, 50-58, 84-85, 91, 100-2, 113-15, 130, 141-42, 145, 148, 158-60, 229, 230, 260, 263; see also Model
Hypothetico-deductive method, 12, 23, 41, 57, 59

Ideational archeology (cognitive, structuralist), 269-74
Idiographic, 31, 35, 36, 266, 267, 269

Implications (of hypotheses), 12, 13, 57, 59, 118, 144, 187, 229, 250
Induction, inductive, 5, 19, 22, 23, 33, 59, 60, 143, 260
Input, 71
Interdisciplinary research, 134-36, 149, 233-35
Irish wake, 106

Jarmo, 116, 124
Joking relationship, 105
Justification, see Confirmation or verification; Context of verification

Knowledge claims, 13, 31, 33, 34, 35, 42-43, 52, 63, 65-66, 266

Law, laws, viii, 2, 4, 6, 7, 11, 12, 14, 17, 18, 25, 28, 29, 30, 35, 39, 41, 51-52, 66, 70, 264, 266-68, 275; statistical (or probabilistic), 4, 18, 27, 28; universal, 4, 18
Lawlike generalization, 6, 11, 12, 14, 29, 31, 33, 45, 52, 63-64, 224, 266-67
Linearization, 76
Locational analysis, 224-25
Logic of discovery, see Context of discovery
Logic of justification, or of verification, see Context of verification
Logic of science, ix, 3

Macrotheory (grand theory, hypertheory), 35, 46, 47, 52, 53
Mammoth Cave, Ky., 50, 237
Mammoth Cave National Park, 50, 55
Marginal zone, 125
Mental templates, 208-10, 231
Method of multiple working hypotheses, see Hypothesis
Microfiche, 240
Middle-range theory, 47, 257, 263-65
Mimbres Foundation, Project, 133, 173, 241
Minitheory, 41, 46, 47, 52, 53, 257
Model, 48, 86-88, 102, 123, 144-47, 260, 262; see also Computer simulation; Hypothesis
Multidimensional scaling, 217, 218, 219-23

Subject Index

Multidisciplinary research, *see* Interdisciplinary research
Multistage design, 172-75, 194

Negative evidence, 157
"Noise," 169; *see also* Random error
Nomological, 16, 21, 25, 28, 31, 34; *see also* Explanation, D-N
Nomothetic, 31, 35, 36, 266, 267, 269
Normandy Reservoir, 244, 245
Normative view, 69

Ontological, 58, 60, 253
Optimum zone, 125
Output, 71

Paradigm, 36, 39; *see also* Disciplinary matrix
Parity (Symmetry) of explanation, 25-26
Particularistic or particularizing, viii, 31, 49, 63, 64, 262, 266, 267; *see also* Idiographic
Phytoliths, 117
Piltdown forgery, 17, 18
Poppy seed test, 171
Possibilism, 120
Prediction, 2, 4, 5, 6, 14, 25-26, 43
Preservation of archaeological sites, 179, 237, 242-47
Principle of generic similarity, 259
Promotion, 76
Publication of archeological reports, 233-42

Random error, 169-70, 175
Realism, realist, 58, 59, 61
Reference classes, 19-21, 23-24
Regular error (bias), 169, 171, 175, 179, 185
Relevant data, 53-55, 160-63, 166
Research design, 167-68
Rodgers Shelter, 127, 128

Salts Cave, 50, 55
Sampling error, 175
Sampling in archeology, 176-85; *see also* Error
Scales of measurement, 188-92, 215, 232

Self-regulation, self-regulating systems, *see* Systems theory
Seriation, 166, 223
Settlement pattern analysis, 123, 130-31, 151; *see also* Locational analysis
Settlement system, 121-22, 151; *see also* Locational analysis
Shellmound Archeological Project, 133
Simulation, *see* Computer simulation
Site catchment analysis, 130, 146-47
Site formation processes, 47, 51, 175, 256, 257-59, 260
Site preservation, 233, 242-47
Stability analysis, 102-3
Star Carr, 115, 162
Statistical relevance, 21-25; in functional analysis, 108-10
Stylistic vs. functional attributes, 210, 254-56
Subjective element (in science), 32, 37-38, 40-41
Systemization, *see* Axiomatization
Systemic approach, or systems approach, 25, 48, 68 ff, 84-85, 151; *see also* Functionalism
Systems theory, ix, 48, 65, 68 ff, 84-85; and cultural change, 84-85; and ecology, 113 ff; and hypothesis testing, 84-85; 100-2; and self-regulating systems, 75, 105-10

Taphonomy, 175, 256, 258
Tehuacan Valley, 116
Tellico Reservoir, 244, 245
Trade, 123, 130, 131; "down-the-line," 90
Trajectory, 78, 80
Transformational error, 175; *see also* Site formation processes
Truth, 6, 43-44
Types, 201-14; monothetic, 202, 218; polythetic, 202, 218

Underdetermined theory, 56
Uniformity of nature, 4, 5

Variable, 192, 196
Verification, *see* Confirmation